D1288253

NEW DIRECTIONS IN ARCHAEOLOGY

Editors

Richard Bradley
Lecturer in Archaeology, University of Reading

Richard I. Ford
Professor of Anthropology and Director of the Museum of Anthropology, University of Michigan

Ian Hodder
Assistant Lecturer in Archaeology, University of Cambridge

Glynn Isaac
Professor of Anthropology, University of California, Berkeley

Rhys Jones
Senior Research Fellow, Department of Prehistory, Research School of Pacific Studies, Australian National University

Martyn Jope
Professor of Archaeology, Queen's University, Belfast

Colin Renfrew
Professor of Archaeology, University of Southampton

Andrew Sherratt
Assistant Keeper, Department of Antiquities, Ashmolean Museum, Oxford

David Thomas
Assistant Curator, Department of Anthropology, American Museum of Natural History, New York

THE ARCHAEOLOGY OF DEATH

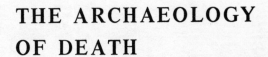

THE ARCHAEOLOGY
OF DEATH

EDITED BY ROBERT CHAPMAN
IAN KINNES
KLAVS RANDSBORG

CAMBRIDGE UNIVERSITY PRESS
CAMBRIDGE
LONDON   NEW YORK   NEW ROCHELLE
MELBOURNE   SYDNEY

GT
3170
A734
1981

Published by the Press Syndicate of the University of Cambridge
The Pitt Building, Trumpington Street, Cambridge CB2 1RP
32 East 57th Street, New York, NY 10022, USA
296 Beaconsfield Parade, Middle Park, Melbourne 3206, Australia

© Cambridge University Press 1981

First published 1981

Printed in Great Britain at the University Press, Cambridge

British Library Cataloguing in Publication Data
The archaeology of death. – (New directions in
archaeology).

1. Funeral rites and ceremonies
– History
I. Chapman, Robert II. Kinnes, Ian
III. Randsborg, Klavs IV. Series
393'.1'0901   GT3170   80-41751
ISBN 0 521 23775 0

For C.J. Becker (K.R.)
Jan Chapman (R.W.C.)

CONTENTS

337167

LIBRARY
MURRAY STATE UNIVERSITY

CONTRIBUTORS

R.J. Bradley, Department of Archaeology, University of Reading,
Reading.

J.A. Brown, Department of Anthropology, Northwestern University,
Evanston, Illinois, U.S.A.

J.E. Buikstra, Department of Anthropology, Northwestern University,
Evanston, Illinois, U.S.A.

R.W. Chapman, Department of Archaeology, University of Reading,
Reading.

D.C. Cook, Department of Anthropology, Indiana University,
Bloomington, Indiana, U.S.A.

L.G. Goldstein, Department of Anthropology, University of Wisconsin-
Milwaukee, Milwaukee, Wisconsin, U.S.A.

I.A. Kinnes, Department of Prehistoric and Romano-British Antiquities,
British Museum, London.

J.M. O'Shea, Department of Anthropology, University of Iowa, Iowa
City, Iowa, U.S.A.

K. Randsborg, Forshistorisk-Arkaeologisk Institut, University of
Copenhagen, Copenhagen, Denmark.

PREFACE

This volume was conceived by the editors in 1978. It was planned at the same time as Robert Chapman and Ian Kinnes were organising a programme for the 1979 Spring Conference of the Prehistoric Society in London. The conference was entitled 'The Archaeology of Death' and gave many of the contributors to this volume an opportunity to meet each other and exchange ideas and information. We would like to thank the Prehistoric Society and its President, Professor John Coles, for providing the occasion for such interaction. Subsequently the editing of this volume, which includes papers not presented at the conference as well as several of those that were, has been organised in the following way: Ian Kinnes has assumed responsibility for primary editing of the manuscripts, while Robert Chapman and Klavs Randsborg have combined to write an introductory paper which sets the papers in this book in a broader perspective. We would like to thank Josephine Say for the efficient and prompt manner in which she put together the bibliography at very short notice. Jan Chapman has provided invaluable secretarial assistance. We would also like to thank the contributors to this book, from whom we have learnt much. The friendship and sheer good company of Richard Bradley has been most beneficial throughout the conception and editing of the book: he was there at the beginning and in at the death! Lastly we acknowledge with gratitude the guidance and patience of Cambridge University Press, and Robin Derricourt in particular.

Robert Chapman
Ian Kinnes
Klavs Randsborg

When an Indian burns himself
He cremates his flesh and bone.
Does he fear holy torment,
Or the pressure of the grave
Upon his flat skeleton?

(Abu al-Ala al-Ma'arri (973–1057),
Birds through a Ceiling of Alabaster,
Penguin Classics, 1975)

We can bury her, burn her or dump her.

(Line remembered from the Undertaker's sketch,
Monty Python's Flying Circus)

Chapter 1

**Approaches to the
archaeology of death**
Robert Chapman and
Klavs Randsborg

What could be more universal than death? Yet what an incredible variety of responses it evokes. Corpses are burned or buried, with or without animal or human sacrifice; they are preserved by smoking, embalming or pickling; they are eaten – raw, cooked or rotten; they are ritually exposed as carrion or simply abandoned; or they are dismembered and treated in a variety of ways. Funerals are the occasion for avoiding people or holding parties, for fighting or having sexual orgies, for weeping or laughing, in a thousand different combinations. The diversity of cultural reaction is a measure of the universal impact of death. But it is not a random reaction; always it is meaningful and expressive.

(Huntington and Metcalf 1979, p. 1)

The archaeology of death is not a new subject. An interest in the mortuary practices of past human cultures has been evident throughout the development of archaeology to its present disciplinary status. Indeed there is little to match the discovery of an impressive new grave assemblage in generating both professional and public enthusiasm and demonstrating 'the universal impact of death'. The recent finds of a Celtic chieftain's tomb in southern Germany and the claimed tomb of Philip II of Macedon in northern Greece support this contention. But such finds sit on the tip of literally thousands of burials known and analysed by prehistoric and historic archaeologists in every part of the world. In addition to their overall frequency, the myriad variable forms in which they occur ('the diversity of cultural reaction') have ensured that data on mortuary practices have played a central role in the study of social, cultural, chronological, ethnic and racial problems.

If we accept the view expressed by Huntington and Metcalf that the cultural reaction to death is not random but 'meaningful and expressive' then we must concern ourselves with the problems of meaning and expression. Of course these problems can be approached at different levels (e.g. 'emic' and 'etic' – Harris 1969). In this volume the central argument is that archaeologists need a body of theory in order to relate the mortuary data at their disposal to patterns of human behaviour within past human societies. Within the last two decades such theoretical perspectives have been found within the New Archaeology and directed towards the study of social organisation and the dynamics of cultural systems. But given the emphasis placed upon the potential of mortuary data, it seems somewhat surprising that there has been only one book devoted to it within the last ten years (Brown 1971*b*). Doctoral dissertations and papers abound and there is an excellent review article by Tainter (1978) but, even though *Approaches to the Social Dimensions of Mortuary Practices* (Brown 1971*b*) went out of print within two years of publication, no further attempt has been made to integrate the wide range of research in a single volume.

This book represents an attempt to refocus archaeologists' attention upon the meaning and expression of cultural reactions to death. In keeping with the series in which it appears, the emphasis is on the new directions of current research. Some continuity with the earlier book is evident in the content of several papers and also in the presence of that volume's editor. The evolution and critical appraisal of the ideas presented in 1971, as well as the subsequent emergence of new approaches, are central to this volume.

In order to relate the studies presented in this book to each other and to past and present research into the archaeology of death, some coherent introduction is necessary. We do not pretend that what follows is an exhaustive presentation of work in the field of mortuary studies. Our discussion centres initially upon prehistoric Europe, since this is the area in which our own research has been pursued, but broadens out subsequently to consider research pursued in North America and elsewhere. We do not see these geographical limitations as restricting the value of the discussion, since we believe that the focus upon problems, approaches and theory gives it a wider relevance. All but one (Randsborg) of the papers published in this volume are concerned with pre-state societies, but we refer also to mortuary practices in more complex societies. We begin by trying to document the problems for which mortuary practices were thought to provide a critical testing-ground at earlier periods in the history of archaeology. Then we examine the anthropological perspectives introduced in the New Archaeology and applied to the analysis of prehistoric cemeteries. The many stimulating problems which have been raised by these approaches are discussed. The wider perspectives of regional analysis, the measurement of biological distance,

palaeodemography, palaeopathology and the emerging field of dietary analysis are added to provide a broad illustration of the range of problems upon which the analysis of mortuary practices is being focussed.

Speculation, chronology and normative thought

In the pre-scientific period of archaeology's development in both Old and New Worlds, antiquaries, travellers and the public at large came into contact with burial mounds and other forms of monumental burial from a very early date. In Europe such mounds were believed to contain the direct ancestors of the local populations and were central to disputes over national boundaries. More often speculation centred upon the identity of the builders (who were to be found in the annals of history or in folk tales), a trend which culminated in the Romantic period of the early nineteenth century. In searching for the particular groups responsible for these mounds (frequently known as Giants' Graves) the early antiquaries and historians often reached what we would now regard as eccentric conclusions. For example the megalithic tomb at New Grange in the Boyne valley of Ireland was at different times attributed to the labours of Egyptians, Danes and Phoenicians (Daniel 1964, p. 24). The Danes were also one of the groups looked to for an origin of the mounds of the Ohio valley in North America (Willey and Sabloff 1974, pp. 30–4).

In the late eighteenth and the nineteenth century, burials became the subject of the first systematic excavations. Pioneers such as Thomas Jefferson in Virginia (Willey and Sabloff 1974, pp. 36–8), Colt-Hoare and Cunnington, Bateman, Mortimer and Greenwell in England, and Worsaae in Denmark (Marsden 1974; Daniel 1964, 1975) began excavation of literally hundreds of burial mounds. The quantity of data on mortuary practices and grave goods (albeit of variable quality) from the excavations carried out throughout the nineteenth century was on such a scale that we are still trying to collate it in comprehensive corpora. Although excavators were still concerned with the identification of the builders of such mounds, the development of the Three-Age system in Denmark helped to put such research in a less speculative context. Indeed it was the work of Worsaae (1843, 1849) on Danish burial mounds which not only helped to verify the Three-Age system, but also established the chronological approach to the analysis of mortuary practices: Worsaae's Law (i.e. those artefacts found together must have been used together) has been described as 'the first use of grave associations to solve a chronological problem' (Rowe 1962, p. 130). It was the extension of this approach, as well as the development of the typological method, that enabled such scholars as Oscar Montelius (e.g. 1885), Paul Reinecke (e.g. 1904–11) and Joseph Déchelette (e.g. 1908) to produce the chronological schemes which provided the basis for the study of European prehistory in the present century.

Mention of these early developments, particularly in Scandinavian archaeology, should remind us that the foundation in the nineteenth century of museums and other 'antiquarian' institutions devoted to local or regional studies greatly aided the collection of data on prehistoric and early historic burials. This early establishment of European museums was of the utmost importance, since it saved enormous amounts of material which would have been lost in the face of the economic expansion of early industrialism, with its intensive agriculture, building of railways and roads and rapid development of towns. For this reason it has proved less difficult to undertake regional analyses of mortuary practices in Europe than in many parts of the world where reliance is placed solely on modern excavations and recently developed regional sampling strategies.

It should be stressed that, for the Neolithic, Bronze and Iron Ages, burial evidence was the most substantial body of data available in the nineteenth century. Known settlements were few outside the regions with monumental or stone structures. Within Europe the notable exceptions (apart from the settlements of the Aegean Bronze Age excavated by Schliemann) were the Danish 'kitchen-middens' and the Swiss lake-side settlements. These were unusual in that the former were easily visible and the latter were well preserved under subsequent rises in lake levels. Elsewhere, and with the exception of the 'tells' of south-east Europe, settlements were only more rarely distinguished by their surface cultural materials. It was not until the twentieth century that more attention was given to settlement excavation, with important implications for the interpretations which had previously been based upon the evidence of mortuary practices. In short we state that the early history of archaeology was very much the history of burial studies.

In addition to the chronological approaches, some inferences about social organisation were made. In general the late-nineteenth-century archaeologists were interested in the same questions as ethnographers and other students of society in the Victorian Age. One example here concerns the relations between the sexes. In Denmark it was noted that Bronze Age women with rich graves 'were not the slaves of the men' and culture must have been on a relatively high level, since African societies with marriage by purchase were considered 'primitive' by those studying the evolution of culture (e.g. Müller 1897, pp. 400ff.). Most observations, however, concerned social stratification and other social roles, as reflected in the presence of certain artefact types like weapons, tools, keys etc. (e.g. Müller 1897, pp. 401ff.).

A greater concern with social organisation as a relevant variable in the understanding of mortuary practices also appeared in early-twentieth-century anthropology (e.g. Hertz 1907; Durkheim 1915), and replaced the later-nineteenth-century concern with primitive religion (e.g. Tylor 1871; Frazer 1886).

In the twentieth century the chronological, social and religious approaches to the archaeology of death have been continued, although there has been much variation in their adoption and frequency within both the Old and New Worlds. Whether or not stratified sites and absolute chronologies are available, typologies and seriations of material from mortuary

contexts continue in use in an attempt to analyse both spatial and temporal variations in culture. The central and West European Bronze Ages provide good examples of this approach. With the advent of multivariate analyses and computer simulations, as well as a general increase in the use of mathematics and statistics in archaeology, more refined examples of seriation and chronological ordering have emerged (e.g. the series of analyses of the La Tène period cemetery at Münsingen-Rain, Switzerland – Doran and Hodson 1975; also Renfrew and Sterud 1969; Graham, Galloway and Scollar 1976). The seriation method of 'sequence-dating' devised by Petrie (1899) to cope with nine hundred predynastic Egyptian graves has been reviewed over half a century later by Kendall (1963), in order to examine statistical problems inherent in the original work. Finally the simulation of cemetery formation has been developed in an experiment in the formulation and evaluation of hypotheses (Doran 1973).

Although the chronological approach has been pursued this century, the first fifty years were dominated by the normative, cultural approach. Within anthropology the reaction against the theory of unilinear evolution led to the rise of diffusion as a mechanism proposed in explanation of changes in material culture in time and space. Under the influence of German ethnologists such as Graebner and Schmidt and Americans such as Boas (e.g. 1940) and Wissler (1922), much attention was given in anthropology and archaeology to the definition of culture-areas and the flow of traits within and between them. Within European prehistory the large amount of mortuary evidence from excavations and museum collections played an integral part in the recognition of regional as well as chronological variations in material culture. The main formulation was that of Childe, who defined and interpreted the 'culture' as follows:

> We find certain types of remains – pots, implements, ornaments, burial rites, house forms – constantly recurring together. Such a complex of regularly associated traits we shall term a 'cultural group' or just a 'culture'. We assume that such a complex is the material expression of what would today be called a 'people'. Only where the complex in question is regularly and exclusively associated with skeletal remains of a specific physical type would we venture to replace 'people' by the term 'race'.   (1929, pp. v–vi)

The types (including burial rites) were 'socially approved' (1956, p. 8) and common to the members of particular societies at particular times:

> Community of tradition imposes on all members of the society in question a common pattern of behaviour. *This must result in the production of standard types, which, if they be artifacts, burial rites or remains of repasts,* archaeology can identify.

(1956, pp. 9–10, our emphasis)

An obvious condition for the association of types is that they shall be in use or occupation at the same time. All types thus associated should then have the same chronological co-ordinate. But repeated association requires no less that they shall be used by the same society, that is *by persons inspired by the same common tradition of wood-working, fighting, dress, domestic architecture and burial rites.*   (1956, p. 16, our emphasis) This then was a 'normative' view of culture (see Binford 1965), that common patterns of behaviour produced spatial regularities in traits, including mortuary practices, and these were crystallised into 'cultures'. Similarities and differences between cultures in such features as inhumation or cremation, individual or collective burial and the forms and average dimensions of graves were interpreted in terms of diffusion or population movement. Binford summarised the assumption behind such an approach as follows: 'the degree of formal similarity observed among independent sociocultural units is a direct measure of the degree of genetic or affiliational cultural relationship among the units being compared' (1971, p. 9). While in North America Kroeber (1927) argued that burial rites should be considered along with 'fashions', it was Childe's opinion that they belonged to the field of religion: in itemising the different aspects of cultures he placed burial rites under the heading of 'Ideology' (1956, p. 131).

Mortuary practices were therefore an integral part of Childe's cultural framework. The later prehistory of Europe was systematically organised in successive editions of *The Dawn of European Civilisation* (e.g. 1925, 1957) into a series of cultures. Study of the distribution of traits allowed the inference of diffusion or population movement. Where such traits and indeed whole cultures occurred over thousands of square kilometres within a short period of time, as in the case of the Corded Ware/Battle-Axe and Bell Beaker cultures, such inferences were thought justified. Physical anthropology came to the support of these inferences with its use of cephalic indices to define different racial groups. When such traits as mortuary practices showed discontinuities from one culture to its successor (e.g. from communal to single burial), inferences of diffusion or population movement were again drawn. Such discontinuities became of particular importance in those areas in which historical and/or linguistic evidence was being used to detect the existence and spread of ethnic or linguistic groups. It has been argued that the spread of pit-graves or ochre-graves, along with battle-axes and other traits, demonstrates the spread of the Indo-Europeans from their southern Russian steppe 'homeland' in the late fourth and third millennia B.C. (e.g. Gimbutas 1973). Similarly the appearance of widespread Urnfield cremations in the late Bronze Age has been discussed in relation to the origins of Celtic-speaking tribes (e.g. Childe 1930). This equation of 'cultures' with ethnic, racial or linguistic groups was carried to its extremes by Germans such as Kossinna (Daniel 1964).

In spite of Childe's insistence that such 'cultures' be defined by many aspects of life, he was compelled to admit that many of them were known solely from their mortuary practices (1956, p. 122). This was certainly the case with the Corded Ware/Battle-Axe culture and the Bell Beaker culture

mentioned above. With the subsequent excavation of many more settlements, it is now apparent that many cultural discontinuities (whether in time or space) were more apparent than real. Recent years have also seen mounting criticism of the general normative, cultural approach (e.g. Binford 1965; Renfrew 1977; Hodder 1978*b*; Chapman 1979), whether in Europe or North America. But the emphasis upon the definition of regularities or 'norms' in mortuary practices still survives in many areas, as can be seen from a recent survey of the European Bronze Age (Coles and Harding 1979). Similarly the simple explanation of such practices in terms of religious beliefs is still in the minds of many prehistorians.

When it came to the social approach to the archaeology of death, the first half of this century revealed a strong inclination towards the broad horizontal (e.g. tribal areas) rather than the local vertical (e.g. social stratification) dimensions of prehistoric societies. While Childe and his contemporaries related their 'cultures' to 'peoples' and examined their interrelationships, as seen in trait distributions, they also used the burial evidence to infer social distinctions within such cultures. Notable here were interpretations of the existence of Bronze Age 'chiefs' or 'aristocrats', based upon such features as large mounds and rich grave furnishings. Examples of these included the Wessex culture barrows of southern England (Childe 1957), the Unetice culture burials of Helmsdorf, Leubingen (fig. 1.1) and Łęki Małe in Germany and Poland (Gimbutas 1965) and the Argaric culture burials in south-east Spain (Blance 1960). But such interpretations treated the rest of these prehistoric societies as being rather homogenous. One exception to this was the work of the German Otto (1955) on the Unetice culture, from the burials of which he inferred the existence of four levels in a social hierarchy. Warriors and archers were inferred from a number of contexts, while in Scandinavia there was a continuation of the discussion begun in the last century on the status of individuals from Bronze Age mounds (e.g. Moberg 1956). For example it was suggested that craftsmen belonged to the lower levels of society, since tools were not included among 'aristocratic' burials (Brøndsted 1939).

A less speculative basis for social inference existed in North America in the form of ethnological and archaeological research into recent Indian tribal customs and cultures. The observations on mortuary practices among these tribes by early travellers, traders etc., were employed in the interpretation of burial mounds and cemeteries, as can be seen, for example, in the series of Bureau of American Ethnology Bulletins published by the Smithsonian Institution (e.g. Bushnell 1920, 1927). These volumes include references to high-status burials, such as those of particular chiefs, and to sub-groups such as clans and phratries within tribes. To illustrate this point we refer to a quotation from the work of F.H. Cushing on the Tarpon Springs mound on the Gulf of Florida:

> (the skeletons) with notable exception — probably those of chiefs and head men — had been dismembered previously to interment, but were distributed in distinct groups that I regarded as communal or totemic and

phratral, and of exceeding interest; for they seemed to indicate that the burial mound had been regarded by its builders as a tribal settlement, a sort of 'Little City of the Dead', and that, if so, it might be looked on as still, in a measure, representing the distribution and relation of the clans and phratries in an actual village or tribal settlement of these people when living. Moreover in the minor disposition of the skeletons that had not been scattered, but had been buried in parts, or else entire and extended, in sherd-lined graves or wooden cists within and around each of these groups, it seemed possible to still trace somewhat of the relative ranks of individuals in these groups, and not a few of the social customs and religious beliefs of the ancient builders. This possibility was still further borne out by the fact that with the skeletal remains were associated, in different ways, many superb examples of pottery and sacrificial potsherds, and numerous stone, shell and bone utensils, weapons and ornaments.   (quoted in Bushnell 1920, p. 117)

From our side of the Atlantic it seems as if this 'possibility' was not actually realised in early-twentieth-century archaeology and more emphasis was placed upon normative cultural studies of mortuary practices. In addition it is worth noting two points: first that early writers in the nineteenth century often concentrated upon the mortuary rites for higher-status individuals such as chiefs (Swanton 1911); secondly that Kroeber's (1927) view of mortuary practices being classed alongside 'fashions', rather than within the field of social expression, was widely influential. The methodological basis for a social analysis of mortuary practices within archaeology had not been formulated.

Thus the archaeology of death had moved from speculative to chronological and cultural approaches by the early 1960s. At the same time evidence from sources in history, linguistics and physical and social anthropology was introduced to help explain both high-status burials and the appearance of major discontinuities in the archaeological record and in mortuary practices in particular. But the development of

Fig. 1.1. An early Bronze Age 'chieftain' from eastern Germany: the wooden mortuary house under a barrow at Leubingen. Source: Piggott 1965, fig. 67.

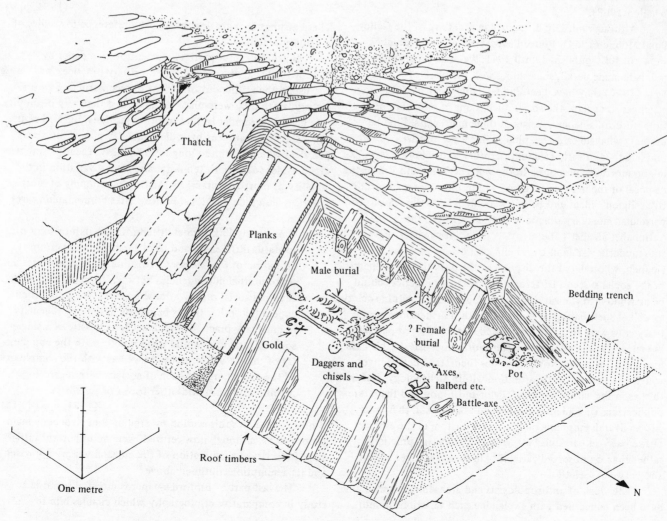

the earlier anthropological perspectives of Durkheim and his followers, linking mortuary practices to social structure, had to wait until the last two decades.

Mortuary practices, society and the New Archaeology

Among the central assertions of the New Archaeology was the denial of any essential limitations on our knowledge of the past. Binford (1968) argued strongly against the pessimistic view, current in the 1950s, that archaeologists could come to reliable conclusions only about the technology and economy of past societies, while social organisation was beyond the limits of reference. In Binford's opinion the adoption of a systemic approach and the search for a theoretical basis upon which archaeologists could construct relationships between material culture and other parts of the total cultural system led the way towards the abandonment of this position. It is important to note that the analysis of mortuary practices played a central role in demonstrating the veracity of this argument. As far as social organisation was concerned, complementary research was undertaken on disposal practices, from both archaeological and anthropological contexts, and on the analysis of structural features and artefact distributions within settlements (e.g. Deetz 1965; Hill 1968; Longacre 1968; Whallon 1968).

Although initially developed in his study of the Galley Pond Mound (1964), Binford's ideas on mortuary practices were not fully published until 1971. We must present his main points in some detail, since along with the work of Arthur Saxe (1970) they have been fundamental to many subsequent attempts to analyse the social dimensions of mortuary practices. Binford's paper consists of three main parts. First he presents what he calls the 'philosophical perspectives' of late-nineteenth- and early-twentieth-century anthropologists working on mortuary practices. In the work of Tylor and Frazer the disposal of the dead was studied within the context of 'primitive religion': ideas and beliefs were invoked as the reasons for particular mortuary practices. Binford refers to this as the 'rationalist-idealist's argument'. A different perspective was subsequently visible in Durkheim's followers, Hertz and van Gennep, who related the disposal of the dead to other aspects of the social system. Differences in mortuary practices could be attributed to the varying status of individuals within society, as well as such factors as mode of death. Furthermore mortuary rites were to be understood like other 'rites of passage', as marking a transition in the status of individuals, in this case into the afterworld. Now it was this theoretical perspective which had received little attention within archaeology. But in this, as in the earlier works of Tylor and Frazer and the later publications of Radcliffe-Brown and Malinowski, there was still an overall emphasis on 'mortuary custom in the abstract or focussed on particular categories of mortuary practices' rather than on observed variability in these practices within and between societies.

The work of anthropologists and archaeologists who have been concerned with explaining such variations in mor-

tuary practices forms the second part of Binford's paper. Such approaches are referred to as 'historical-distributional' and were exemplified in the cultural studies of mortuary practices outlined above. Binford's critique of these approaches in relation to mortuary practices forms an integral part of his general attack on the practice of culture history (cf. Binford 1965, 1972). He summarises the assumptions of this approach as follows:

> (1) Culture is a body of custom which arises in the context of the conceptual-intellectual life of peoples; it distributionally varies directly as a function of the patterns of transmission and communication among peoples, and with the differential capacities or opportunities for intellectual experience . . .
> (2) The customs of a single sociocultural tradition were originally uniform and formally distinct . . .
>
> Multiple practices observed among sociocultural units result from cultural mixing or hybridization in the past . . .
> (3) For practical purposes, the degree of formal similarity observed among independent sociocultural units is a direct measure of the degree of genetic or affiliational cultural relationship among the units being compared.
>
> (1971, p. 9)

These assumptions are documented by reference to studies of mortuary practices.

Binford devotes particular attention to a paper by Kroeber (1927), who argued that mortuary practices may be less useful than other cultural traits in reconstructing cultural history, since they were unstable and owed that very instability to a behaviour similar to that of other fashions. Binford refutes the instability argument by indicating examples of mortuary practices which exhibited long-term stability. Clearly there was much evidence for both temporal and spatial variation in the stability of mortuary practices. As for the grouping of mortuary practices alongside 'fashions' Binford cites ethnographic cases which

> consistently link formal differentiation in mortuary rites to status differences and to differences in the group affiliation of the deceased. This linkage demonstrates a set of mutual dependencies between forms of mortuary rites and social organizational features. We would then expect that other things being equal, the heterogeneity in mortuary practices which is characteristic of a single sociocultural unit would vary directly with the complexity of the status hierarchy, as well as with the complexity of the overall organization of society with regard to membership units and other forms of sodalities.
>
> (1971, pp. 14–15)

Binford concludes this section by arguing that Kroeber's main propositions, although now refuted, were an important initial stage in a critical examination of the cultural-history approach and its assumptions outlined above.

The last part of Binford's paper is directed towards a study in comparative ethnography which enables him to evaluate the success or failure of the culture history approach to the study of mortuary practices. He begins by arguing that the forms taken by symbols in mortuary practices should not be confused with what is actually being symbolised. Thus different disposal methods (e.g. inhumation, cremation) may have had a different significance in different societies (cf. Haglund 1976). Simply to compare these symbols and deduce some formal relationship between several societies, as is done in the culture-history school, becomes an illusory exercise. But what aspects of social organisation may be symbolised?

It is proposed here that there are two general components of the social situation to be evaluated when attempting to understand the types of social phenomena symbolized in any given burial situation. First is what we may call, with Goodenough . . . the *social persona* of the deceased. This is a composite of the social identities maintained in life and recognized as appropriate for consideration after death. Second is the composition and size of the social group recognizing status responsibilities to the deceased. We would expect direct correlations between the relative rank of the social position held by the deceased and the number of persons having duty-status relationships vis-a-vis the deceased . . . Also we would expect that the facets of the *social persona* symbolically recognized in the mortuary ritual would shift with the levels of corporate participation in the ritual and hence vary directly with the relative rank of the social position which the deceased occupied in life.

(Binford 1971, p. 17)

The main dimensions of the social persona which are recognised in mortuary practices are age, sex, social position, social affiliation and conditions and location of death.

Preliminary tests of these propositions are provided on a sample of 40 non-state societies taken from the Human Relations Area files. First a calculation was made of the average number of dimensional distinctions for four different subsistence types, hunter-gatherers, shifting agriculturalists, settled agriculturalists and pastoralists, which Binford argued represented 'a very crude index' of societal complexity. The results (table 1.1) show an interesting difference between settled agriculturalists and the other three. Secondly, the frequency with which the dimensions of the social persona were recognised in the mortuary practices of these different subsistence types was tabulated (table 1.2). The results gave some support to Binford's contention that, with increases in social complexity, the dimensions of social position and affiliation assume greater importance in mortuary practices. Thirdly Binford discussed correlations between the different dimensions of the social persona recognised in mortuary practices and the form which those practices took (table 1.3).

This analysis led Binford to employ his conclusions relating 'the form and structure which characterize the mortuary practices of any society' to 'the form and complexity of the organizational characteristics of the society itself' (1971, p. 23) to attack each of the three assumptions of the culture

Table 1.1. *Source: Binford 1971, table II.*

Subsistence category	Average number of dimensional distinctions per category
Hunters and gatherers	1.73
Shifting agriculturalists	1.75
Settled agriculturalists	3.14
Pastoralists	1.66

historian (see above). Mortuary practices are no longer to be used as indications of cultural diffusion or 'fashions', but rather they should be analysed within the context of variations in society and social complexity.

A similar concern with the potential of mortuary practices for social analysis was visible in Saxe's doctoral dissertation (1970), although he was less concerned with using this body of data to strike at the roots of traditional archaeology. Like Binford he argued that mortuary practices could be analysed within the context of the social system and emphasised that this approach required a concern with processual rather than formal regularities (1970, p. 1). The formal comparison of disposal methods told us little about the organisation of mortuary practices and what they actually symbolised. Saxe also adopted a cross-cultural perspective to test eight hypotheses regarding the organisation of mortuary practices in three societies: the Kapauku Papuans of New Guinea, the Ashanti of West Africa and the Bontoc Igorot of Luzon (Philippines). This more detailed study must be seen as essentially complementary to Binford's broader examination of the ethnographic record. Both used the concepts of role theory (e.g. social identity and social persona). Saxe's formal analysis of the mortuary practices of these three societies was employed to define disposal types which represented different social personae: in the case of the Bontoc nine such personae were recognised, such as old respected men, married/unmarried males/females and children less than seven years old. The eight hypotheses received variable support from these three societies, but what is important is that these modern test cases confirmed the social approach to mortuary practices argued by Binford.

It is important to note that the Binford/Saxe hypotheses and philosophical perspectives have formed the basis of many social analyses of mortuary practices undertaken in the last decade. One of Saxe's hypotheses, relating disposal areas to corporate groups, has been further tested by Goldstein (1976, this volume), while Tainter has expanded upon Binford's ideas to link energy expenditure in mortuary practices to the rank of the deceased in a sample of 103 ethnographic cases (1973a, 1975a). This proposition has also received support from contemporary American society. Rathje (1979, pp. 5—6) reports the results of work on Tucson cemeteries which show correlations between the deceased's job/income level and the form of the grave marker. Although sample size was small, a study

Table 1.2. *Source: Binford 1971, table III.*

Dimensional distinctions	Hunter-gatherers	Shifting agriculturalists	Settled agriculturalists	Pastoralists
Conditions of death	1	0	6	1
Location of death	1	1	0	0
Age	2	1	7	1
Sex	12	4	10	3
Social position	6	5	11	0
Social affiliation	4	3	10	1
Total cases	15	8	14	3

Table 1.3. *Source: Binford 1971, table IV.*

	Conditions of death	Location of death	Age	Sex	Social position	Social affiliation
Body						
(1) Preparation	–	–	–	–	2	–
(2) Treatment	2	1	–	–	2	2
(3) Disposition	2	1	3	–	2	1
Grave						
(4) Form	1	–	1	–	3	1
(5) Orientation	–	–	–	3	–	9
(6) Location	3	–	7	–	8	15
Furniture						
(7) Form only	–	–	–	16	5	–
(8) Quantity only	–	–	–	–	9	–
(9) Form and quantity	–	–	–	–	7	–

of the mortuary practices of Mexican-American families also provided examples of the cause of death (e.g. breast cancer, drug overdose) being more important than the deceased's socio-economic status in deciding the energy expended on the funeral. Lastly it was suggested that in periods of political or economic stress the presence of the deceased's family and religious affiliations on the grave marker would increase. Another contemporary example of the use of grave markers to symbolise such attributes of the deceased comes from rural cemeteries of the last hundred years in Hungary: differences of size, shape (fig. 1.2) and colour were and are still employed to symbolise religious affiliation, age, sex, marital status, social status, profession and way of death (Zentai 1979). In accordance with Binford's expectations the use of such symbols varies between communities, so that the same dimension (e.g. age) may be symbolised by different forms (e.g. different colours of grave posts).

The social perspectives of mortuary practices have by no means convinced all archaeologists. Some, including a large number of British archaeologists, still prefer to view the disposal of the dead within the context of 'intangible' religious beliefs. Thus Piggott has stated that 'grave archaeology from the start presents us with evidence which is the product of complex mental situations and emotional states now irrecoverable' (1973, p. 10; cf. Wilson 1976, p. 3) and places this study 'within the field of religion' (1973, p. 14). Those archaeologists who follow this line of interpretation also show unease with the use of ethnographic evidence and derive support from a cautionary paper by Ucko (1969). Among other things he pointed out that burial practices are not necessarily indicative of afterworld beliefs, that grave goods do not always reach the grave, that absence of grave goods does not necessarily imply low status or poverty, large funerary structures do not always reflect rulers or chiefs and that body orientation varies in many ways. This variation observed in ethnographic studies disturbed many archaeologists (e.g. Hunter 1975, p. 80), all of whom seem to have neglected Ucko's two most important generalisations. First there may be many similarities in the disposal of the dead which do not reflect contact between people (1969, p. 275). Secondly 'in the vast majority of cases known ethnographically, a culture or society is not characterised by one type of burial only, but . . . on the contrary, one society will undertake several different forms of burial, and . . . these forms will often be correlated with the status of the deceased' (1969,

p. 270). In both cases Ucko is echoing the conclusions of Binford and Saxe.

Within the social approach to mortuary practices attention has been focussed upon the detection of ranking in prehistoric societies by analysis of their individual cemeteries (Tainter 1978; Brown, this volume). Concern with a more regional approach has been limited (e.g. Randsborg 1975*a*, *b*). James Brown (this volume) documents three major arguments that have been employed in the analysis of ranking. First there is the effort-expenditure principle proposed by Binford (1971) and expanded by Tainter (1973*a*, 1975*a*, 1978), who proposes that 'higher social rank of a deceased individual will correspond to greater amounts of corporate involvement and activity disruption, and this should result in the expenditure of greater amounts of energy in the interment ritual' (1978, p. 125). This energy expenditure will be reflected in the complexity of body treatment, the location and construction of the burial container and the extent and duration of ritual mortuary behaviour. Problems arise in the actual measurement of energy expenditure (Tainter 1978, p. 128; Goldstein, this volume), in the possible noise generated by parallel status relationships (Goldstein, this volume) and in the possible confusion of rank differences with stages in the interment ritual of individuals (Brown, this volume; Tainter 1978, p. 128). Secondly there is the argument that certain artefacts and attributes symbolise authority within society and that when these can be shown to cross-cut age/sex/personal quality distinctions, then some form of ranking is indicated (e.g. Stickel 1968; Larson 1971; Peebles 1971; Shennan 1975; but note also examples where such symbols do not cross-cut sex differences, but ranking is still indicated – e.g. Randsborg 1975*b*). Apart from the problems of preservation of such symbols in the archaeological record, the reliance upon this sole dimension of mortuary practices has been criticised. Indeed Tainter has published results of a cross-cultural survey which show that less than 5% of a sample of 93 societies used grave goods to symbolise status differences (1978, p. 121). Thirdly there is the demographic structure of skeletal populations and its agreement with or departure from that which would be expected in a 'normal' population.

Techniques used in the analysis of prehistoric mortuary practices have ranged from relatively simple tests of significance of association between age, sex and grave goods (fig. 1.3; e.g. Milisauskas 1978; Saxe 1971), to the nearest-neighbour analysis of burials within cemeteries to detect the nature of their spatial patterning (e.g. Peebles 1971; Tainter 1976) and computer programmes for cluster analysis (fig. 1.4; e.g. Shennan 1975; Hodson 1977), monothetic-divisive analysis (e.g. Tainter 1975*b*; King 1978), principal-components analysis (van de Velde 1979) and formal analysis (fig. 1.5; e.g. Saxe 1970; Brown 1971*a*). The use of entropy measurement, derived from information theory, has been recommended by Tainter both as an aid to formal analysis (1978) and in the detection of the degree of organisation reflected in the mortuary practices of past social systems (1977*b*, 1978). There have also been case-studies of the relative efficiency of these different techniques applied to the same data. Tainter (1975*b*) concludes that monothetic-divisive methods are most successful in isolating burial clusters, but Mainfort (1977) is less conclusive: while monothetic-divisive methods distinguished high-status burials they were less successful in dividing up the medium- to low-status burials, a pattern which was exactly reversed by the use of cluster analysis. In geographical range these analyses have covered hunter-fisher-gatherers from California (e.g. King 1969; Stickel 1968; King 1978) to the Sudan (Saxe 1971) and ranked societies from the eastern United States (e.g. Brown 1971*b*; Peebles and Kus 1977; Greber 1976; Mainfort 1977; Rothschild 1979; Brown, this volume; Goldstein, this volume) to Bronze Age Czechoslovakia (Shennan 1975).

Many of these studies have been concerned with using these techniques to place prehistoric societies on an evolutionary scale, such as Service's 'bands', 'tribes' and 'chiefdoms' and Fried's 'egalitarian', 'ranked' and 'stratified' societies (e.g. Brown 1971*b*; Peebles and Kus 1977; Chapman 1977, 1980). Such an approach has come under criticism as being concerned with rather general classification as opposed to detailed analysis and actual measurement of social variation (Tainter 1977*a*, 1978).

From this discussion it can be seen that the philosophy and methodology of the social approach to mortuary practices

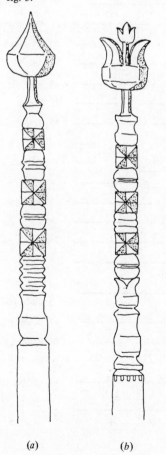

Fig. 1.2. Examples of knobbed headboards from Alsora Kosol (Transylvania): (a) male, (b) female. Source: Zentai 1979, fig. 3.

(a) (b)

played an integral part in the emergency of the New Archae-ology. Within that tradition comparative ethnography has pro-vided the source for hypotheses relating the disposal of the dead to the organisation of human societies and quantitative analyses have been applied to an ever-increasing number of individual cemeteries. The detection of co-varying patterns of age, sex and grave goods within such cemeteries has led to a proliferating discussion on the degree of ranking exhibited by

past societies, whether or not an evolutionary typology was applied. While this concern with social analysis has been an invigorating corrective to the excessive concern with economic archaeology which characterised some areas of the discipline in the 1960s, a more critical evaluation is now necessary. Such an evolution is already in evidence for some of the major theor-etical and procedural bases of the New Archaeology (e.g. Schiffer 1978; Dunnell 1979) and there seems no reason why it should not be directed towards mortuary analyses. Specifi-cally, which problems remain unsolved and undiscussed and which new areas of research promise to further our under-standing of the nature of past societies?

Formation and transformation

One of the basic assumptions of the New Archaeology was that human behaviour left a fossilised record in the form of spatial patterns of variation and co-variation of artefacts

Fig. 1.3. Association of burial data with age and sex groups from the late fourth-millennium bc cemetery at Tiszapolgar-Basatanya (Hungary). Note the examples of highly significant associations with males and females. Source: Milisauskas 1978, fig. 6.25.

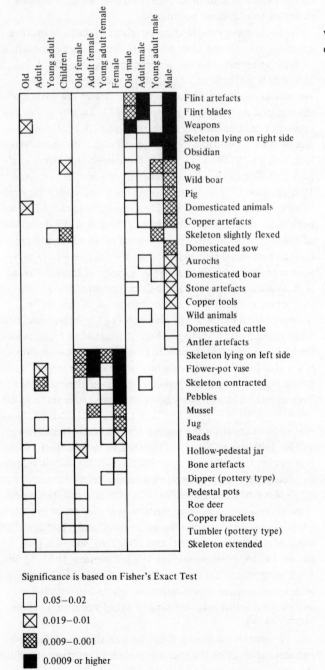

Fig. 1.4. Single-link cluster analysis of functional artefact-types regularly associated in 'good' graves from the early Iron Age cemetery at Hallstatt, Austria. Source: Hodson 1977, fig. 3.

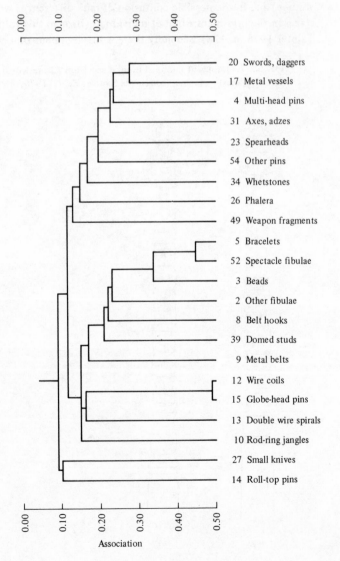

and features on archaeological sites. Thus the key to perceiving this behaviour lay in the use of appropriate quantitative analyses through which patterning could be isolated. More recently there has been a greater concern with the nature of the archaeological record and its formation (e.g. Schiffer 1976). How are we to understand patterning in the archaeological record if we lack an understanding of the many processes, both cultural and non-cultural, through which it came into existence? As usual Binford expresses the problem directly:

> Every archaeologist must accept the following challenge: archaeological observations are contemporary facts and they are static facts. Our job is to make meaningful observations about the past from contemporary facts and to make meaningful statements about dynamics from static facts. In order to accomplish this, the archaeologist must have a strong body of theory — middle range theory — which guides him in making statements about dynamics from observed statics. In short, we must have a strong and well-founded understanding of the formation processes of the archaeological record.
>
> (Binford and Bertram 1977, p. 77)

The conceptual basis of middle-range theory has been elaborated by Schiffer (1972, 1976) in his distinction between the present archaeological context and the past systemic context. The transformation from the latter to the former by the operation of various cultural and non-cultural processes is discussed at length. The analyses of such formation processes have been pursued in the context of refuse disposal and its associated spatial patterning (e.g. South 1979) and the formation of lithic assemblages (Schiffer 1976) and faunal assemblages (e.g. Binford 1978).

In this context it seems surprising that there has been little explicit concern with the formation processes of mortuary practices. The disposal of the dead, and burial in particular, represents what O'Shea (this volume, p. 39) refers to as 'the direct and purposeful culmination of conscious behaviour, rather than its incidental residue'. Indeed Schiffer (1976, pp. 31—2) includes disposal of the dead alongside discard, loss and abandonment in one of four types of cultural formation processes. Quite correctly he notes that the attempts to relate methods of disposal of the dead to social organisation represent a welcome advance in the archaeologist's understanding of cultural formation processes. But as O'Shea argues, 'the existing theory of mortuary differentiation has concentrated on statements which specify the relationship between the organisation of a living society and its practices for the disposal of the dead. It fails to predict the additional relationship between

Fig. 1.5. An example of formal analysis. Key diagram of burial attributes from the Spiro civic-ceremonial centre of the Mississippian period in the southeastern United States. Source: Brown 1971*a*, table 1.

Burial behaviour			Grave behaviour					
Degree of skeletal articulation (diminishing from bottom to top)	Disposition of skeletal remains	Numbers in burial	Arrangement of burial	Inclusion within facility	Occurrence as solitary or group burial	Sex	Age group	Burial type
Disarticulated	unspecific	single	specialised	with container	isolated and grouped	male?	adult and child	XIa, XIb, XII
		single and multiple	specialised	with container	grouped	?	adult	XIII
			unspecialised	without container	N/A	male and female	adult	VIa, VIb
	specific	single?	specialised	without container	?	male?	adult	X
		single and multiple	unspecialised	without container	N/A	male and female	adult	VII, VIII, IX
Partly disarticulated	unspecific	multiple	unspecialised	without container	isolated	male and female	adult	IV
	specific	multiple	unspecialised	without container	isolated and grouped	male and female	adult	V
		single	unspecialised	without container	isolated and grouped	male and female	adult	II
					isolated	male and female	adult and child	IIIa
Articulated	specific	single	unspecialised	without container	isolated	male and female	adult	I

these mortuary practices and their archaeological observation, which is, of course, the evidence on which any social reconstruction will be based' (p. 40). In an important contribution to the study of transformational processes, he presents his analysis of five cemeteries dating to the late eighteenth and early nineteenth centuries in the North American Central Plains. Both 'horizontal' (e.g. descent groups, societies) and 'vertical' (ranked) social divisions were known from ethno-historical sources. In all cases the principal-components and cluster analyses of the cemeteries were able to distinguish social ranking, but horizontal divisions were less successfully isolated. O'Shea argues that this difference in archaeological visibility is due to the fact that the horizontal groups were distinguished by their pre-interment rituals, body preparation and the inclusion of mainly organic items as grave goods. In contrast ranking was expressed in elaborate grave construction and the types and quantities of grave goods, which were inherently more likely to survive in the archaeological record. The potential ambiguity involved in the interpretation of horizontal differentiation is made clear (cf. Tainter 1978, p. 131) and also arises in the context of attempting to dis-

tinguish important social distinctions from unconstrained or idiosyncratic patterning.

In addition to the non-preservation of aspects of mortuary practices (e.g. skeletal materials, clothing, organic grave goods), it has also been long known that disposal methods do not all have equal chances of preservation in the archaeological record. Tree burials and simple exposure are obvious examples (plate 1.1). Among the southern Kikuyu bodies of certain types of individuals will be dragged out into the bush for hyenas to consume; alternatively houses containing dead individuals may have their doors blocked, a hole cut in the back and the hyenas allowed to enter and remove the corpses during the night (Leakey 1977). Archaeological examples of periods for which the burial record is incomplete or absent (e.g. large areas of the British Iron Age – Whimster 1977) are well known and must be evaluated against the effects of other formation processes to determine whether their frequency is representative or distorted (for sampling bias, see Goldstein, this volume).

There are many cases where the deceased's possessions or offerings to the deceased are not placed within the grave.

Plate 1.1. A scaffold burial: Indians offering food to the dead. Source: Schoolcraft 1851, plate 3.

These come within the bounds of Schiffer's S-S processes 'which do not result in cultural deposition or in modification of extant deposits' (1976, p. 29). Several of Ucko's examples of burials which do not reflect the actual status or funeral rites of the dead can be seen within this context, rather than simply as isolated ethnographic cautionary tales. These include the LoDagaa and Lober of Ghana and the Yoruba of Nigeria: among the latter the most important cult priests are accorded magnificent funerals, with a great display of valuables, but these are not then included among the grave goods (1969, p. 267). One must also remember examples of periods during which goods may be inherited rather than consumed in graves: during the seventh century in England, Anglo-Saxon barrows show a decline in the deposition of grave goods which can be attributed, through the use of literary evidence, to their inheritance by the heir(s) of the deceased (Shephard 1979, p. 58). Clearly, erroneous conclusions can be reached when such examples of particular formation processes are not considered. Thus Tainter (1978) notes the case of the Modoc of northern California, who would be revealed to the archaeologist measuring types and frequencies of grave goods as an apparently egalitarian society: unfortunately goods are removed from the funeral pyre by individuals attending the last rites and evidence for ranking by these criteria becomes less visible.

Other cultural formation processes which deserve formal consideration relate to both past and present activities. For the past, problems of secondary interment or multiple phases of mortuary activity must be disentangled. Within the Old World considerable problems are posed in the isolation of the sequence of constructional and ritual activities associated with megalithic tombs (see Kinnes, this volume). But even with less complex modes of disposal problems may arise. Are we always sure that the groups of burials distinguished by such techniques as cluster analysis reflect different social groups or personae, rather than different stages in what Meehan (Haglund 1976, pp. 11–17) refers to as 'compound' rather than 'simple' disposal methods? Even if the archaeologist successfully solves these difficulties he may still come to grief if the units of time within which he works when analysing mortuary practices are too broad. Even a single cemetery may exhibit changes in social organisation and its representation within the period of its use. As Goldstein (this volume) writes, 'the time depth must be regarded with respect to the rate of social change in the prehistoric society. What we may interpret as different ranks may in fact represent changes in funerary behaviour through time' (pp. 56–7). Periods of rapid social change have to be viewed through a currently inadequate chronological filter in many areas of the world.

When one moves to the discovery and analysis of the present archaeological record of mortuary practices, the evaluation of data recovery and the nature of the available samples are of continued importance. Activity here ranges from the estimation of excavation strategies and their reliability (e.g. Chapman 1980) to the study of current knowledge of different disposal types and the sometimes intense problems posed by their differential preservation and often random methods of discovery over a period of at least a century. Within Neolithic western Europe, monumental tombs are inherently more likely to be known to the archaeologist than the isolated flat graves which may be located within close proximity (e.g. Bakker and van der Waals 1973). Common methods of discovery such as ploughing may well result in the disproportionate representation of different burial methods. Analysis by Balkwill (1976) of later prehistoric flat graves in the Rhineland has revealed that preservation from disturbance and the likelihood of discovery were both related to the depth of the inhumations and cremations below the ground surface (fig. 1.6).

Clearly then, different types of formation processes affect the nature of the archaeological record. The task which the archaeologist faces, as Schiffer puts it, is 'one of modeling the transformations wrought by formation processes on systemic materials to produce the archeological structure' (1976, p. 43). Within behavioural archaeology this has been done by using either flow models to show the 'life history' of both organic and inorganic materials or behavioural chains to show different stages of cultural activities and their archaeological residues. In the context of mortuary practices and their interpretation in terms of past human behaviour, we clearly have to consider the generation of archaeologically recoverable patterns. At the same time, if we are genuinely interested in the erection of a body of theory which may be used to formulate archaeologically testable hypotheses, then we must also focus attention upon the process of decision-making which lies behind the successive stages in ritual and burial. Formal analysis was introduced into archaeology in the hope that it might fulfil such a function (Brown, this volume). But its application to model the mortuary practices of contemporary or recent societies (Saxe 1970; Brown 1971*a*) raises distinct problems. It has also become abundantly clear that traditional ethnographies of mortuary practices have considerable defects (see also the section on spatial patterning and society below). Periods of fieldwork which are of short or intermittent duration cannot hope to yield information on the full range of decision-

Fig. 1.6. Frequency of depth recorded for 56 graves from 55 later prehistoric flat-grave cemeteries in the Upper Rhine valley. At a depth of 1 m, 80% of cremations but only 50% of inhumations will have been discovered. Source: Balkwill 1976, fig. 9.

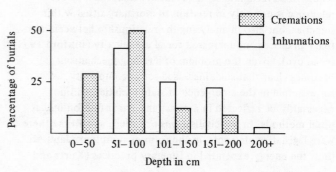

making processes which take place within societies when individuals of different rank and status die. Reliance on a limited number of informants raises the problem of inadequate samples of individual models of cultural behaviour practised within any social group. Problems such as these, leading to a tendency to underestimate the variations of behaviour in mortuary practices, and the decisions upon which these variations depend, have been discussed recently by Levine (1977). In a period of nineteen months he observed eleven funerals and attempted to model the decision-making processes of each using flow charts. He was concerned particularly with the large number of factors which determined which individuals took decisions about the funeral (e.g. age, status, residence). While he concluded that different types of mortuary rituals may be correlated with aspects of social identities (as predicted by Binford and Saxe), it was by no means a straightforward relationship. For one thing the people in charge of the funeral activities may vary over a period of several days. What is of interest to the archaeologist here is the extent to which this variation may affect his ability to differentiate between individuals and groups within societies. The scope for further fieldwork designed to examine decision-making processes and their relationship to social identities is evident.

Any consideration of decision-making processes must also include examination of cultural values and attitudes towards death. Huntington and Metcalf make this point when they write that 'in all societies . . . the issue of death throws into relief the most important cultural values by which people live their lives and evaluate their experiences' (1979, p. 2). They follow Geertz in arguing that 'death and its rituals not only reflect social values, but are an important force in shaping them' (p. 5). The importance of such factors as these has been emphasised recently by Okely, in her discussion of the mortuary practices of British gypsies (1979). Her most significant conclusion is that 'an archaeologist examining graves needs to be alert to the possibility that the identity, social structure and ideology of the living may have been inverted or disguised in death' (1979, p. 86). In Saudi Arabia it has been noted that dead kings are buried simply under stone piles rather than being distinguished by any rich or monumental interment. This practice must be seen in the context of the more extreme Islamic emphasis on the way death acts as a 'levelling' force (Huntington and Metcalf 1979, p. 122). In Africa the unified Islamic burial rite has been outlined by Alexander (1979). Where observations such as these have their most direct relevance is not only in relation to mortuary ritual within societies, but also in analysing the relationship between mortuary practices and increased social complexity (Binford 1971, see above). Given the problem of levelling mechanisms it becomes clear that such increased social complexity, as seen for example in the emergence of state societies, will not necessarily be reflected in a direct and linear fashion in disposal methods. In the civilisations of Greece and Rome there were legislative attempts, in the form of sumptuary laws, to limit the energy expended in funerary practices (Kurtz and

Boardman 1971; Toynbee 1971). Even in modern American society, with its noted cultural heterogeneity, there are many uniform features in funeral practices which can be understood in terms of attitudes towards death and dying (Huntington and Metcalf 1979).

Now consideration of attitudes towards death and processes of decision-making inevitably involves us in the question of cognition. Indeed social anthropologists such as Okely are working within a framework different from that of the archaeologist. This gives rise to the question whether this framework of cognitive analysis is of relevance to the archaeologist. On one level we would argue that this has yet to be demonstrated and that the student of material culture is ill equipped to formulate testable hypotheses about attitudes towards death in past societies. But on another level altogether, a productive approach to the analysis of past mortuary practices cannot ignore the lesson that social divisions are not necessarily directly and unambiguously reflected in mortuary data. The evaluation of social complexity on the basis of relative numbers of burial types should be re-examined in this light. Within Danish prehistory there are periods when the social ranking finds explicit recognition in mortuary practices and other periods when it does not (Randsborg 1980). What matters here is that the archaeologist evaluates the degree to which the mortuary data do reflect the social structure by analysis of complementary data (e.g. settlements and settlement patterns, metal hoards etc.). This appears to be a far more profitable line of argument than to take examples of inversion or levelling to castigate social archaeologists with charges of stunning naivety and excessive, unfounded optimism. It will also take the archaeologist further along the road towards an understanding of the meaning and expression of cultural reactions to death.

Spatial patterning and society

The spatial patterning of graves within cemeteries and cemeteries within settlement landscapes forms an important dimension of the mortuary practices of any community. This patterning should be studied alongside the form of the interment, the treatment of the body, the nature and frequency of the grave goods and the demographic and biological attributes of the interred population in a multidimensional analysis. Although some attempts have been made to pursue a spatial analysis at the intra-cemetery level, the definition and analysis of the cemetery location within human-settlement landscapes have attracted little attention. But even when spatial patterning is defined (whether by quantitative or visual methods – Goldstein, this volume), there remains the problem of its meaning in terms of human behaviour. The following discussion makes no claim to solve this problem, but it does suggest what we consider to be profitable areas of enquiry.

At the intra-cemetery level we must examine spatial patterning both within and between graves or interments. Within graves the spatial dimension and its symbolic meaning has only recently begun to receive attention. Pader (1980) has followed the example of recent work in the study of material culture symbolism and attempted to apply it to mortuary remains. Her analysis of the early Anglo-Saxon cemetery at Holywell Row (Suffolk, England) in terms of both the grave assemblages and the positioning of grave goods and skeletons within the grave is of interest for two reasons. First she shows how in some cases the *form* of grave goods used may vary but the spatial *structure* within the grave remains the same. Secondly Pader demonstrates that non-random spatial clusters of graves could be defined on the basis of the positioning of goods and skeletal material within graves, while consideration of grave assemblages alone revealed a random distribution. Clearly here is another dimension of mortuary practices which requires analysis.

Archaeologists have used both visual and numerical techniques to isolate spatial patterns within cemeteries. Visual recognition of clusters or rows of graves within central European early Bronze Age cemeteries has been interpreted in terms of familial groupings (Coles and Harding 1979). Distribution of kinship, sex or status groups in different spatial patterns within Iron Age European cemeteries has also received comment, as well as linear or centrifugal patterns in the overall layout of graves within cemeteries (Hodson 1979). Nearest-neighbour analysis has been used in a number of studies to isolate non-random patterning in the distribution of grave types and assemblages (e.g. King 1969; Peebles 1971; Tainter 1976). Whatever techniques are used, analysis along single dimensions of mortuary practices will be insufficient. What the archaeologist is aiming for is the definition of spatial patterns which can be interpreted as the results of conscious or unconscious human behaviour. Consequently environmental constraints (e.g. topography, soil depth, water table etc.) on grave location must be considered in order to avoid confusion with social constraints. As for the latter there are certainly good examples from ethnography of different areas within cemeteries being allotted to different social groups (e.g. Ucko 1969). On the other hand little attention has been given to cemeteries which remain in use over generations, if not centuries: what is the nature of the changing relationship between the availability of space within the cemetery and the decisions taken by the living community about the form and location of interment of different age, sex and status groups? Indeed by such decisions the community may or may not choose to reflect social affiliation or status through the spatial dimension. Where they do the results may sometimes be seen as clear, unequivocal statements of social or kinship relationships. In rural Hungarian cemeteries the different generations of individual families are mapped out in rows which radiate out from the ancestral grave, while the inter-marrying of families may be represented by linear patterns (fig. 1.7; Zentai 1979).

There is no inherent reason why there should be a one-to-one correlation between cemeteries and settlements. The association of a settlement with a single cemetery is only one example of the possible range of associations known from ethnographic and archaeological sources. There are many cases

from ethnography which show interment of different status groups and categories of social personae at discrete locations (e.g. Ucko 1969). Saxe (1970, p. 160) writes of the Ashanti that 'unless the archaeologist were to excavate the total settlement system or a stratified sample of it he would not find the separate disposal areas which in concert represent the range of corporate land-holding groups and social personae'. Clearly assessment must be made of the range of disposal types and areas used by individual communities. The archaeologist's use of age and sex data from excavated burials will certainly help him to predict the existence of unknown or invisible disposal types. The increasing intensity of modern archaeological survey has also ensured that earlier settlement landscapes (including field systems, settlements and cemeteries) are becoming available for study. We will return to the potential of this evidence later. Cases may also be cited where more than one residential unit may make use of a particular cemetery. For

Fig. 1.7. Map of cemetery at Kunsziget, Győz-Sopron county, Hungary. I–III mark family groups laid out in generational rows with the founders in apical position. IV shows a linear grouping, resulting from the intermarriage of two families in the nineteenth century: the two family heads are in graves 1 and 3. Collateral relatives are on the right side and blood relatives on the left. Source: Zentai 1979, fig. 1.

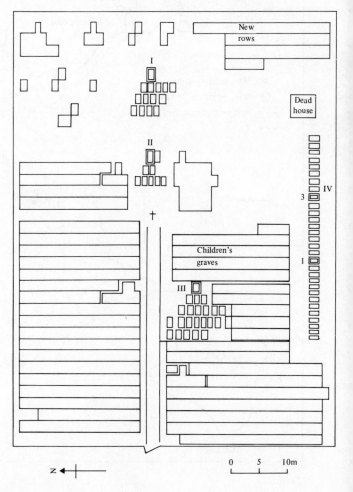

example the Kaloko cemetery (North Kona, Hawaii) services
the dead from four discrete residential areas up to half a
kilometre away (fig. 1.8; Tainter and Cordy 1977). Archaeological evidence exists for the same type of association elsewhere. In the Sancton area of the Yorkshire Wolds in England
an early Anglo-Saxon cremation cemetery was located
immediately beyond the cultivable land of several settlements
and the excavator has argued that it was used by all of these
communities (Faull 1976, p. 233). What is then interesting is
that inhumation cemeteries were later attached to the individual settlements, perhaps with the communal cemetery continuing in usage. Thus the archaeologist is able to look at

longer-term changes in the numbers and distribution of disposal areas in relation to the settlement landscape.

It is one thing to discover such patterning, but further
problems remain. What factors determine the location of
cemeteries or monumental tombs in the settlement landscape?
What choices and constraints govern the precise locations, the
distance and direction from contemporary settlements and the
relationship to patterns of economic exploitation and land
division? A rapid survey of traditional ethnographic sources
for America and Africa suggests that insufficient information
was collected on the location of disposal areas and the factors
governing the choice of their location. For example in the

Fig. 1.8. Archaeological features, including common cemetery and residential clusters (Groups A–D),
at Kaloko, North Kona, Hawaii. Source: Tainter and Cordy 1977, fig. 1.

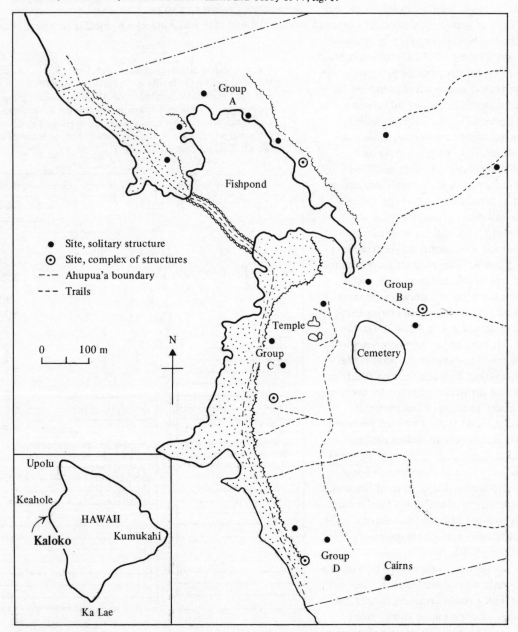

Bureau of American Ethnology Bulletins published by the Smithsonian Institution, there are occasional references to the location of cemeteries (e.g. on hill-tops, behind villages, on the edges of woods), few details on distance from settlements or the sharing of cemeteries by different residential groups and scarce information on the actual choice of location. One might expect consideration to have been given to prevailing patterns of land use, so that disposal areas did not compete for space with critical resources. Where this expectation is not fulfilled, whether in an ethnographic or an archaeological context, we may be justified in the inference that the determinants of burial location were not dominated by economic necessity. Topographical constraints on the location, form and size of cemeteries must also be borne in mind. Similarly visibility and intervisibility of interment sites and settlements deserve fuller examination.

Above all else a satisfactory approach to cemetery location will only arise from a balanced view of both symbolic and functional factors. The symbolism of funerary sites and monuments has been discussed by archaeologists in rather general ways, as, for example, in Renfrew's reference to European megalithic tombs as 'territorial markers' (1976). It is worth reminding ourselves at this point of a recent definition of symbols:

> Symbols are objects, acts, relationships or linguistic formations that stand ambiguously for a multiplicity of meanings, evoke emotions and impel men to action. They usually occur in stylised patterns of activities, such as ritual, ceremonial, gift exchange, prescribed patterns of joking, taking an oath, eating and drinking together, acts of etiquette and various cultural traits that constitute the style of life of a group. (Cohen 1974, p. 23)

Although symbolism featured in early publications using the social approach to mortuary practices (Binford 1971), we feel that it is only now beginning to receive fuller consideration (e.g. Pader 1980). But the symbolic factors influencing the location of disposal areas have yet to receive archaeological attention. Examples from ethnography are of interest here. Saxe has noted that the ruling clan of each Ashanti village has its cemetery located at its village centre, with pathways radiating from it (1970). Thus the Ashanti conception of the social order is expressed symbolically in the location of the ruling cemetery. Archaeologists interested in the generation of models for cemetery location might fruitfully look also at cosmological beliefs in ethnographic contexts. For example Hall has quoted an account of the Blackfoot Indians, who placed their graves on the opposite side of the river from each village, because of their belief in the power of water as a boundary to ward off spirits and ghosts (1976, p. 361). In a similar vein examples can be quoted of societies who buried their dead on uninhabited islands near the shore (Hall 1976, p. 361; Bosi 1960, pp. 137–8). Once again we have moved into an area of cognitive analysis but it is surely right that we look to the ethnographic record if we wish to erect a theoretical framework for the analysis of the spatial patterning of mortuary practices.

Analysis on both local and regional levels cannot fail to make use of the results of both intensive and extensive surveys, which have provided some of the most exciting developments in field archaeology in the last decade. The emerging potential for detailed analysis of the settlement landscapes with their settlements, cemeteries and land boundaries is now becoming apparent. This tradition of field archaeology has a long ancestry in north-west Europe, but the point has now been reached when analysis should begin to relate the landscape of the dead to that of the living. To take one example, the excellent fieldwork of Klindt-Jensen on the Iron Age settlement of north-east Bornholm (Denmark) provides the basis for the analysis of the location of graves in relation to farmsteads (fig. 1.9): in this case the graves appear to be located beyond the infield cultivated area and not in direct association with the farmsteads. British prehistoric land boundaries and field systems have been synthesised recently (Bowen and Fowler 1978) and the long-awaited attempt to relate prehistoric cemeteries to their settlements can be seen, for example, in Bradley's discussion of the middle Bronze Age in southern England (this volume). Similar associations of settlements, cemeteries and land divisions can be seen in other areas of Britain (e.g. the Iron Age complex at Wetwang on the Yorkshire Wolds – Dent 1978) and Europe (e.g. the Roman Iron Age landscape at Flögeln, Lower Saxony, Germany – fig. 1.10; Zimmerman 1978). For the early historic period in southern England, Bonney has noted the location of large numbers of early Anglo-Saxon burials on what appear to be existing land boundaries dividing different communities (e.g. 1976). The importance of burial mounds in marking conceptual or physical boundaries between settlements can also be seen in their use in early-seventh-century property laws in Ireland (Charles-Edwards 1976). But above all it is the observed relationships between different categories of evidence, such as burials, settlements and land divisions, which may lead to hypotheses concerning broader changes within societies through time (Bradley, this volume), including access to property and resources and inheritance patterns.

Most of the discussion so far has assumed the existence of cemeteries or disposal areas. But they are not known from every period and area of the prehistoric past. Is their absence simply the result of poor preservation and inadequate fieldwork or are there reasons why some societies bury their dead in formal disposal areas and others do not? An answer to this question was suggested by Saxe (1970), who found evidence in three ethnographic contexts for burial in formal disposal areas being associated with the existence of corporate groups which have 'rights over the use and/or control of crucial but restricted resources'. This hypothesis has been further extended by Goldstein (1976, this volume) in a cross-cultural study of thirty societies. Goldstein restates Saxe's hypothesis but generally her work supports his and she found no exceptions to the hypothesis. On the other hand she does note that the absence of formal disposal areas does not necessarily imply the absence of such corporate groups, since they may have expressed their descent from the dead ancestors by other symbolic or ritual practices. Saxe and Gall (1977) have also published the first positive test of this hypothesis (for details see Chapman, this volume). But although this hypothesis has been generated from ethnographic contexts, there are still few attempts to apply and test it on archaeological data. The papers by Chapman and Bradley in this volume should be understood as

Fig. 1.9. Farmsteads and graveyards on north-east Bornholm (Denmark) in the Iron Age (late first millennium B.C. to first millennium A.D.). The graves were found partly on the coast and around the central settlement area (including the fields), but not at the house sites. Source: Klindt-Jensen 1957.

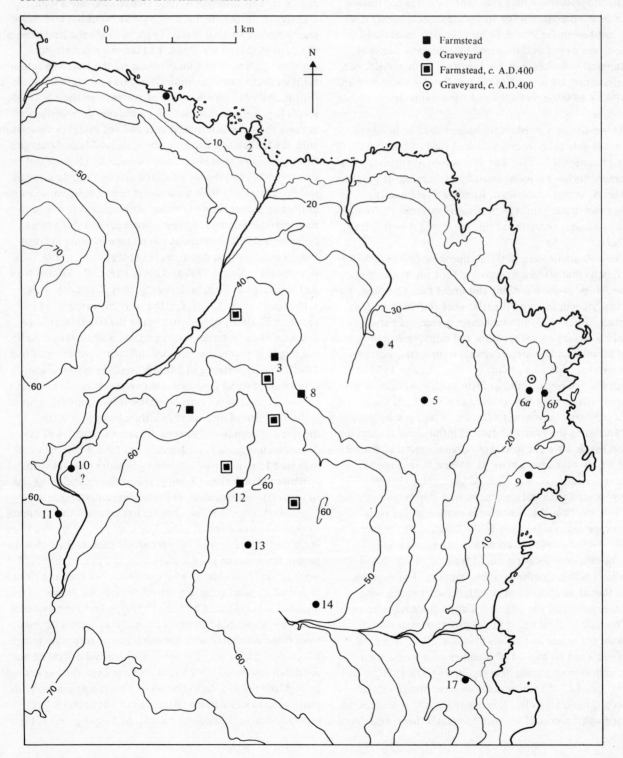

contributions towards this aim. While neither author would yet claim to have tested the hypothesis, they both offer new interpretations for changes in culture and society in the later prehistory of western Europe. Resource control and formal disposal of the dead have also been briefly mentioned in the context of the early Anglo-Saxon period in England (Shephard 1979).

Demography and distance

Any analysis of mortuary practices must be multi-dimensional in approach and execution (Goldstein, Buikstra, this volume). Indeed what has been particularly challenging and potentially most productive about the archaeology of death in the last decade has been the development of several different dimensions. There have been not only consider-ations of social factors using strictly archaeological data, but also exciting changes in the analysis of skeletal materials by physical anthropologists, in many cases working within the framework of a combined research strategy with archaeologists. This is a welcome development from the relegation of the physical anthropologist to the status of an appendix writer. Demography and biological distance are two aspects of skeletal populations which have received increasing attention. Although they are not the subject of papers in this volume it is import-ant that they be included in any general survey of approaches to the archaeology of death.

The study of palaeodemography revolves around two basic questions: what were the sizes and structures of past populations? An initial problem is that unlike normal demography, in which data on complete populations are com-piled before analysis of its structure, palaeodemography works with incomplete data and not from overall population statistics towards details of structure. But if this limitation be accepted, what information can we hope to obtain about past popu-

Fig. 1.10. Island of Flögeln, Kr. Cuxhaven, Lower Saxony (Germany). Celtic fields, settlements and cemeteries dating from the first to fifth century A.D. Source: Zimmerman 1978, fig. 1.

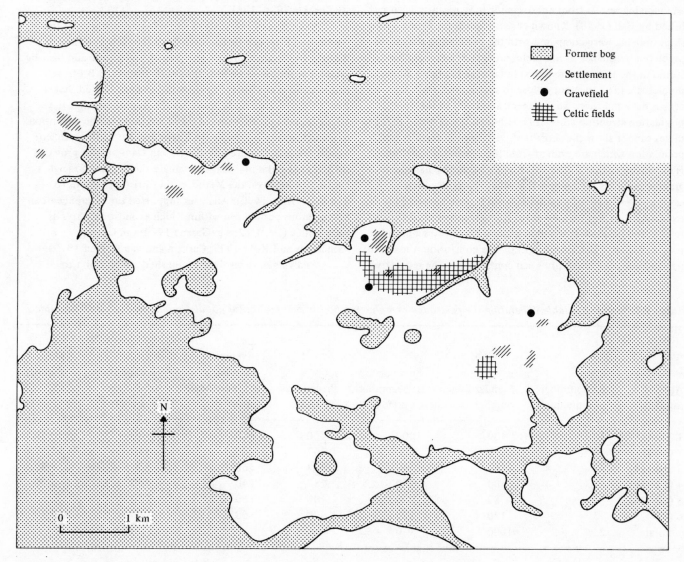

lations? It must be remembered that the difficulties involved in ageing and sexing skeletal materials must be considered before more complex analyses are undertaken. The new technique of citrate estimation for sex determination offers the possibility of easing at least some of these difficulties in the near future (Dennison 1979). But given the basic age and sex structure of skeletal populations the use of life tables has provided estimates of population structure. This approach is based upon stable-population theory and its assumptions have been summarised by Weiss (1973). Life tables can be constructed from census data from living populations and skeletal data and incorporate survivorship rates, the probability of death for each age group, the average number of individuals left alive and the life expectancy for each age group (table 1.4; Acsadi and Nemeskeri 1970; Weiss 1973; Ubelaker 1974; Asch 1976). Criticism of this method has been made on the grounds that infants are often under-represented in skeletal populations, that short-term fluctuations in rates of population growth may affect any conclusions and that stochastic variations in populations of small size may lead to significant errors (for discussion see Moore, Swedlund and Armelagos 1975). However, encouraging results from a test sample have recently been published by Hall (1978). Known census records for Union Township, Indiana, were compared with the population structures predicted by the use of life tables on data drawn from headstones in the town's cemeteries. In fact the life-table model predicted a life expectancy close to that known from the census data and there was a general similarity in the overall population structure (fig. 1.11), although it was noted that life tables cannot show the short-term variations in fertility and population which are evident from the census information. Hall concludes that if 'the anthropologist using palaeodemographic methods remembers that what is produced is a smoothed estimate of population structure and average life expectancy, rather than an exact reconstruction of historical reality, the palaeodemographic method constitutes a useful tool' (1978, p. 728). In the light of this conclusion, the use of palaeodemographic methods can contribute to the reconstruc-

tion of population size and structure in the same way as can estimates based upon settlement and economic evidence (for a review, see Hassan 1978).

The analysis of fertility has been pursued by Angel in several papers (e.g. 1975) in which he has calculated the number of births per female by examining the degree of pitting, grooving and distortion on the pubic symphysis. Recent research indicates that doubt may be cast on any exaggerated claims to calculate the exact number of children born to any one female (e.g. Kelley 1979).

The measurement of biological distance has also made progress during the last decade. Multivariate analyses of metric and non-metric traits of the cranium, dentition and the post-cranial skeleton have appeared (e.g. Berry 1968; Wilkinson 1971; Berry 1974; Suchey 1975; Bartel 1979). Debate about the relative merits of metric and non-metric traits has been active but may be approaching its conclusion with the recent argument by Cheverud, Buikstra and Twichell that 'cranial non-metric and metric traits share a moderate to high degree of developmental determination' and that 'it seems there is no biological reason to favor either kind of trait in population studies' (1979, p. 196).

Examples of the analysis of biological distance at the population level can be found in both the New and the Old Worlds. In Britain there are analyses of prehistoric and historic samples spanning some four thousand years (e.g. Brothwell and Krzanowski 1974). For the southeastern United States Wolf (1976) found no support for the hypothesis that the Mississippian culture's spread owed anything to the expansion of a single group of people. In Egypt and Nubia the archaeological research initiated by the Aswan Dam project provided sufficient skeletal material to evaluate the degree of racial continuity between the Meroitic and Christian periods (c. 350 B.C.–A.D. 1400). Analyses supported the inference of an homogenous population within which evolutionary trends were visible (fig. 1.12; e.g. Greene 1972; van Gerven, Armelagos and Rohr 1977; Carlson and van Gerven 1979).

Analyses have also been published which claim to

Table 1.4. *Sample life table illustrating the palaeodemographic method in a hypothetical population. Source: Hall 1978, table 1.*

x Age intervals	d'x Raw number of individuals	dx Standardised number	lx Survivorship at beginning of period	qx Probability of death	Lx Average number of individuals alive	Tx Total number of years left	e_x^o Mean number of years left
1 (0–4)	10	400	1000	.400	800	2140	10.70
2 (5–9)	4	160	600	.267	520	1340	11.17
3 (10–14)	4	160	440	.364	360	820	9.32
4 (15–19)	2	80	280	.287	240	460	8.20
5 (20–24)	2	80	200	.400	160	220	5.50
6 (25–29)	3	120	120	1.000	60	60	2.50
Total	25	1000	0		0		0

demonstrate small-scale genetic and social relationships within populations (fig. 1.13). Family groupings within tombs have been suggested for sites as far apart as Eneolithic Buccino in southern Italy (Holloway 1974) and the Classic Maya site of Lubaantun (Hammond, Pretty and Saul 1975). Analysis of metric and non-metric traits has been used to isolate residence patterns. Pioneering work by Lane and Sublett (1972) on cranial traits has tried to assess the degree of genetic homogeneity or heterogeneity within and between males and females

in five Indian cemeteries in New York State (*c.* A.D. 1850–1930). Assuming adequate sample sizes and that each cemetery contains localised populations, then it is argued that if 'the maximal resident kin groups are the relevant social units between which genetic trait variations develop', then it may be possible to distinguish whether it was males or females who changed residence after marriage. The authors argued that there was a high probability of male residence and female movement. It is interesting to note that ethnohistorical sources dating from the nineteenth century suggest predominantly patrilocal residence. Work on the same theme has been published by Spence (1974).

Fig. 1.11. Stationary population models of selected burial cohorts and census distributions from Hendricks County and Union Township, Indiana. Frequency in the age groups plotted on the y-axis and 10-year groups on the x-axis. Source: Hall 1978, fig. 5.

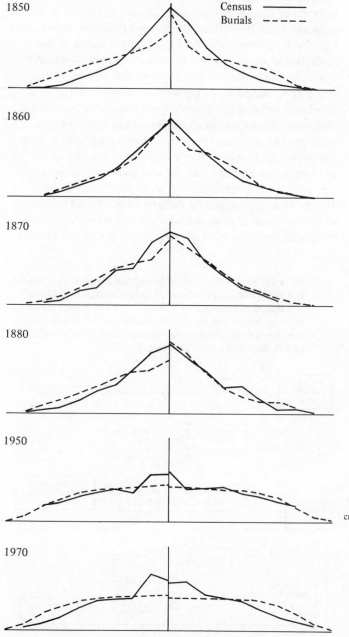

Fig. 1.12. A model of the masticatory-functional hypothesis of craniofacial change in post-Pleistocene from the Mesolithic (*c.* 10000 B.C.) to the Christian period (*c.* A.D. 1100). Micro-evolutionary change stemming from dietary change within an homogenous population. Source: Carlson and van Gerven 1979, fig. 2.

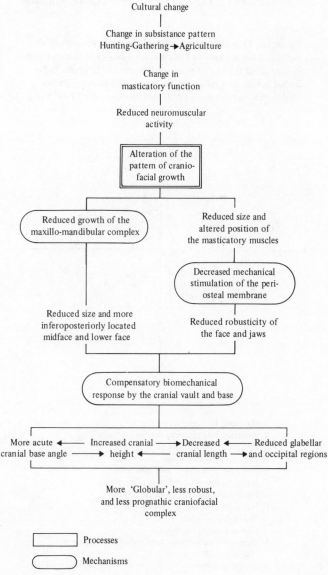

Pathology and diet

The subject of the pathology of past human populations has a considerable antiquity and a voluminous amount of literature has appeared. In the present century human skeletal material has yielded many examples of disease diagnosed by the palaeopathologist, including tuberculosis, arthritis and tumours (e.g. Wells 1964; Brothwell and Sandison 1967; Janssens 1970). But much of this work has been piecemeal, with the pathologist being consulted as a specialist to examine skeletal materials at the analysis stage of a research strategy. What has been rarer until recently has been the involvement of the student of palaeopathology in the planning and execution of research designs. Furthermore the popularity of ecological and systemic perspectives in archaeology in the last twenty years has encouraged attempts to relate pathological data to information about such variables as population density and structure, subsistence, settlement patterns, social organisation and trade (e.g. fig. 1.14). A number of recent publications indicate the potential of this research and the results obtained so far (Buikstra 1977; Lallo and Rose 1979; Lallo, Armelagos

and Mensforth 1977). The main efforts in this field have been seen in research on the transition from hunter-fisher-gatherer to agricultural societies in the Illinois valley, centred upon the work of the Northwestern University Archeological Program.

Central to recent research has been the identification and interpretation of evidence for stress suffered by human populations as a result of nutritional deficiencies. This evidence may be readily visible in some cases, as in the pathology known as porotic hyperostosis, which affects the cranium and takes three different forms (i.e. osteoporotic pitting, spongy hyperostosis and cribra orbitalia — El Najjar *et al.* 1976; Lallo, Armelagos and Mensforth 1977; Cybulski 1977). One cause of this condition is iron deficiency anaemia, which has been discussed in the references cited above, especially in relation to the dietary changes resulting from the adoption of maize agriculture. Other evidence for stress, such as arrests in and disturbance of enamel formation (e.g. Rose 1977; Rose, Armelagos and Lallo 1978; Hillson 1979) and transverse lines (Harris Lines) in long bones (e.g. McHenry 1968), is visible by use of radiographic techniques (see Cook, this volume). One might think that the incidence of these stress indicators would provide a direct indication of the level of stress and nutritional deficiency suffered by the prehistoric population under study. This would not be a valid assumption. In all cases consideration must be given to the nature of the skeletal sample available for study. It may be that it represents only part of the population, interred in a disposal area separate from other segments of the community (e.g. an age/sex/status group). This problem is discussed by Buikstra (this volume) in relation to the incidence of stress indicators and their implications for the quality of life in the Archaic period in the Illinois valley.

Fig. 1.13. Two-dimensional plot of the first two canonical variates from a stepwise discriminant analysis of skeletal populations from urban and rural settlements in Harappan India. Social patterns of endogamy are suggested as being partly responsible for the results obtained. Source: Bartel 1979, fig. 3.

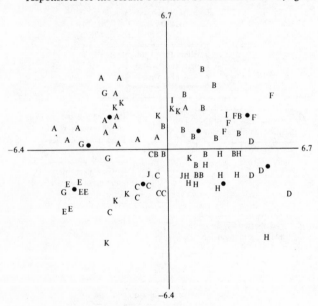

A Harappan R37 cemetery males
B Harappan R37 cemetery females
C Harappan Area G males
D Harappan Area G females
E Harappan cemetery H male inhumations
F Harappan cemetery H female inhumations
G Harappan cemetery H male jar burials
H Harappan cemetery H female jar burials
I Mohenjo-Daro males
J Nevasa Chalcolithic females
K Mean measurements for rural Indian populations and
    Harappan AB area
● Group centroids

Fig. 1.14. Schematic model of biocultural change during middle and late Woodland periods in the lower Illinois valley. Identifiable directional changes indicated by + and −. Broken circles indicate changes associated with middle–late Woodland interface. Open circles indicate modulations within late Woodland period. Source: Buikstra 1977, fig. 2.

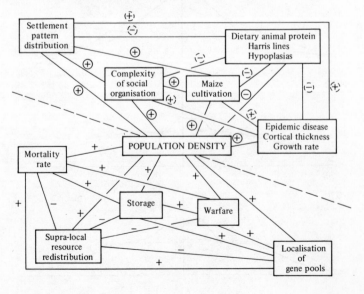

In addition it should be emphasised that the incidence of stress indicators in a skeletal population is affected by the age at death, a problem which is discussed in detail by Cook (this volume). Indeed the papers by Buikstra and Cook are important precisely because they temper excessive optimism about the potential of contemporary pathological research with a productive evaluation of the interpretative snares which lie in wait for the incautious archaeologist.

Concern with nutrition and disease and their relationship with population levels and reproductive performance, as well as the other variables mentioned above, has stimulated the development of methods for analysing dietary patterns from skeletal materials. This has been done by the measurement of the trace elements in human bone. These elements may be essential in the diet for the services they provide in the maintenance of the body's normal biological functions: such elements include iron, manganese, chromium, zinc and cobalt (Schroeder 1973). Furthermore if one knows the trace-element content of different types of food (e.g. table 1.5), then there is the possibility of using the content of bone to examine dietary changes and periods of nutritional stress. Work undertaken so far has concentrated upon the measurement of elements to obtain an indication of the relative parts played by animal protein (zinc, copper) and vegetal foods (strontium, magnesium, manganese) in the total diet (e.g. Gilbert 1975). At the same time equally stimulating research is focussing not only on society-wide diet but also on the variations that might be related to age, sex and social-status groups. Lambert, Szpunar and Buikstra have undertaken atomic-absorption analyses of skeletal material spanning the transition from hunting, fishing and gathering to agriculture in the Illinois valley (1979). Although they indicate problems such as the absorption of trace elements in the bone from the surrounding soil matrix, and although unambiguous results

were not consistently forthcoming, there was some basis for inferring differences in diet according to age, sex and social status. Similarly at the middle Formative site of Chalcatzingo in Mexico, strontium analyses of skeletal material suggest differential access to animal protein according to the position of groups within the social hierarchy (Schoeninger 1979).

Conclusions

During the course of this paper we have attempted to survey different approaches to the archaeology of death. While acknowledging the antiquity of archaeological interest in mortuary practices, this discussion has built consciously upon the most recent of these approaches, which focussed upon social dimensions. We have outlined what we perceive to have been the bases of that approach and further discussion appears in other papers in this volume (Brown, O'Shea, Goldstein, Chapman). At the same time we have presented some of the shortcomings revealed in the decade since the social approach was crystallised in the *American Antiquity* Memoir (Brown 1971*b*). This critical evaluation is aimed at developing the body of theory and approaches underlying current research into mortuary practices.

Among the shortcomings of social analyses published in the last decade we have discussed the insufficiently explicit attention given to the formation and transformation of the archaeological record, the inadequate treatment of symbolism, the relative neglect of spatial patterning in the location of disposal areas and the absence of a regional perspective in the analysis of mortuary practices. The paucity of formal testing of hypotheses derived from ethnographic contexts is also visible. This is true of archaeological use of Saxe's hypothesis 8 (1971; Goldstein, this volume), the operationalisation of which requires closer attention. For example how can we rank differing degrees of formality and how can we define which resources

Table 1.5. *Essential trace elements in various types of foods in average values ppm. Source: Schroeder 1973, table V-9.*

Type of food	Chromium	Manganese	Cobalt	Copper	Zinc	Selenium	Molybdenum
Sea foods	0.17	0.05	1.56	1.49	17.5	0.57	0.10
Meats	0.13	0.21	0.22	3.92	30.6	1.07	2.06
Dairy products	0.10	0.70	0.12	1.76	8.6	0.02	0.14
Vegetables							
Legumes	0.05	0.44	0.15	1.31	10.7	0.02	1.73
Roots	0.08	0.78	0.13	0.69	3.4	<0.02	0.23
Leaves and fruits	0.03	3.47	0.14	0.42	1.7	<0.02	0.06
Fruits	0.02	1.0	0.14	0.82	0.5	<0.02	0.06
Grains and cereals	0.31	7.0	0.43	2.02	17.7	0.31	0.33
Oils and fats	0.15	1.83	0.37	4.63	8.4	–	0.00
Nuts	0.35	17.7	0.26	14.82	34.2	0.72	?
Condiments and spices	3.3	91.8	0.52	6.76	22.9	0.24	0.45
Beverages							
Alcoholic	–	–	0.03	0.38	0.9	–	0.08
Non-alcoholic	–	3.8	0.01	0.44	0.2	0.35	0.03

337167

LIBRARY

MURRAY STATE UNIVERSITY

are critical? In addition the archaeologist must assess the degree
to which the absence of cemeteries in any one period is real or
the result of the current state of archaeological knowledge.
Binford's hypothesis relating increased heterogeneity in mortuary practices to increased sociocultural complexity has also
received insufficient archaeological testing on data taken from
long time spans in different areas. In considering the formation
and transformation of the archaeological record we have cited
examples from modern state societies in which the degree of
sociocultural complexity is not directly and unambiguously
reflected in mortuary practices. The potential ambiguity
involved in the interpretation of mortuary practices is discussed specifically by O'Shea (this volume). In addition we
would note that the archaeological record for later prehistoric
Europe reveals examples of societies of increased complexity,
in which mortuary practices do not appear to have been
employed to reflect these developments. The stratified societies
of the pre-Roman Iron Age in England are a case in point.
Indeed the mortuary practices of more stratified, state societies
deserve closer scrutiny from the social archaeologist, both in
terms of their local development and in relation to their
regional contexts. One of us has noted elsewhere that the
regional patterning in mortuary practices in Viking Age Denmark indicates the social hierarchy as well as the spatial distribution of power and authority within the kingdom
(Randsborg 1980).

The mention of these problems should act as a spur to
future research. Alongside such work we have reviewed the
fields of palaeodemography, palaeopathology and dietary
analysis, all of which have emerged in the archaeology of death
in the last decade. Given the stimulus of holistic, ecosystemic
research derived from the New Archaeology (e.g. fig. 1.14),
the physical anthropologist has been integrated more formally
into the analysis of mortuary practices. The results of this
integration and the developing techniques of skeletal analysis
comprise some of the most exciting and stimulating avenues of
interdisciplinary work. As we have suggested above, more
categories of information do not lead by themselves to any
immediate increase in our understanding of past societies. If
anything the history of interdisciplinary research reveals that
the picture tends to become much more complex and requires
more subtle treatment. However, such a realistic assessment
should not detract from our main general conclusion. The
archaeology of death is of crucial importance in current
archaeology, as it has been in the past, and the developments
of the last decade of research, as well as those reported in this
volume, are among the most stimulating within our discipline.

Acknowledgements

A first draft of this paper was read by Ian Hodder, Ian
Kinnes, John O'Shea and Susan and Stephen Shennan. We
warmly acknowledge their comments, although they would
not necessarily agree with all that we write. In addition we
also acknowledge the stimulus provided by the other authors
in this volume.

Chapter 2

**The search for rank
in prehistoric burials**
James A. Brown

Introduction

In the revival that burial studies have enjoyed in the last
few years, the detection of hereditary inequality has clearly
become one of the dominant objectives of sociological analysis.
This is hardly surprising since the character of the archaeological
record tends to encourage the search for traces of social rank.
Where great aggregates of wealth are concentrated in the graves
of a minority, visions of hereditary status distinctions are
readily evoked. A certain forcefulness emanates from the great
contrasts between rich and poor graves. Intuitively, the general
guiding principles are plain when the archaeological manifestations of rank are extreme (Childe 1963). The pyramids of
Old Kingdom Egypt, the royal tombs of Third Dynasty Ur and
the gold treasures of Iron Age European graves testify to the
marking of rank by the extremely expensive constructions,
costly artefacts and symbolic exclusiveness of the graves — far
in excess of typical expenditures among contemporary burials.
But these unsystematised principles fail us in cases of moderate
contrasts in wealth and grave expenditures. At what point are
we warranted in inferring hereditary inequality? Granted that
wealth differentials bear on any argument in favour of hereditary inequality, are there other means for establishing the
presence of social rank in an ancient culture? Furthermore,
rank might be so variously expressed in burials as to offer
contradictory indications, or be so weakly expressed as to be
invisible archaeologically. The investigation of prehistoric
social rank is not as straightforward as it might seem at first.

Is it really of much significance to be able to detect degrees of hereditary inequality in the archaeological record? I think the answer to this question is Yes. In the first place, the degree of social ranking is a measure of the size and complexity of a social system. Secondly, the emergence of hereditary inequality accompanies the rise of rulers and increased potential for the elaboration of social systems. As yet we do not have adequate knowledge of its beginnings among many societies. Flannery (1972, p. 402) in a much-cited passage stated that 'one of the thorniest problems in cultural evolution is the origin of hereditary inequality − the leap to a stage where lineages are "ranked" with regard to each other, and men from birth are of "chiefly" or "commoner" descent, regardless of their own individual capabilities'.

The renewed interest in the emergence of social ranking has conferred great importance on the archaeological record, because the latter vastly augments the limited number of historical and modern situations in which the social, economic and ecological conditions promoting social complexity can be studied. In fact, the circumstances surrounding the origins of ranking in the earliest Old World civilisations are accessible only through archaeology.

This paper gives an archaeological perspective to the problem of investigating hereditary inequality, drawing on the work of Saxe (1970) and Binford (1971). My concern is primarily with petty hierarchies in which the presence and scope of inherited status are subject to question. The archaeological literature on the subject of social rank in burial studies is substantial, with more attention devoted to this subject than any other (Braun 1979; Brown 1971a; Goldstein 1976; Greber 1979; Hatch 1976; King 1978; Peebles 1972, 1974; Peebles and Kus 1977; Randsborg 1974; Rathje 1973; Renfrew 1972; Rothschild 1979; Shennan 1975; Tainter 1975a, 1977a, 1977b; Terrell 1978; Trubowitz 1977; Wright 1978).

Other social dimensions studied have been sex roles (Rothschild 1975), regional differentiation and local descent group differentiation (Gruber 1971; Tainter 1978; van de Velde 1979).

In consideration of the scope of the problem and the voluminous literature on the subject in anthropology alone, I choose to concentrate on the logic that allows social statements to be made about the archaeological record. Key to this logic is careful attention to what I see as the critical steps in the chain of inference from theory to data. These steps include, (1) a general theoretical position that harnesses the study of social status to that of evolutionary problems, (2) a specific theory connecting social relations with the material world, and (3) a battery of arguments that create a model of patterned human behaviour at some time in the past from the static traces of that behaviour found in the archaeological record.

Social rank

A short review of the subject of social ranking in simple societies is useful before we consider prehistoric examples.

The two contexts in which hereditary inequality is found illustrate quite clearly the need to distinguish social ranking from authority associated with political leadership. The presence of social ranking does not presuppose such centralised leadership and most cases respond to a set of factors different from those promoting centralised leadership as defined by Service (1975).

Fried (1967, p. 109) defines a ranked society as 'one in which positions of valued status are somehow limited so that not all those of sufficient talent to occupy such statuses actually achieve them'. The independence of social rank and authority has been documented among small independent self-sufficient village-based groups with stable subsistence bases. These societies display basic features of social ranking without authority extending beyond the local community (Drucker 1939, 1955, p. 117; Codere 1957). Ranking appears to emerge as a result of competition for marriage mates and control of wealth among groups that are autonomous, but not biologically self-sufficient (Rosman and Rubel 1971; Friedman 1975). This competition between groups has been argued to be a feature emanating from the need to recruit new individuals (Friedman and Rowlands 1977). At any rate, the competitive social contests that are embodied in feasts and showy consumption of material goods (e.g. the potlach) give a structure to inter-group social relations that otherwise would be absent (Friedman 1975).

In more complex ranked systems in which central authority spans many villages the chiefly family enjoys privileges that are unavailable to the masses. The reward that accrues to villagers for complying with chiefly demands is incommensurate with their effort. It is mainly intangible, and characteristically it is the chiefly establishment that benefits most from the relationship (Earle 1978). In contrast, the efforts of the independent villagers in acephalous societies receive more tangible reward through enhanced personal prestige and beneficial redistribution of valued resources (Friedman and Rowlands 1977).

Origins of ranking

Until recently, it was widely held that surplus above subsistence needs was a necessary condition for the emergence of chiefs and social stratification (Childe 1936, pp. 106−7; see Cancian 1976, pp. 227−8). Rulership and inherited status rested on the back of others' work. Egalitarian societies, on the other hand, were maintained by the common necessity for work. This meant that the origins of rank had to be sought in the economic consequences of food production. However, the necessary-surplus argument was effectively demolished by the discovery that social rank existed quite independently of a definable surplus (Sahlins 1972). Rulership is not instituted by the work of others (Brunton 1975). Nor did a 'drive' towards creating a surplus exist among technologically simple societies. Furthermore, the leisure time available did nothing to promote surplus production or any other social and cultural innovation that could undermine an egalitarian ethos.

The potential for social rank is present in all egalitarian societies. Rank only requires the proper social circumstances to emerge from ever-present differences in personal abilities and achievements (Fried 1967). In simple societies this potential for social hierarchy and inherited authority is held in check by levelling mechanisms that dampen the acquisition of personal wealth and power through social custom and ceremony (Flannery 1972).

With the downgrading of surplus as a key variable, it quickly came to be seen as an effect rather than a cause. Rappaport (1971) and others (e.g. Flannery 1972) argued that the demands of elaborate ritual stimulate production in technologically simple societies and Sahlins (1972) proposed more specifically that in chiefly societies leadership is the source of stimulation of surplus production.

With this new approach came the realisation that social stratification and other aspects of social hierarchy are not the results of a single evolutionary process, but are the product of the joint operation of several processes. These processes are still being examined (e.g. Service 1975; Netting 1972; Earle 1978).

Two different theories have been advanced to explain the emergence of social ranking, stratification and central leadership. One is the circumscription theory of Carneiro (1970), the other is the managerial theory espoused by Service (1975) and Wright (1977). These are not rival theories but argue from different aspects of the connections between individuals and their resource base. Basically they explain the emergence of social stratification, but in the process social rank and centralised leadership are taken care of too. They are much more limited in the scope of their explanations than their advocates have often held, but within these limitations they forge convincing arguments.

The core argument of circumscription theory turns on the power acquired through control of critical resources to which there is restricted access (cf. Chapman, this volume). Restriction here means a curtailment of equal opportunity to acquire, make use of, or allocate critical resources, such as fishing shoreline or patches of arable land in an otherwise infertile country. By extension, strategic position in an exchange network can be included since it operates in the same manner (Dalton 1977; Brunton 1975). The geographical positioning of a group plays a dominant part in forcing such curtailment, since it is so inelastic in response to increase or shifts in demand (Harner ,1970). In addition, the control over the technical means for producing valued goods has the same effect (Frankenstein and Rowlands 1978). One of the first social responses to a curtailment of access is the acquisition of hereditary rights to the resource in question. At the most basic level it is an investment by a group or community in those rights. Tribal fishing rights are a common example. Of significance is the distinction between heritable rights, the formation of centralised leadership and population density (Brunton 1975), although these factors commonly co-vary under favourable circumstances (Vincent 1978).

The managerial arguments in the theories of Service and Wright offer a different perspective. Service (1975, pp. 72–8) advanced a specific model founded on the assumed application of the bureaucratic function in embryonic leadership roles. He posited that leadership emerges to solve a critical-resource allocation problem. For him the situation that most clearly acts to promote the rise of such figures of authority is their management of the redistribution of pooled resources to alleviate recurrent local shortages among neighbouring self-sufficient villages. Although Service's argument carried force, recent ethnographic research has disclosed that this redistributive function is not fundamental to central leadership (Earle 1978), and therefore the range of applicable managerial models requires expansion. Here Wright's (1977) systems approach is helpful, since he points out that any threat to the security of the food supply or the safety of the community from outside encroachment is sufficient to promote the investment of decision-making authority in the hands of a single individual (Peebles and Kus 1977). Netting (1972) has described conditions under which local subsistence insecurity and limited subsistence supply were alleviated by the allocation of authority to a single individual with greater powers of ritual knowledge and managerial foresight. In groups for which a measure of agricultural security is necessary, ritual leaders, sorcerers and diviners are elevated to positions of leadership (Netting 1972). By extension, the power of Big Men leaders can be broadly interpreted as enhancing the relative prestige and security of their followers. The strengthening of this authority seems to feed on the sanctification of authority in the absence of powers of coercion. Obviously, where authority and control over access to valued resources coincide, leadership is considerably consolidated, the result being the emergence of the classic chiefdom as a more stable social type, combining power and authority.

All of this leaves population growth out of consideration. Good reasons are cited by Cowgill (1975) and Flannery (1972) for regarding population change as a sufficient, but not a necessary, determinant of social ranking. Although population growth frequently precedes the emergence of social and cultural complexity (Flannery 1972, p. 406), there are important exceptions that show growth to be a secondary factor responding to more basic variables of social organisation and subsistence-settlement logistics.

Therefore, the role of population pressure advocated in circumscription theory (Harner 1970) is actually secondary to the social-opportunity argument that occupies a key position in that theory.

Archaeological approaches

Early work in the study of burial patterning was content to classify mortuary sites into evolutionary types. That was sufficient when the methods of demonstrating social structure in archaeological data were not readily agreed upon, but this classification has a serious fault. Since the arguments that must be made for membership of a burial system in one or another evolutionary type, such as a chiefdom, hinge on the number of distinctive traits present, it is evident that only well-developed examples will be assigned with confidence. However, as Renfrew (1972, 1974) has observed, relatively few cases possess a majority of the traits associated with the archetypal chiefdoms. This means that many 'exceptional' cases will be created. The utility of this classificatory approach can rightly be questioned on grounds of inefficiency (Tainter 1978). But, more basically, it constitutes a second-rate substitute for examination of the effects of co-variation of the underlying variables, which for present purposes are rank, authority and power.

In terms of variations in rank, classification is a poor research objective because the gradations in scale of social hierarchy are more important than the type of hierarchy. For this reason, archaeological research should shift to models and methods for detecting gradations of rank irrespective of the institutional contexts in which it might be expressed. Rather than concerning ourselves with whether a particular burial population belongs to a prehistoric chiefdom (or state), it is more rewarding to assess the degree of ranking and to determine the ecological contexts of social hierarchy.

Theoretical perspective

The most useful theoretical perspective for the task of bringing the social theories of Service (1975), Fried (1967) and others to bear on material culture has been developed by Saxe (1970) and Binford (1971). In conformity with most modern students of the subject they reject the idea that any intrinsic meaning is attached to a specific rite, grave type or form of interment, or that any of these mortuary forms has any specific ethnic affiliation (Ucko 1969). Beyond this assumption, they make two further ones: first, that the social persona (or overall status composite) of the deceased will be symbolised in funerary and mortuary behaviour; and second, that the funerary rites and burial will be affected by the size and composition of the body of individuals recognising some social tie or linkage with the deceased. From these principles they develop a systematic theory that allows variations in social and political spheres to be adequately recorded. From this emerge composite measurements of social complexity, among other features. For instance, Saxe (1970) proposed that the number and kinds of dimensions of the social personality that will be given recognition in the mortuary behaviour of a society will vary with the organisational complexity of the social system. The theoretical approach of Binford and Saxe basically regards burial custom in whatever form it might be expressed as somewhat arbitrary, but nonetheless subject to certain constraints.

Least-effort constraints

In the first place, custom should discriminate categories of the dead deemed significant to the society of the survivors. The number of such categories in any society varies greatly in a regular manner. The categories do not proliferate needlessly, but the number should relate closely to the critical distinctions required to set apart significant groups within a society. Thus the effort to maintain cultural distinctions should have social benefit. Cost-benefit considerations will affect the scale of the funeral and mortuary processing. It is to be expected that the cost should be balanced against the degree to which disruption of normal social relations can be tolerated. Secondly, the overall cost in effort and wealth accorded to burial will be economically apportioned to achieve a measure of discrimination in accordance with the array of disposal forms. At its foundation this theory is based on an economy of symbols.

The potential amount of wealth and effort that different societies can allocate to the funerary rite varies to such an extent as to be very obtrusive archaeologically. Just as variable is the proportion of the total wealth so expended from society to society. But within the range available to each society the relative apportionment of effort should depend upon the relative importance of the deceased. A budgeting concept underlies this formulation.

The budget model is only an approximation of archaeological reality, however, since each death is different within each status category. All told, some variation in disposal practices can be realistically expected because of differing opportunities for acquiring appropriate grave goods and the effect that disputes among the survivors might have on burial ritual.

Focus of mortuary ritual

Death is a critical event to the survivors. In small-scale societies the loss is proportionately greater than in larger societies. In the former, the death of an adult who is the main productive member of the household probably will elicit strong responses from the household members, but the overall magnitude of the bereavement will vary in direct proportion to social scale, since the proportion of the population involved at this basic level of bereavement will constitute a lesser portion of a large society than of a small-scale one.

In small-scale societies in which authority is parcelled out and status lacks value within a sphere of social relations, the main characteristics of the deceased to be accorded symbolic distinction will be age, sex, personal achievement, and personality. Circumstances of death seem to be included as well (Binford 1971). These characteristics loom larger in small societies than in larger ones, because they are affected greatly by the power of centralised leadership and the ownership of land and means of production. Since survival is the central concern of small societies, the effort expended on any burial will not be disproportionate. But in accordance with the relatively great impact that each death has in such a society, special attention will be accorded to such factors as the circumstances and location of death. As the sphere of authority widens and power gravitates towards individuals, leadership will supersede other statuses and dominate the mortuary symbolism. The widening of authority beyond the lineage entails an increase in the field of allegiance that leads to greater effort and wealth being applied to the funeral and the burial. The existence of a spatial base in the control of critical resources means that power will be symbolised through exclusive access to specific burial locations. It is at this juncture that children can become the object of elaborate treatment that is archaeologically visible. If the loss of children to a community or lineage can be argued to be critical to the future of a heritable claim, then children can be expected to be singled out for elaborate treatment when the birth rate is low or the family circle is narrow.

Contrary to some statements in the literature, wealth distinctions are not as indicative of specific social variables as are the rights to symbolically special burial locations. Nor is the elaborate treatment of children an indication simply of the inheritance of power or authority in a society. Characteristics of funerals and burial such as wealth expended and treatment of small children seem to be related to other social and demographic variables.

From these considerations six expectations follow:

(1) as long as hierarchical aspects of society are minimal, distinctions chosen for symbolic treatment will be based on age, sex, personal ability, personality, circumstances of death and social deviance;

(2) societies exhibiting minimal hierarchy will record symbolic distinctions with a minimum of wealth, the average depending upon availability;

(3) as the hierarchical aspects of society increase, burials will record gradation in treatments among otherwise equivalent statuses;

(4) as the hierarchical aspects increase, children will be accorded relatively more elaborate attention in proportion to the decline in the opportunity for replacement of the following generation;

(5) as authority increases the amount of wealth and effort expended on the burial will increase;

(6) as power increases the attachment of the powerful exclusively to locations indicative of their power base will emerge.

Discrimination of rank

The means by which the above theories connect with the archaeological record depend upon the use of three major arguments that translate archaeological remains into patterned human activity. They have been employed more often in conjunction than separately, and the result has been a strong argument bridging the archaeological facts and the behaviour they represent.

The effort-expenditure principle

This key argument, which is a refinement of the principle of least effort (Zipf 1949), has received extensive treatment by Tainter (1975*a*, 1977*a*, 1977*b*, 1978; Tainter and Cordy 1977). He argues that the greater the social rank of the deceased, the greater the expenditure of energy (and wealth) in the interment ritual (including burial). Conversely, it is possible to state that the existence of major quantitative

differences in the effort and wealth expended in the mortuary processing will be indicative of graded status distinctions. To Tainter (1978) these grades constitute ascribed (inherited) status although Braun (1979) has contested a connection with inherited status without clearly distinguishing the inheritance of control over resources from inherited authority. Braun's argument applies only to the latter condition.

One is reminded of the theoretical statement of Binford (1971) to the effect that the quantitative differences in the treatment of the dead are basically dependent upon the size of the social sphere or the number of individuals involved in the funerary rite. Large numbers are possible only in chiefly societies, but there may well be a considerable range at the lower end of the scale, among acephalous societies. This is especially true in dense populations or for autonomous groups that occupy tightly packed territories where inter-group competition is rife. In this light Braun's (1979) and Saxe's (1970) comments are particularly relevant, to the effect that grading in wealth accorded the dead at burial is characteristic of statuses acquired through competition among equals.

A review of the ethnographic literature by Tainter (1978, pp. 116–17) shows that various forms of effort and wealth distinctions are employed to distinguish rank. They are: (1) complexity in the treatment of the corpse; (2) the position and construction of the interment facility; (3) the extent and duration of the funeral; (4) differences in the material contribution to the ritual; and (5) selective sacrifice of humans. Although Tainter claims that the first three are confined in their use to rank distinctions, wealth differences must reflect a wider range of factors, including distinctions between grades of achieved status (Braun 1979).

The utility of the effort-expenditure argument is that it permits the recognition of social rank from the widest range of mortuary data, thereby offering a methodology applicable to situations of poor preservation and scanty grave goods (Tainter 1978). The monumental stone constructions of Bougainville offer a case in point. The relative size of stone monuments distinguished the graded statuses known ethnographically in a situation in which the burials were poorly preserved (Terrell 1978).

There is a methodological weakness in effort-expenditure measures. There is no certainty as to the reliability of a scale of effort expenditure that includes different material expressions. For instance, the difference between the use of natural limestone slabs and logs is difficult to assess since the difference in procurement effort represented by each is subject to widely varied estimates.

Symbols of authority

It has been argued that the disposition of symbols of authority among the dead will be indicative of the composition of the group within which authority is normally vested. Peebles (1974; Peebles and Kus 1977) has proposed that authority can be said to be inherited when artefacts and attributes indicative of authority and power within a prehistoric society 'cross-cut' distinctions based on age, sex and personal ability. It is assumed that the distribution of these symbols will be consistent with other criteria for defining this burial set (Peebles 1974). Peebles and Kus (1977) and Braun (1979) argue that such a set of symbols must be present to establish definitively the presence of rank, although authority is clearly what is warranted. Unfortunately the vagaries of preservation do not always allow negative evidence to be used safely (cf. O'Shea, this volume) and the absence of appropriate symbols may not indicate the absence of inherited authority.

Demographic structure

The biological component of burials is another exceedingly useful means for ascertaining the social composition of a particular burial type. In principle, a natural population is present when the sex ratios are approximately equal and the mortality profile falls within the range for pre-industrial populations (cf. Buikstra 1977). Hence, any statistically significant departure from these 'normal' age/sex expectations points to differential recruitment of a particular age and sex category into specific status groups and interment types. Possible applications for the problem at hand can be foreseen. Competing social hierarchies can be expected to divide the total population into two or more segments, depending on the size of the local population. Where authority is inherited, however, the segments will be very disproportionate. This follows from the observation that the 'ruling' elite should constitute a distinct minority of the population. Division of the population into ranked groups should result in subpopulations containing all age classes and both sexes. A much-used touchstone for stratification is the presence of grave wealth in child graves (Flannery 1972, p. 403; Saxe 1970). However, such associations must be interpreted with reservations since inherited prestige of ranked lineages can be symbolised by this means as much as inherited authority. Nonetheless, the cases where symbols of authority, such as crowns and head-dress ornaments, are deposited with infant and adult graves alike constitute strong evidence for inherited status (Peebles and Kus 1977).

Some measurements of these arguments

In the application of the methods summarised above, students of mortuary practices have made use of several techniques that have exploited strong points in their data sets. The techniques have been of use in identifying ranking among burials. Greber (1976) has applied Kendall's (1948) ranksum index to the problem of determining average relative order of the burials in three classic Ohio Hopewell mounds. The index is calculated on the sum of the rank order of each burial on several variables, including burial space area and the number of objects of each material category. In her measure there is an implicit use of the effort-expenditure model.

Randsborg (1974), in a study of regional status differentiation in Bronze Age Europe, has made use of differences in the weights of gold and bronze artefacts to determine an ordering among burials. These metals are, of course, ranked in relation to each other as well, which provided Randsborg with a further means of ordering burials in terms of grave goods.

Another approach to the effort-expenditure model has been advanced by Rathje (1973). He has proposed that a social system with rigid levels of status, to the exclusion of achieved-status gradations between them, should be represented by clear levels of burial wealth. The effect of an achieved component in the social system would be to promote a continuum with few breaks and with weakly defined levels in the amount of effort expended in the burial (see Hodder 1978a, pp. 237–9).

Studies of artefacts as symbols of authority have not developed to the extent that the relative-ranking techniques have. The hazards of content analysis are known all too well to require elaboration but certain students of burial studies have employed interesting strategies to differentiate artefacts which are potential symbols. Braun (1979) has divided the series of Hopewellian grave goods into those whose contexts were exclusively burials and those that were found in middens as well. He reasoned that grave goods that were not also found in residential refuse were more likely to function as symbols of authority. This procedure is useful for burial sets in which the type of status that is inherited is in question, owing to the lack of items obviously symbolising authority. In the various Mississippian period studies, this lack is not as critical, since head-dress and other items of costume are easily recognised as symbols of rank and authority (Brown 1971a; Hatch 1976; Peebles 1974; Peebles and Kus 1977).

One other technique should be mentioned, and that is formal analysis (Brown 1971a; Saxe 1970; Tainter 1978). In the early investigations of rank and status this technique was part of a methodological strategy to isolate the distinctions among disposal types. It was a method for finding differences, and in the hands of Saxe (1970) it has been generalised into a calculus for elucidating the structure and organisation of an array of burials in a single society, called a disposal-of-the-dead domain. Without going into details, this method allows the comparison of different burial domains in terms of relative entropy and degree of organisation (Saxe 1970; for a discussion of entropy, see Goldstein, this volume). Of utility here is Saxe's proposition that high status in a domain of burials will be represented by more positive attributes than low status. Although Saxe's method has a strong theoretical basis, it has been difficult to apply to archaeological situations in total. His theoretical approach to burial studies is in terms of decision making. In the three ethnographic studies he has used, a decision-making approach worked well, but it is now clear that this approach is only suitable for the analysis of a behavioural model and not of untranslated archaeological data. However, despite the uncertain applicability of formal analysis, the propositions in Saxe's theory have proved of great value in constructing arguments about the social dimensions of mortuary practices.

Examples

With these theoretical statements behind us it is appropriate to consider specific case studies. At this point a model must be created to relate physical interments and their contexts (tombs, mounds etc.) to phases of burial programmes, which are treatment sequences of the corpse (and skeleton if secondary burial is involved) particular to specific status categories. The practical result of this modelling is to connect dissimilar burial 'types' with a single, culturally recognised burial treatment sequence. For instance, bone bundles can be a consequence of additional handling of the bones of the dead in a programme that begins with and essentially focusses on primary interment. Some of the most universal burial types are secondary burials or corpse treatments involving a number of distinct processing steps (e.g. cremation). Three good examples of multi-phased programmes are illustrated below.

The central purpose of this model is to construct a representation of the burial phases of the funeral process. Generally, a defensible model requires the integration of scattered pieces of evidence from a wide series of mounds and cemeteries belonging to a single sociocultural system. Failure to construct such a model carefully before analysis of the burials and their associations risks the creation of false social groups out of the remains of the various phases of a single burial programme.

To illustrate the points made so far, I wish to review three cases from the prehistoric record in the eastern United States. The first example demonstrates the internal consistency of the separate measures of power, authority and social ranking, in a period when hierarchical settlement systems and archetypal chiefdom organisations were common (Peebles 1974; Peebles 1978; Peebles and Kus 1977; Steponaitis 1978). The other two examples illustrate the independent behaviour of these measures, in a manner that reveals some of the potential that burial studies have for revealing variations in social rank as distinct from other variables.

The Spiro phase of the Caddoan area

This period (A.D. 1200–1400) in the North Caddoan cultural tradition of the western Ozarks and adjacent Arkansas River valley displays basic features of economy and technology indicative of complex social systems of the Mississippian type (Brown 1975; Brown, Bell and Wyckoff 1978; Brown n.d.*a*). The geographical location of this tradition at the western fringes of the well-watered Eastern Woodlands was presumably the reason for population concentrations which were relatively meagre by contemporary standards. The location probably exposed the agricultural economy to high drought risks that promoted a dispersed settlement system. Separate from the ordinary villages there were sparsely occupied civic-ceremonial centres. Three tiers of civic-ceremonial centres can be identified by the size and complexity of the earthworks. The Spiro site is the largest of several, widely separated 'first-rank' centres. The second level were clustered within 16 km of Spiro in the approximate centre of the greatest concentration of arable land. The greatest concentration of known habitation sites occurs here as well (Brown *et al.* 1978).

It is not surprising that settlements were usually small and very dispersed. The unconcentrated distribution of population is also reflected in the vacant type of civic-ceremonial centre. The concentration of arable land in the river valleys (which constitute a small percentage of the land) acts to circumscribe access to the soils basic to the subsistence economy. The scarcity of critical resources is the variable essential to the appearance of certain manifestations of power in the North Caddoan area.

The Spiro phase supplies a consistent picture of a hierarchical social organisation. The iconographic materials nicely bear out the burial data on the cultural role performed by the key symbols of authority (Brown 1971*a*, 1975; Phillips and Brown 1978).

At the Spiro site, which occupies the apogee of the civic-ceremonial-centre hierarchy, the main mound presents a situation unusual in burial studies. High-status burials were neatly laid out on the floor of a large mortuary, with extraordinary amounts of grave goods for the period under consideration. The associations of burial treatment, elaborate facilities, grave goods and symbols of rank and authority leave little doubt as to the social significance of this mortuary. The analysis of burials in terms of skeletal treatment, disposal types, and post-mortem handling has disclosed a number of facts that support a behavioural model of Spiro burial practices. The skeletal remains had been subjected to varying amounts of post-mortem processing and ranged from complete articulation to partial disarticulation and loose bones. Examination of the archaeological contexts showed that the least disarticulated remains were from those burials that were probably moved around – presumably from near-by mortuaries. Completely disarticulated burials of selected bones were from burials subjected to more extensive curation, and also originally housed in near-by mortuaries (Bell 1972). This series of burial types comprises a graded series ranging from minimal to protracted handling. This grading happens to correspond with important grades in status, in which the lowest-ranking burial type is subjected to the least post-mortem handling and the highest burials to the greatest. The highest-ranking group is confined to the special mortuaries of the Craig mound at Spiro and at other centres. The intermediate group is also found at Spiro and other centres, presumably wherever charnel houses were maintained. The least treated are found in grave plots of varying size in or near habitations. These are the rudiments of the mortuary model that was constructed from various lines of evidence (Brown 1971*a*, 1975; Bell 1972).

Indicators of power were present. Elite burials were found in the remains of a richly furnished mortuary, much larger than any other structure of this type in the area and distinct in furnishing and location from contemporary cemeteries. Litter burials are not found outside the Spiro site, even taking into account the perishable wooden poles. At one secondary centre, the older elite treatment by cremation was retained for an individual with copper head-dress emblems of authority the same as ones found at Spiro (Finklestein 1940). The symbolic content of the emblems of authority is strongly indicative of the use of military force and the importance to the social order of organised warfare in Spiro-phase society. All the emblems are elaborations on weaponry, mainly club forms, but including the distinctive bi-lobed arrow emblem that is taken from an arrow in a drawn bow (Phillips and Brown 1978).

Demographic data exist that confirm the inherited nature of elite status for the apical Spiro lineage. Although age and sex data are incomplete owing to loss and breakage of burials over the years, the evidence that can be marshalled reveals adults in the litter burials, and at least one is a male. Basket burials include both adults and children under the age of twelve. The presence of a complete population in the charnel house satisfies a minimal requirement for inherited status (cf. Peebles and Kus 1977). It is all the more convincing since this age distribution is different from that of the lower ranks. Children are not found among the latter. Hence the attributes of high rank in the Spiro system isolate a group of burials that includes young individuals not otherwise visible in the charnel-house burial population.

The burials exhibiting the greatest amount of post-mortem care and treatment were found with the grave facilities evincing the greatest expenditure of effort. Thus, two indicators of disproportionate effort were associated at the Spiro site. The elaborate grave facilities and the very disarticulated burials were confined to the two high-ranking burials from the Great Mortuary and other special locations. The highest ranking had litters constructed of long cedar poles lashed together in a square framework with projecting ends. These litters ranged in size from 2.1 × 1.8 m to 0.75 m square along the sides of the framework. They contained the disarticulated remains of the deceased and piles of grave goods, including cloth cloaks, conch-shell cups, copper artefacts, shell and pearl beads and various sociotechnic artefacts. These facilities resembled badges of office so closely as to leave little doubt that they were reserved for the highest status in the Spiro system. Burials of the next rank were more modest, comprising basket boxes which contained disarticulated remains and a much smaller set of shell and copper grave goods. Head-dress parts and status emblems (sociotechnic axes) were regularly found in these baskets.

The grave goods constituted a large and conspicuous display of wealth interred with the dead. Copper objects, marine-shell cups, mica sheets and pearl beads were important wealth items in the Mississippian systems and were interred in these graves in great number (Brown n.d.*b*). They were acquired from distant sources through trade. The grave goods also contained ritual objects important in this society, namely shell cups. Moreover, the symbols of authority recognised at Spiro and throughout the Mississippian sphere, were present here and solely with the elite dead. They included the copper and copper-covered wooden head-dresses and the hair ornaments whose importance in this society is documented from icon-ographic evidence (Brown n.d.*b*). In short, the symbols of paramount authority that were concentrated with the three grave types identified with the high-ranking Spiro dead were also found sparingly with high-ranking burials at the outlying centres of Norman and Reed, but not in local cemeteries.

Major aspects of social ranking in Spiro society are disclosed in the above account. But additional features are revealed in the mortuary treatment of the elite throughout the Spiro domain. This elite had access to the privilege of burial with recognised forms of wealth in marine shell and copper. But the amount of wealth interred with the elite was graded according to the rank of the civic-ceremonial centre's charnel house (Brown 1975). Access to mortuary treatment privilege was confined to individuals (probably of both sexes) who had attained the age of twelve (Brown n.d.*b*).

The Harlan phase of the Caddoan area

The earlier Harlan phase in the North Caddoan area (A.D. 1000–1200) was a simpler society with ample evidence of ancestry to the Spiro phase in technology and settlement. The Spiro site was the largest of the centres, but was on an equal footing in terms of settlement complexity. The settlement hierarchy was confined to a two-tier system, and the upper-level centres were evenly spread throughout the western Ozarks. All had the same basic layout and they differed only in site size and, by inference, in the size of the support population within the service territory. With this available information, one would predict that indicators of power and perhaps of authority would be weaker. But does social ranking also extend back in time?

In accordance with expectations, indicators of power and special burial treatments exclusive to a central apical centre were absent. However, the elaborated axe and weaponry insignia of authority were present. The total amount of wealth expended in mortuary rites was smaller and the quantity of items representative of long-distance exchange was also small. Significantly, there were fewer burial treatments and associated programmes, and cremation occupied the apogee of burial treatments. At the Harlan site, the second largest of the upper echelon centres, investigation of the burial mound disclosed that cremations were located in the centre of each stratum of the three cones that composed this mound (Bell 1972). Inhumations of the articulated, partly disarticulated and bundle types were distributed around the central cremations that account for a distinct minority of the dead (Bell 1972, pp. 142–5). In association with these cremations were most of the copper artefacts and all the conch-shell cups (fig. 2.1). Although cremation was a high-status treatment here, it was evidently available to each of the separate groups having rights to interment in the different burial cones. The groups were evidently affiliated to the mortuaries found buried under small mounds that compose the centre. In fact, the number of such mortuaries corresponded with the number of distinct strata in each of the burial cones, thereby supporting the inference that each mortuary and burial layer pair was part of a cycle of treat-

Fig. 2.1. The Harlan burial mound. Source: Bell 1972. fig. 7B. (a) profile, (b) lower layer of Lobe C.

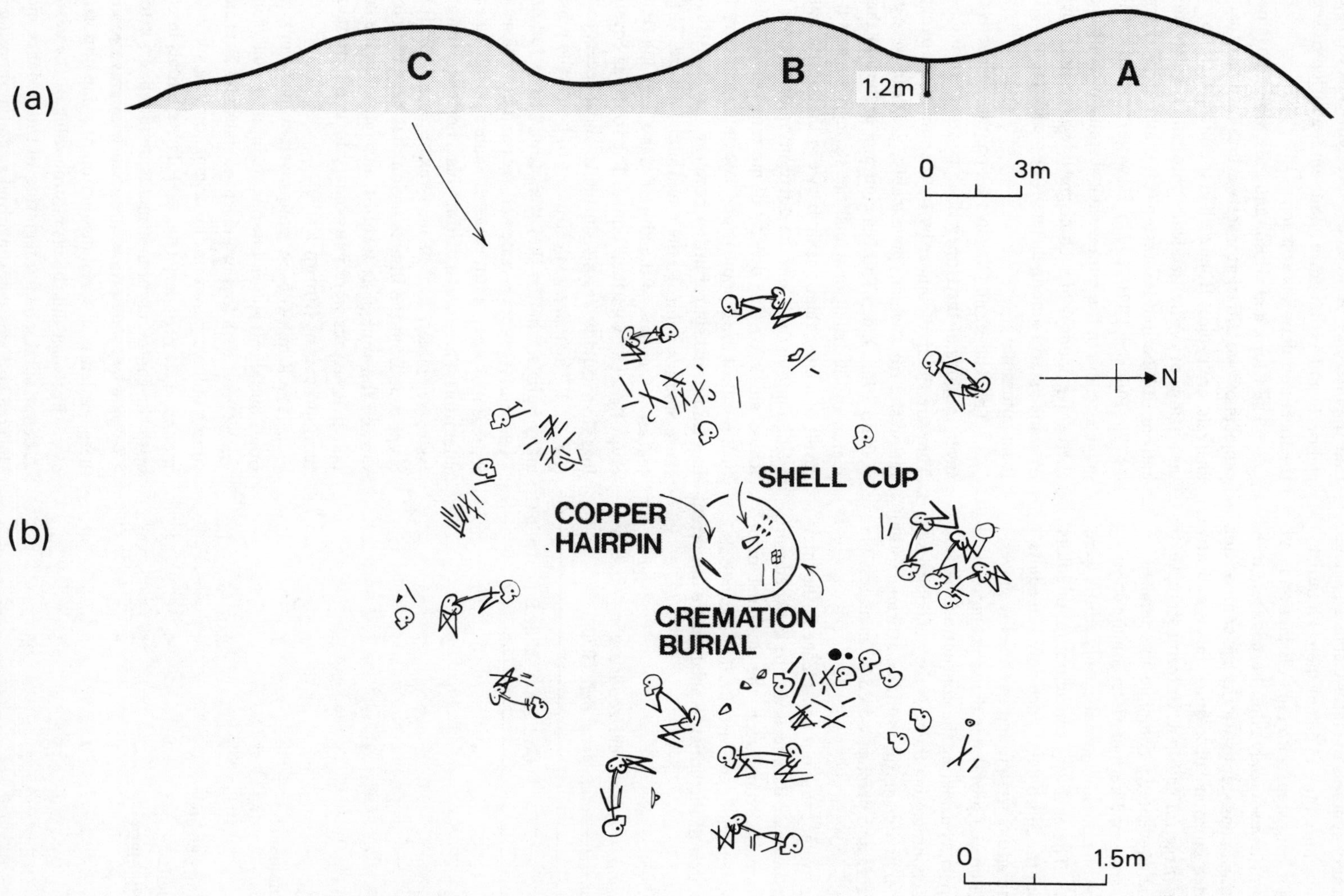

ment in a burial programme. The three cones suggest that three descent groups were attached to this civic-ceremonial centre. The middle (Unit B) of the three groups was distinctly wealthier than the others. The grave goods in the cremation burials of this group consisted of copper head-dress parts elsewhere used as sumptuary symbols of status (table 2.1). The cremated category accounted for 11.8% of the total burial population, and this is consistent with rank distinction in a complete population. However, only adult burials seem to be represented and, though consistent with the age composition of the burials accorded mortuary processing, this is indicative of no differential privilege for children. Unfortunately, the condition of the bone prevented a complete and detailed study. Accurate age and sex determinations could not be made, but except for one possible juvenile, only adults were identified in the field. The exclusive concentration of adults can be expected from the Spiro data, since only sub-adults (over age twelve) and adults were found in non-elite graves (Brown 1971a). The crucial problem is the age composition of the cremated burials, considering the concentration of authority symbols accompanying them. If they encompassed children and adults, inherited status would be affirmed, otherwise non-inherited access to prestige would be an admissible conclusion.

In review, it is evident that our confidence in the interpretation of the Harlan-phase data rests on our knowledge of the succeeding Spiro phase. Nonetheless, the combined information on wealth distributions, the distribution of symbols, and the age composition of the burial population are important

Table 2.1. *Distribution of select grave goods among the lobes of the Harlan site burial mound. After Bell 1972.*

	Unit A	Unit B	Unit C
Copper items:			
Head-dress plate*	–	1	–
Sheet fragments	1	2	1
Hair pins*	2	2	1
Globular beads	2	–	–
Tube	1	–	–
Sheathed rattle†	–	1	–
Maskette ear ornament*	–	1	–
Marine shell items:			
Shell cups†	–	2	1
Other status-defining objects:			
Earspool ornaments*	2	9	12
Massive sculptured pipe†	–	1	–
Sociotechnic axes	1	2	–
Utilitarian objects:			
Axes	5	1	3
Pottery vessels	27	23	15

*status emblems   †ritual equipment

features of the system that enlighten us as to the degree of status grading in the Harlan phase.

The Illinois Hopewell case

The third case presents a challenge of a different sort in that the interplay between the differential distribution of elaborate and exotic grave goods among different segments of the local population is at issue.

The Klunk and Gibson mounds, which have been the subjects of two different investigations into mortuary-patterning analysis, are typical Hopewellian mounds, with no concrete indications of centralised leadership, and scarcely any indications of inherited leadership (cf. Braun 1979; Tainter 1975a, 1977b; Buikstra 1976, 1977). However, the differences in grave size and in the number and scarcity of copper and marine shell grave goods is of such magnitude as to raise the possibility of graded status among different domestic groups within a local community.

The Klunk and Gibson sites contain respectively ten and seven mounds of the Hopewellian period (110 B.C.–A.D. 400). They are situated on near-by bluff spurs overlooking a habitation site from which, presumably, the dead were drawn (Perino 1968, n.d.). This is a common pattern in the Illinois region and distributional analyses strongly suggest it to be the result of a close relationship between the location of Hopewellian populations and the distribution of mounds (De-Rousseau 1973). The density of mounds can thus be argued to be a result of local populations' continuing to bury their dead in a traditional spot. Furthermore the very construction of these mounds points to their communal nature. The common feature at the base of the mound was a large log-framed burial crypt flanked by earthen ramps. The roof was covered with logs that could be readily shifted to allow access to the interior (fig. 2.2). Their size was sufficient to house the remains of many burials, whether they were found to be full or not. These burial crypts revealed all ages and both sexes to be represented when a full range of examples was taken into consideration. There was a distinct bias, however, towards adult males (see table 2.2). The many examples of this Hopewellian crypt type from the Illinois region that have been excavated showed the same basic features, and reinforce the conclusion that these crypts were a customary form of communal mortuary processing (Brown 1979).

The Klunk-Gibson groups were unusual in including two other burial categories, interments in individual 'tomb'-like graves lined with logs or limestone slabs and interments in simple unlined graves on the original mound surface and in the mound at its periphery (fig. 2.2). These burials in comparison with the central crypt interments, required less effort to make and were less elaborately furnished with grave goods. We have here, evidently, a social distinction of some importance.

But what did the crypt processing of the dead involve? A behavioural model integrating all the evidence indicates that the standard treatment involved an initial reposing of the corpse in extended position on the crypt floor with a cover of

Table 2.2. *Age, sex and selected artefact distributions in the Gibson and Klunk middle Woodland mound groups.
After Buikstra 1976.*

Burial categories	Sub-adult	Adult		Copper artefacts	Sea-shell artefacts	Platform pipes	Ceramic vessels	Lamellar blades
		Male	Female					
Crypt processing programme:								
Central crypt	10	19	7	7	5	12	–	–
Ramps	4	16	10	–	–	–	2	–
Mixed programme:								
Mound fill	34	23	24	1	1	–	1	1
Sub-floor pits	87	54	68	2	–	–	7	9
Non-crypt programme:								
Original surface	25	22	15	–	–	–	4	3

Fig. 2.2. Klunk Mound 6. Source: Perino 1968.

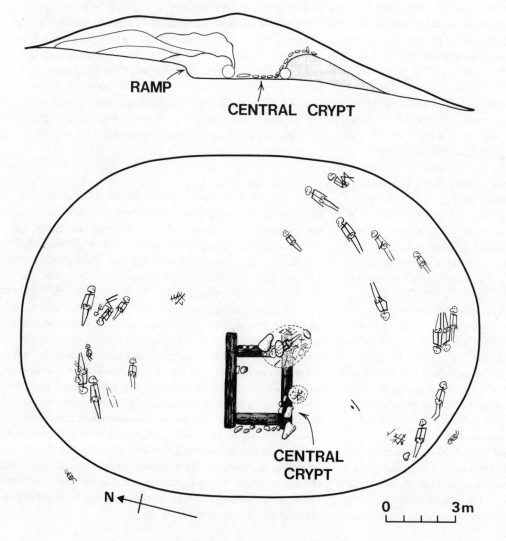

RAMP

CENTRAL CRYPT

CENTRAL CRYPT

N

0   3m

mats secured by cannon-bone skewers. After the corpse had decayed, the skeleton was left in place unless the space was needed for fresh corpses. In that case the bones were gathered together and piled in the corners of the crypt, or sometimes the bones were cast out onto the earth ramp flanks. At this stage, what was initially an extended skeleton was reduced to scattered bones and an occasional body part. Since scattered bones were also found in the mound fill, perhaps the surfaces of built-up mounds in the group were used as a refuse area as well. All told, three different interment categories can be linked to phases in the reduction of a single burial programme: extended, bundled and scattered bone burials. To lend further confusion to the situation, two and possibly three different locations were involved.

In contrast to the model of the crypt-processing programme, the peripheral burial programme involved extended and flexed burials in the lined graves and only flexed interments in the unlined examples. There exists no evidence to suggest exhumation or further post-mortem handling of the dead. Hence there is a distinct disparity in the social commitment to curating and handling the dead in the two programmes. However, it is easy to exaggerate the difference in effort expenditure as Tainter (1975a) has done (Brown 1979). The investment in the crypt seems impressive, but a comparison of the number of dead potentially processed through this facility, against the low level of maintenance required in its upkeep, diminishes first impressions (Brown 1979). What is interesting is the exclusion of the peripheral burials from the normal crypt processing. There was, however, a provocative distribution of grave goods that corresponds with the breakdown of the Klunk-Gibson dead by burial programme (table 2.2). Grave goods of foreign origin (principally the objects of copper and marine shell) were concentrated in the crypt, whereas certain classes of locally available items (e.g. ceramic vessels, *Anculosa* beads, clay and bone objects) were concentrated among the peripheral burials (Tainter 1975a; Buikstra 1976; Braun 1979). Here we see a well-behaved co-occurrence of effort investment in grave facility and buried wealth. However, this wealth does not include anything that convincingly constitutes a symbol of authority, since most items occur in midden deposit as well (Braun 1979). Thus the existence of anything approaching inherited authority is doubtful. From this evidence I would argue that there existed in the Klunk-Gibson communities a distinct order of prestige and privilege that departed from the typical local Illinois Hopewell status systems. Within the paradigm I have set forth, there are two alternative interpretations: either that prestige is primarily achieved within a society differentiated only by ordinary social inequality, or that prestige is primarily vested in a distinct group within the community.

There are some important additional considerations. First, the Klunk-Gibson mounds belong to a mortuary type associated solely with local communities. They are not greatly differentiated in size and construction. None, consequently, constitutes an example of a burial precinct super-ordinate to a region. In fact, mounds of quite different type on the floodplain have been argued by Struever and Houart (1972) to constitute supra-local mortuary centres. Second, the population density is not exceptional for intensive foragers and horticulturalists (Asch 1976; DeRousseau 1973). These data largely confirm the conclusion that inherited authority is absent.

The third consideration is the discovery by Buikstra (1976, 1977) that the higher-status individuals in the crypts enjoyed significantly better health from infancy than the adults in the peripheral graves (Buikstra 1976, p. 37; cf. Cook, D.C., 1976). This information accords with a model of socially determined, differential access to critical resources at times of food shortage. If this is translated into the paradigm introduced above, such a history of privilege is readily understandable as an inherited right. However, this data set requires further analysis, since the age and sex ratios of the two burial-programme sets are different (table 2.2). Although this fact has been used by Braun (1979) to argue for achieved status, inadequate allowance was made for the situation in which privilege was vested in a dominant group lacking claims to centralised leadership. In support of this, the considerable consumption of long-distance trade goods in burial and in living activities attests conspicuous consumption that is typical of groups vying with each other for highest prestige. Friedman and Rowlands (1977) have argued that such jockeying for prestige affects the economic future of the local group by recruiting new individuals through marriage and other means. In conclusion, the Illinois Hopewell case confirms the independence of social power and authority by showing an inherited status component with no vestige of centralised leadership.

Conclusion

The search for rank has been shown to be a complex problem which can be studied objectively when three logical steps in such an enquiry are clearly distinguished. In this essay care has been exercised to expand the basic arguments that archaeologists are currently employing on these three levels. For general theory I have found it useful to distinguish between social rank, power, and authority, because they seem to operate independently at the level of small-scale societies, where the presence of social rank is an issue in the prehistoric record. Secondly, the sociological variables of rank, power and authority are related to the material world through the middle-range theory of Saxe and Binford. At this level it is important to distinguish between the funeral and burial events themselves. The third step involves the creation of a site- or culture-specific model that translates the physical remains into patterned human behaviour. Three basic arguments have been employed to translate the archaeological record, namely, the effort-expenditure principle, the symbol-of-authority argument, and the age/sex-distribution argument. Used in combination they enable forceful statements to be made about the social organisation of prehistoric groups.

The three examples illustrate the independent operation of rank, authority and power in North American prehistory. The earliest case of the Illinois Hopewell lacks demonstrable indications of centralised leadership among groups in which inherited rank is indicated. Later in the Mississippian period inherited status is present in an early Caddoan phase, with variable degrees of evidence for centralised leadership. Strong indication of such leadership is present only later, in the Spiro phase, when a hierarchical settlement pattern emerged in the North Caddoan area.

The problems connected with the search for social rank have generally turned on the question whether there are grades in burial treatment etc. indicative of achieved or ascribed status. Rank has been argued to encompass more than the situations in which central leadership obtains. At the latter extreme the exclusive association of badges of premier status with a cross-section of the population should constitute a distinct minority of the burial population. In the case of competing autonomous groups, ranking is not exhibited by such symbols.

In my review I have pointed out a number of easily categorised pitfalls that await the archaeologist conducting this type of research:

(1) The apical social order may be missed. Several levels are required for investigation of social ranking and stratification, since relative differences are important. Typically, different locations will be used to mark out status differences, hence the archaeologist should be prepared to link up burials in different locations into a single burial system before searching for rank.

(2) Symbols of authority may not be identified. Some investigation must be made into the employment of artefacts as symbols of authority. Investigators must be particularly alert to emblems of rank such as costume (particularly head-dresses), elaborated weapons and other artefacts with ritual connections of great power.

(3) Complex burial processing may create false impressions of disposal programmes. Care must be exercised in interpreting the complexities of the burial programme, lest different phases or stages in burial processing be mistaken for different statuses.

Chapter 3

**Social configurations and
the archaeological study
of mortuary practices:
a case study**
John O'Shea

Introduction

The study of mortuary behaviour, and its use as a basis
for reconstructing past social organisation, is unique in
archaeology because of the emphasis which has been placed on
the formulation and use of theory. The developing archaeological theory, which attempts to correlate the social con-
figuration of a society with its practices for the disposal of the
dead, has a broad anthropological base: a terminology derived
from role theory (Saxe 1970); a conceptual framework from
formal semantic analysis in linguistics (Brown 1971a); and test
cases from comparative ethnography (Binford 1971; Goldstein
1976). Yet although such theory is intended for use almost
solely in archaeological contexts, archaeological evidence has
contributed little either to the formulation or to the testing of
the general theory. Nor has much attention been focussed on
the formal application of such a theory to archaeological cases
(cf. Chapman, this volume). Instead, it has been assumed that
if an ethnographical relationship can be demonstrated, a
corresponding archaeological relationship will be observed as
well.

Mortuary evidence is an extremely valuable archaeological resource, since it represents the direct and purposeful
culmination of conscious behaviour, rather than its incidental
residue. However there are still transformations intermediate
between the mortuary practices employed by a society and the
evidence of such practices which comes to be observed archae-

ologically (fig. 3.1). Firstly, although many of the observable elements of mortuary treatment are the direct and purposeful result of patterned behaviour, other aspects of the funerary ritual are not, for example ritual activity occurring prior to interment. Elements of this type can only be observed through non-purposeful, incidental attributes of the behaviour which are evidenced in the grave. Secondly, there is the range of transformations reflecting the failure of preservation and archaeological recovery. Finally, there are the limitations inherent in the archaeologist's ability to discriminate and explain the mortuary patterning which is present.

The existing theory of mortuary differentiation has concentrated on statements which specify the relationship between the organisation of a living society and its practices for the disposal of the dead. It fails to predict the additional relationship between these mortuary practices and their archaeological observation, which is of course, the evidence on which any social reconstruction will be based.

Other than recognising that information is lost, it is possible that there are no regularities in these transformational processes. Alternatively, if there are regularities in these transformations, recognition of them could vastly enhance the accuracy and reliability of archaeological reconstruction of past social organisation.

This paper will consider the existence of such regularities

by examining two specific questions: (1) do all social distinctions have an equal chance of being observed through archaeological analysis; and (2) how does a society's system of mortuary differentiation change through time? Although different in kind, both questions seek systematic relationships between the archaeological manifestations of a society's mortuary practices and those mortuary practices themselves. The first considers whether certain types of social differentiation are systematically lost or accentuated by their archaeological formation processes; the second searches for regularity in the manifestation of temporal change on the mortuary complex. This second is of special importance since the archaeologist's ability to infer social information from mortuary remains is itself dependent on the passage of time, during which the sample of the society's dead is accumulated (Peebles 1971, p. 69).

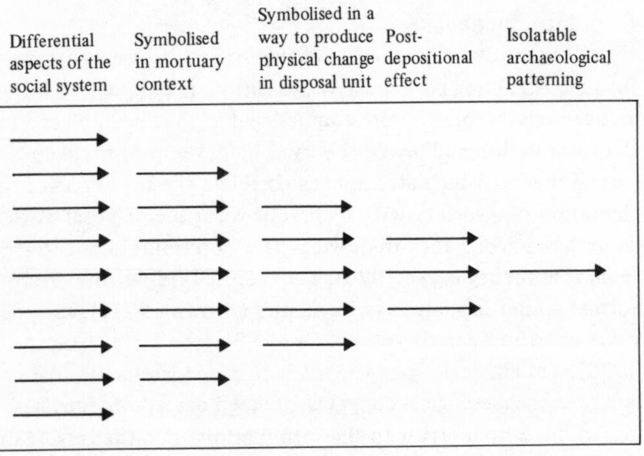

The sample

Since these questions are concerned with the actual forces of archaeological transformation, it was necessary to deal directly with archaeological materials as the basis of the analysis. It was also essential to compare, in some manner, these objectively derived archaeological results with known features of mortuary treatment and social organisation. In the present case, archaeological remains were analysed from a series of cemeteries for which the ethnic identity and societal organisation were known ethnographically. The sample was further structured so that sites produced by the same ethnic group, but at slightly different times, were selected, allowing for comparison across both temporal and ethnic boundaries.

The sample consisted of five cemetery sites dating from the late eighteenth and early nineteenth centuries on the Central Plains of North America. Two of the sites are associated with the Arikara of central South Dakota who spoke a Plains Caddoan dialect; two are from the Chaui band of the Pawnee, also speakers of a Caddoan language; and the fifth is associated with the Omaha, speakers of the Dhegian-Siouan language, who lived in the vicinity of northeastern Nebraska. Three of the sample cemeteries were excavated prior to the second world war by W.P.A. labour, while the other two (Leavenworth and Larson) were excavated in the 1960s as part of the general salvage efforts associated with the Oahe reservoir (table 3.1).

Fig. 3.1. Filtering processes affecting mortuary evidence.

| Differential aspects of the social system | Symbolised in mortuary context | Symbolised in a way to produce physical change in disposal unit | Post-depositional effect | Isolatable archaeological patterning |

Table 3.1. *Details of the archaeological sample.*

	Site name	Years occupied	Number of graves	Number of burial areas	Year excavated
PAWNEE	Linwood	1777–1809	54	3	1939
	Clarks	1820–45	70	8	1940
OMAHA	Big Village	1810–19	50	2	1939–40
ARIKARA	Larson	1750–80(?)	680	1	1966–8
	Leavenworth	1800–32	235	5	1965–6

Plains ethnohistory

Of equal importance to the selection of the archaeological sample was the ethnographic documentation of Arikara, Pawnee and Omaha social organisation. Such documentation provided a reference for comparison with the archaeological findings, and a means for predicting the kind and form of burial distinctions which 'should' be observed in the archaeological remains.

Despite differences in language and ethnic origins, the Arikara, Pawnee and Omaha exhibited considerable similarity in material culture and subsistence strategies. All three groups practised a mixed economy based on the riverine cultivation of maize, beans and squash, along with the seasonal hunting of large mammals, principally bison (Willey 1966, p. 310). Archaeological evidence, supplemented by folk histories, suggests the Pawnee to be the oldest Plains inhabitants, dating perhaps from as early as A.D. 800 (Ludwickson 1975). The Arikara, close relatives of the Pawnee, appear to have moved into South Dakota somewhat later, and perhaps as late as the early 1700s (Deetz 1965, p. 5). The Omaha are certainly relative newcomers to the Plains and appear to have crossed the Missouri river only in the early 1700s (Smith 1974, p. 21).

The internal organisation of these three societies was surprisingly similar given their disparate ethnic origins and length of time as Plains inhabitants. Each of the societies was divided into three stable, ranked groups: chiefs, eminent men and commoners. Among the Pawnee, membership of these levels was strictly hereditary (Murie 1916, p. 643), although an individual's relative position within the ranked group was affected by personal achievement (Dunbar 1880, p. 261). The ranking system of the Omaha exhibited some hereditary ascription similar to that of the Pawnee, but allowed a greater potential for mobility in the rank of a family or individual (Dorsey 1882, pp. 215–18; Howard 1965, p. 81). Among the Arikara, rank was achieved, sometimes through personal exploits but most commonly through the disposal of large quantities of wealth through gifting (Denig 1961, p. 62). Technically such a system is non-hereditary, but the incredible drain on a family's resources, as well as the tendency toward endogamy among families of high rank (Holder 1970, pp. 60–1), suggest that the system had strong hereditary tendencies. Each of the three societies, then, exhibited a distinct, although weakly defined, system of hereditary ranking which perhaps could be best characterised as a petty hierarchy.

In addition, a number of non-political, achieved positions existed within Plains society. These included membership in secret or social societies, participation as a shaman or doctor, and the holding of temporary offices such as hunt leader or war chief.

Considerable variation was also noted in the kin-based organisation of these three societies. Here, and throughout this paper, the term 'horizontal differentiation' will be used to describe these social differences, which tend to cross-cut age and sex categories and rank distinctions. 'Vertical differentiation' will refer to those distinctions which tend to elevate certain individuals above others in the social system; it is synonymous with social ranking. The most notable differences between the three groups were reflected in their patterns of descent and post-marital residence (the Omaha were patrilineal whereas the Pawnee and Arikara were matrilineal) and in the principal kin-based subdivisions of the communities: a moiety organisation for the Pawnee (Lowie 1954, p. 99); moiety and clan divisions among the Omaha (Fletcher and La Flesche 1911, p. 135); and only band distinctions for the Arikara (Curtis 1909, p. 61). These general categories of social organisation are summarised in table 3.2.

Table 3.2. *Principal units of Plains social observation:*
+ observed, − not observed.

	Pawnee	Omaha	Arikara
Moiety organisation	+	+	−
Clan structure	−	+	−
Patrilineal descent and residence	−	+	−
Matrilineal descent and residence	+	−	+
Band organisation	+	−	+
Hereditary social ranking	+	+	−
Age-grade societies	−	+	+

With this brief review of Plains ethnography we can suggest, using the general theory of mortuary differentiation, certain expectations concerning the patterns of mortuary differentiation which should be observed in the cemeteries of the three groups. Table 3.3 summarises the general categories, and specifies the demographic affinities and likely artefact and spatial elements which should characterise such social categories. Clearly, these are only the most general social subdivisions, and we would also expect to observe a number of more specialised statuses within the sample. These expectations will be reviewed in the light of archaeological analysis.

Plains mortuary practices: ethnohistorical accounts

Along with the ethnographic documentation of Plains social organisation, it is also possible to consider Plains mortuary practices as observed by ethnographers and contained in historical sources. In this way we can obtain another perspective on the relationship between the abstract theory of mortuary differentiation and a particular class of data – in this case ethnographic observation.

For the purposes of documentation, mortuary behaviour was divided into normative practices (i.e. treatment which virtually all individuals receive) and differential, or non-normative practices (i.e. treatment given only to a specified subset of the population).

Information on the normative burial treatments of these

Table 3.3. *Social categories and their archaeological attributes.*

Social category	Sex	Age	Pervasive-ness	Symbolic designators	Possible spatial element
			Rank differentiation		
Chieftain	Male	Adult (mature)	Lowest	Supralocal prestige symbols. Most energy intensive mortuary treatment. Wealth	Yes
Ranked males	Male	Adult	Low	Local sociotechnic symbols. Wealth	No
Ranked females	Female	Adult	Low	Wealth	No
Ranked sub-adult	–	Sub-adult	Low	Local sociotechnic arte-facts. Adult ascribed artefacts	No
Priest or doctor	Male (usually)	Adult (mature)	Low	Local sociotechnic symbols. Ritual implements	No
Wealth	Male/female	Adult (usually)	Varies	Artefact quantity and variety, especially exotic trade items	No
			Horizontal differentiation		
Moiety (Omaha and Pawnee)	Male/female	Even distribution	50%	Possible formal differ-entiation (location, orientation). Sociotechnic artefacts. Cross-section of vertical dimensions	Yes
Clan (Omaha)	Male/female	Even	10% each	As above; specific socio-technic symbols	Yes
Societies (non-kin based)					
Omaha	Male/female	Adult	Low	Local sociotechnic symbols	No
Arikara	Male/female	Adult	Low	Local sociotechnic symbols	No
Pawnee	Male (usually)	Adult	Low	Local sociotechnic symbols	?
Circumstantial	Male/female	Sub-adult/adult	Low	Interment away from usual area. Alternative burial treatment. Normal inclusions	Yes
Deviants	Male/female	Adult	Low	Alternative mortuary treat-ment. Interment away from the usual area. Atypical inclusions or absence of grave inclusions	

three tribes was abundant, and suggested that single, primary inhumation in grouped cemeteries was the common mode of burial disposal for all three. Burial posture varied from flexed, among the Pawnee and the Arikara (Bushnell 1927, p. 79; White 1959, p. 162), to extended among the Omaha (La Flesche 1889, pp. 6–7). A preferred burial orientation was observed for the Omaha and Arikara (White 1959, p. 88; Curtis 1909, p. 63), and wooden burial structures were common to all three groups. The burial coverings of the Pawnee and Omaha were relatively elaborate constructions with ridge-poles and gabling (James 1823, p. 2; Dorsey 1904, p. 215), while the typical Arikara covering consisted simply of flat planking over the grave.

The documentation of differential aspects of mortuary treatment was not uniform: the best available evidence was for the Omaha and the poorest for the Pawnee. For the latter, only three categories of treatment were documented: an increase in the elaboration of the burial ritual and mourning activities according to rank (Hughes 1968, p. 356); normative burial for those of lower rank; and alternative rites accorded to deaths under abnormal circumstances or to social deviants (included within these categories were war victims, who on occasion were buried in unused cache pits – Bushnell 1927, p. 80 – and sorcerers, who were decapitated and buried in isolated graves away from the community cemetery – Dorsey 1904, p. 218). Since the normative treatment also prescribed the inclusion of personal possessions in the grave with the deceased, it may also be inferred that basic adult/sub-adult and male/female distinctions would be observed (White 1959, p. 136).

A similar pattern of mortuary distinction was documented for the Arikara, with the addition that elaborated mortuary treatment was restricted to adult males (Curtis 1909, p. 63). Primary age and sex distinctions were symbolised by the inclusion of personal artefacts and ornaments worn in life (Fletcher 1908, p. 86). The Arikara also appear to have used scaffolding as an alternative means of disposal (Abel 1939, pp. 211–12), although it is unclear on what occasions this was employed.

The funerary activities of the Omaha are known in great detail, both through the extraordinary interest in Omaha burial shown by members of the Long expedition in 1820, and through the ethnographic writings of Francis La Flesche, himself a member of the Omaha tribe. As with the two previous groups, basic age and sex distinctions were symbolised through the inclusion of stereotyped sets of age- and sex-specific artefacts (La Flesche 1889, p. 9). Symbols of the clan to which an individual belonged were also included in the grave (Fletcher and La Flesche 1911, p. 588). Special burial treatment was provided for members of the various Omaha secret societies and for wealthy and influential members of the community (Fletcher and La Flesche 1911, pp. 553–4; James 1823, p. 2). Males of high rank were accorded particularly elaborate burial rites, involving the whole of the community and often culminating in the sacrifice of a horse on top of the grave.

Several alternative modes of disposal were known. The most common was the burial of individuals, particularly infants, in trees or on scaffolds when the tribe was on its annual bison hunt (Bushnell 1927, p. 51). (This was not always the case, as the body of the son of Big Elk, a principal chief of the Omaha, was returned for burial at the main settlement.) Other alternative practices divide into those reflecting the circumstances of an individual's death, for example individuals killed by lightning, and those reflecting social deviancy, including suicides and murderers.

It should be clear from this brief summary that, even in the best documented case, the observed mortuary distinctions appear to communicate a very limited sub-set of the social differentiation known to exist in the living society. From this we can conclude not only that a limited number of social distinctions were actually being recognised through the funerary treatment of a society but also that ethnographic observation often may be insufficient to record the total range of mortuary differentiation actually practised by a society. We will return to this suggestion after a consideration of the archaeological analysis.

Plains mortuary practices: archaeological analysis

The analysis of the archaeological samples considered the patterned variation in the formal attributes of burial, followed by an evaluation of the use of artefacts in the funerary treatment.

The formal attributes considered were as follows: grave dimensions, location within discrete burial areas, the posture of interment, the orientation and facing of the body, the presence of a burial covering, and evidence of alternative disposal programmes.

The analysis of artefact distribution began with the specification of an 88-element generalised typology and an observation of the distribution of each type, with reference to the age and sex of the individual with which it occurred, as well as to the location and quantity of each occurrence. Artefact occurrence was then analysed via an R-mode principal-component analysis to distinguish regularly co-varying sets of grave artefacts. This was followed by a Q-mode cluster analysis to distinguish similar groups of graves, and so identify the underlying structure of the mortuary population. Artefact occurrence data were supplied for the clustering procedures in two alternative forms: (1) in the form of a simple incidence matrix indicating the presence or absence of each particular type within each grave; and (2) as factor scores generated from the already mentioned principal-component analysis. The detailed results of these investigations are available elsewhere (O'Shea 1978).

By employing these techniques it was possible to isolate patterning within the funerary complex and to divide the cemetery population into a series of partially overlapping sub-sets. The specific characteristics of each sub-set, including its demographic affinities (Taylor 1969, p. 112) and the means by which it was differentiated in the mortuary ritual, were used to assess its possible social significance. This was done by comparing the observed characteristics of each sub-set with those 'expected' for a series of social distinctions modelled from living societies (in much the same manner as the mortuary expression of social categories was generated for the three tribal groups in table 3.3).

Two important indicators in these comparisons were energy expenditure and the occurrence of known sociotechnic artefacts (cf. Brown, this volume). If discrete levels of energy expenditure within the cemetery population could be demonstrated, it was considered likely that they corresponded with graded levels of social ranking in the living society (Tainter 1977a, p. 333; O'Shea 1978, pp. 18–19). Similarly, the occurrence of ethnographically-defined sociotechnic artefacts was expected to communicate rank-related distinctions if they exhibited a limited or constrained distribution.

Such a procedure permitted the identification of those social distinctions which were communicated through the observed mortuary differentiation. The procedure was used to identify community-wide classes of social differentiation, and did not attempt the specific explanation of more particularised social status which are more susceptible to idiosyncratic variation both in their representation and observation.

Pawnee mortuary practices
The Linwood site

Single, primary inhumation was the normative burial treatment at the Linwood site. Males were oriented to the north-west, females to the south-east, and all individuals were placed in a flexed posture. A number of differential practices were observed in both the formal burial treatment and in the patterns of artefact inclusion.

Three clear rank levels were observed within the mortuary complex. The first, composed solely of adult males, was differentiated by burial in a non-normative, extended posture, by the presence of a wooden burial structure, and by the occurrence of a variety of sociotechnic objects, particularly catlinite pipes. These individuals also possessed the greatest quantity and variety of burial inclusions. The second rank level was divided into two distinct sub-groups: (1) adult males with wooden burial coverings, who also possessed a large number of grave offerings (particularly important trade implements such as gun parts) as well as an occasional sociotechnic item; and (2) a single sub-adult (from the orientation, probably male), who was provided with a wooden burial covering. The third rank level included all other individuals. These graves tended to have fewer artefacts, especially of the types which were constrained in their distribution to specific age or sex categories. The artefacts which they did possess tended to be clothing ornamentation as opposed to tools or larger body ornaments.

In addition to these apparent rank divisions, an alternative disposal programme was observed, which entailed the interment of disarticulated and incomplete remains. The poor state of skeletal preservation precluded the determination of the manner in which disarticulation occurred. Individuals afforded this alternative treatment were not spatially segregated within the cemetery area, nor was the treatment limited to any age or sex category. Grave offerings found with these individuals corresponded with those of the third rank level.

The Clarks site

A similar, although not identical, pattern of mortuary differentiation was observed at the Clarks site. Primary, single inhumation in a flexed posture with a northerly orientation and topped with a wooden burial covering was the normative treatment employed at the Clarks site. As at Linwood, burials were found in a number of discrete burial areas.

Three basic rank levels were distinguished. The first level was composed of a small number of adult males, whose graves contained the greatest quantity of constrained artefact types, most of the sociotechnic objects encountered, and the only examples of catlinite pipes. The second level was subdivided into three categories: (1) adult males whose graves contained at least one sociotechnic object and who also possessed task-related sets of male implements; (2) adult females with grave inclusions similar to those of the ranked males, with the exception that the tool kits related to female activities; and (3) a small number of sub-adults, who were interred with at least one sociotechnic object, and who were also frequently buried with an implement normally restricted in its distribution to adults (i.e. non-normative artefact use). The third rank level included all other individuals found in the cemetery areas. These individuals were interred with fewer artefacts and principally those of an ornamental nature. No evidence for an alternative disposal programme was observed at the Clarks site.

Pawnee social differentiation

Mortuary differentiation observed in the archaeological analysis of the two Pawnee sites suggests that a similar system of social differentiation was in operation in both, although considerable variation was apparent in the specific channels through which distinction was communicated.

Table 3.4 summarises the general results of the archaeological analysis regarding the detection of social units, compared with both the ethnographically known structure of Pawnee society and the reconstruction based solely on the ethnohistorical accounts of mortuary treatment.

As can be seen, neither the archaeological nor the ethnohistorical reconstructions provided a reliable view of horizontal differentiation within Pawnee society. In contrast, social ranking among the Pawnee was reflected from both archaeological examples, but not from the ethnohistorical documentation. In summary, archaeological analysis did provide an accurate representation of Pawnee social ranking. Horizontal differentiation, known to exist in Pawnee society, was not detected in the mortuary remains of either of the two sites. Furthermore, ethnographic accounts of Pawnee mortuary treatment,

Table 3.4. *Ethnographic and archaeological observation of Pawnee mortuary differentiation.*

Type of differentiation	Source of observations			
	Ethnographic		Archaeological	
	Society	Mortuary practice	Linwood	Clarks
Horizontal				
Moiety organisation	+			
Matrilineal residence/descent	+			
Societies	+			
Male/female	+		+	+
Adult/sub-adult	+			+
Vertical				
Chieftainship	+	+?	+	+
Ranked males	+	+?	+	+
Ranked females	+	+?		+
Ranked sub-adults	+		+?	+
Wealth	+	+	+	+
Deviancy	+			
Alternative burial practice	+	+	+	

although accurately reflecting the normative aspects of Pawnee mortuary treatment, were inadequate to predict the nature of either vertical or horizontal structure in Pawnee society.

Temporal change in Pawnee mortuary treatment

Since both cemeteries analysed were produced by the same ethnic group, but separated in time by at least eleven years (Linwood was abandoned in 1809, Clarks founded about 1820 – Wedel 1936, p. 31), variation in the observed mortuary treatment may be attributable to the effects of time, either directly in the form of drift (Binford 1963), or indirectly by reflecting time-dependent changes in the society at large. Such changes in mortuary treatment may be seen as alterations in the means of symbolising a particular social distinction, or as an alteration in the social distinctions chosen to be symbolised. Both types of change were observed in the Pawnee cemeteries.

Considerable variation in the use of formal mortuary treatment was observed between the two sites. At Linwood, formal treatment served a number of differential functions and these included: a sex-based difference in burial orientation; two varieties of mortuary elaboration – burial coverings and non-normative extended burial posture; and an alternative disposal programme of disarticulated burial. At the Clarks site, however, formal treatment served solely normative functions. No evidence was observed for sex-specific orientation, burial elaboration or an alternative disposal programme.

The use of artefacts within the mortuary ritual was similar at both sites, highlighting task-specific sets of implements, especially those associated with male activities, and also emphasising related sets of clothing and body ornaments. The most notable differences in artefact use between the two sites were: (1) a more constrained pattern of artefact distribution relative to age and sex at the Clarks site; and (2) a greater emphasis on age distinctions at the Clarks site. These findings are summarised in fig. 3.2.

Despite changes in the occurrence of specific artefact types, the overall organisation of material culture within the burial context was very similar, as is shown in the fall-off curves of the eigenvalues derived from the principal component analyses (fig. 3.3). These curves, especially when contrasted with that derived from the Omaha cemetery, suggest that the degree of organisation of artefact inclusion was virtually identical, a conclusion which was confirmed by a comparison of the specific factors themselves. Furthermore no change was observed in the varieties of artefacts employed within the burials as compared with those encountered in the excavation of the settlements.

In summary, temporal change in Pawnee mortuary treatment, as evidenced in the analysis of the Linwood and Clarks sites, was observed primarily in the means by which particular social distinctions were given symbolic representation. These results also suggest a trend toward a greater emphasis on age distinctions at the Clarks site, and an apparent discontinuation of an alternative disposal programme, both of which may suggest changing emphasis within the social system of the Pawnee.

Arikara mortuary practices
The Larson site

Normative burial treatment at the Larson site consisted of single, primary inhumation. Individuals were interred in a flexed posture, orientated in a northwesterly direction and covered by a wooden burial covering. Adults were distinguished from sub-adults in both size and depth of grave.

Three basic rank levels were discernible at the Larson site, although they were not as distinct as in the Pawnee examples. The first level was composed entirely of adult males who possessed the largest quantity of artefacts, especially ones of sociotechnic importance and other artefacts whose distributions were constrained and of low overall pervasiveness. The second level was composed of two clear subdivisions: (1) adult males with large quantities of grave offerings, particularly task-related implement sets, quantities of native-made ornamentation, and an occasional sociotechnic object (it should be stressed that the difference between these individuals and

those in level one is really a quantitative rather than a qualitative difference in burial elaboration, perhaps conforming to the higher and lower ends of a single continuum); and (2) a smaller number of adult females, and sub-adults with a large number of grave inclusions, in particular imported *Olivella* shell beads. The final level was composed of the majority of the interred individuals. They were buried with only a few artefacts, these being primarily ornamentation, although some implements of native manufacture, such as projectile points, stone scrapers, and bone quill flatteners were found occasionally with these individuals.

A number of alternative burial postures were encountered at Larson, although they did not seem to correlate firmly with any other clear distinctions in either spatial location or artefact assemblage. The exception to this was that two individuals were interred in an extended posture and decapitated, and also possessed large, intricate spearpoints. Several other individuals, also mature males, were buried with these artefacts, which in at least one case seems to have been the cause of death (O'Shea 1978, p. 113). These graves clearly represent some special social category, but certainly do not constitute an elevated rank level. They may rather be war captives or sacrificial victims who have been ritually interred. An identical case will be mentioned in the Omaha cemetery. It is possible that some form of exposure was practised among the Arikara, although the testing of this possibility was beyond the scope of the present study (but see Ubelaker and Willey 1978).

The Leavenworth site

Normative treatment at the Leavenworth site consisted of primary, single inhumation in a flexed posture, but without

Fig. 3.2. Temporal changes in Pawnee artefact usage.
A. Constraint on artefact occurrence relative to age and sex: + constrained, − not constrained.
B. Comparison of the occurrence of specific artefact types.

A

LINWOOD

AGE	+ SEX −	
+	M. Adult 3	Adult 4
		Sub-adult 2
−	Male 4	41

CLARKS

AGE	+ SEX −	
+	M. Adult 8	Adult 7
	F. Adult 2	Sub-adult 7
−	Male 4	21

B

Artefact type	Linwood	Clarks
Glass trade beads	No constraint	Sub-adults
Whole mussel shell	No constraint	Adults
Metal bangles	Males	No constraint
Strike-a-light	No constraint	Males
Metal hardware	Males	No constraint
Metal projectile points	Male? (n=1)	Adult, male
Metal button	Sub-adult	No constraint
Small brass bells	Adult	No constraint
Sandstone shaft smoother	No constraint	Adult, male
Stone projectile point	No constraint	Adult, male
Stone pipe	Male	Adult, male

Fig. 3.3. Comparison of the eigenvalue fall-off from the principal-component analyses of Pawnee artefact inclusions.

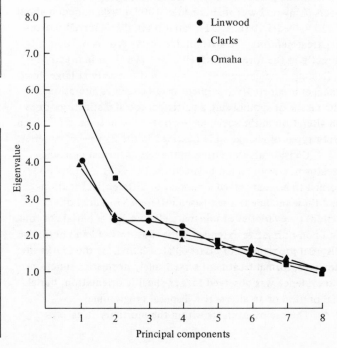

any clear preference in orientation. Wooden burial coverings seem to have been provided for all individuals, and the excavators suggest that the dead were wrapped in bison robes for interment because of the large quantities of robe fragments encountered during excavation (Bass, Evans and Jantz 1971, p. 178).

Clear rank distinctions could not be discerned in the Leavenworth mortuary evidence. The burial population was somewhat artificially divided on the basis of the quantity of artefacts found within each grave, but the division lacked the discrete occurrence of badges or other sets of artefacts which provide qualitative distinctions. Such differences may have been due solely to the economic potency of the individual (and his family) rather than to the existence of two clear rank levels. The higher of the two groups included those individuals with a greater variety of artefacts in their grave assemblages, greater quantities of trade materials, and an occasional native-made implement. Membership in this first group was not restricted to any age or sex category, although slightly more males than females and adults than sub-adults possessed assemblages of this kind. Interments in the lower level, in addition to containing fewer artefacts, tended to contain more irregular sets of trade ornaments, with few, if any, implements or objects of ritual significance.

As was observed at Larson, a few individuals were found in alternative burial postures, although these did not seem to correlate with any other element in the mortuary treatment. However, all of these individuals did have burial assemblages corresponding with the lower of the two rank levels. There is also the untested possibility at Leavenworth that exposure was used occasionally as an alternative form of disposal.

Arikara social differentiation

The patterns of mortuary differentiation obtained from the archaeological analysis of the two Arikara sites were strikingly different in the picture of Arikara social organisation they presented. Table 3.5 presents the comparison of archaeological and ethnographic reconstructions of Arikara social organisation. As was seen in the Pawnee example, neither ethnohistorical observation nor archaeological analysis was able to provide a true picture of the horizontal structuring of Arikara society. However both types of evidence presented a clear representation of Arikara rank organisation.

At Larson, the earlier site, virtually all of the major social categories were recognised from the archaeological results. At Leavenworth, however, a much more limited range of mortuary patterning was discerned. This appears to be the result of a radical realignment of Arikara funerary behaviour, rather than a failure of archaeological observation. This point will be discussed again with regard to temporal changes in Arikara funerary practices.

To summarise the Arikara examples, although archaeological analysis and to a slightly lesser degree ethnohistorical reconstruction of Arikara mortuary patterning did identify the principal rank features of Arikara society, horizontal aspects of the societal structure could not be recognised.

Table 3.5. *Ethnographic and archaeological observation of Arikara mortuary differentiation.*

Type of differentiation	Source of observations			
	Ethnographic		Archaeological	
	Society	Mortuary practice	Larson	Leavenworth
Horizontal				
Matrilineal residence/descent	+			
Societies	+			
Male/female	+		+	+
Adult/sub-adult	+		+	+
Vertical				
Chieftainship	+	+	+	
Ranked males	+	+	+	
Ranked females	+		+	
Ranked sub-adults	?		+	
Wealth	+	+	+	+
Deviancy	?		+	
Alternative burial practice	+	+	+	+

Temporal change in Arikara mortuary treatment

Over the approximately twenty-year period separating the abandonment of Larson and the founding of the Leavenworth site in A.D. 1800, radical changes occurred in Arikara mortuary treatment. Change was not limited to the manner in which social distinction was expressed, but affected all aspects of Arikara mortuary custom, even its normative practices. Over this time, the use of a single burial area was replaced by use of multiple areas, and the consistent pattern of burial orientation was discontinued. Other formal elements of mortuary treatment, however, seem to have remained constant.

It is in the use of artefacts that the real divergence in Arikara mortuary treatment was observed. The use of artefacts was much less constrained and stereotyped at Leavenworth, as can be seen in fig. 3.4. While 62% of all types occurring at Larson show some manner of constraint in their dis-

tribution relative to age or sex, only 36% showed constraint at Leavenworth. This change was plainly visible in the eigenvalue fall-off curves from the two principal-component analyses. These contrast a steep fall-off at Larson, suggesting a high degree of organisation in artefact occurrence, with a nearly level curve produced by the Leavenworth analysis (fig. 3.5). Indeed, the magnitude of change observed seems to suggest a fundamental alteration in the way artefacts were perceived and used within the funerary rites of the Arikara. The existence of such change was further suggested by the fact that at Larson there was little correspondence between artefacts regularly found in the cemetery and those found in the village excavation, while at Leavenworth there was an almost total overlap of the artefact types found in these two contexts.

If these changes are considered within the context of changing mortuary symbolism, one observes a shift from the use of relatively well-defined and stereotyped sets of grave inclusions reflecting primary social distinctions, to a situation characterised by an almost random intermixing of artefact inclusions, and in a quantity corresponding perhaps with the economic potency of the individual and his family. This shift from a coherently organised use of material culture within the mortuary context to a much more idiosyncratic system of burial inclusion may reflect a de-ritualisation of material culture within the mortuary context, and a breaking down of the existing ritual order controlling mortuary treatment.

In summary, major changes were observed in Arikara funerary treatment during the twenty years separating the use of the two sites. Change was pervasive and was observed even in the basic normative practices employed by the Arikara.

Fig. 3.4. Temporal changes in Arikara artefact usage.
A. Constraint on artefact occurrence relative to age and sex: + constrained, − not constrained.
B. Comparison of the occurrence of specific artefact types.

A

LEAVENWORTH

	+ SEX −
+ AGE	M. Adult 2 / Adult 6 / Sub-adult 6
− AGE	Male 5 / Female 2 / 35

LARSON

	+ SEX −
+ AGE	M. Adult 11 / Adult 11 / Sub-adult 8
− AGE	Male 3 / 20

B

Artefact type	Leavenworth	Larson
Glass trade beads	Unconstrained	Sub-adults
Animal teeth	Female	Sub-adults
Bird beak	Unconstrained	Adult, male
Small mammalian crania	Unconstrained	Male
Rib shaft wrench	Unconstrained	Adult, male
Quill flattener	Unconstrained	Adult, male
Gun parts	Unconstrained	Sub-adult
Polished bone tube	Male	Adult, male
Perforated shell pendant	Unconstrained	Adult, male
Metal bracelet	Unconstrained	Sub-adult
Metal bangle	Sub-adult	Unconstrained
Metal container	Unconstrained	Adult
Bifacial spearpoint	Adult	Adult, male
Sandstone shaft smoother	Unconstrained	Adult
Unretouched flakes	Unconstrained	Adult
Stone projectile point	Unconstrained	Adult, male
Stone knife	Unconstrained	Adult

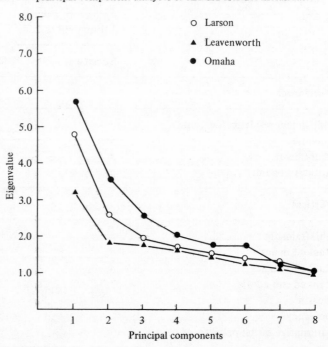

Fig. 3.5. Comparison of the eigenvalue fall-off from the principal-component analyses of Arikara artefact inclusions.

Omaha mortuary practices

The Big Village

As only a single Omaha burial sample was available for analysis, it was not possible to evaluate the nature of temporal change in Omaha funerary treatment, although it provided a valuable third test of the reliability of archaeological and ethnohistorical reconstruction of past social organisation.

The normative burial treatment observed at the Big Village consisted of primary single inhumation. Individuals were placed in an extended posture on their backs (the floor of the grave was occasionally sloped with the effect that the individual's head and shoulders were slightly elevated, resulting almost in a sitting posture) and were orientated toward the north-west.

Some differentiation was observed in the formal aspects of the funerary treatment. This included the interment of adults in graves which were significantly larger and deeper than those for sub-adults, and the possible use of wooden coverings as a burial elaboration.

Three rank levels were clearly defined in the Omaha mortuary evidence. The highest level was composed solely of older adult males. These individuals were provided with substantial wooden burial coverings, and had a number of known sociotechnic objects as well as massive quantities of trade-derived materials. The second rank level was subdivided into three groups: (1) adult males who were interred with quantities of trade-derived body ornamentation, male implement sets, and at least one sociotechnic object; (2) adult females who were buried with the largest quantities of trade goods known for females, female implement kits, and most interestingly, some elements of ornamentation normally restricted to males; and (3) a few sub-adults, frequently with wooden burial coverings, who were interred with elements of adult implement sets and occasionally with a sociotechnic object. The final rank level included the remainder of the individuals of the mortuary population, who were typically interred with more-frequently occurring and unconstrained artefact types, mainly clothing ornaments.

In addition to these rank levels, at least three alternative types of interment could be recognised. The first of these was cremation. A single individual (young adult, male) was found to have been cremated. The second alternative practice was the interment of semi-disarticulated remains (following the terminology of Sprague 1968). This was observed in two cases, both adolescent males and both with grave inclusions consistent with the third rank level (i.e. clothing ornamentation). These individuals may not reflect an intentional alternative disposal programme, but rather the result of the well-known Plains practice of dismembering war victims (cf. Morgan 1953, p. 69). In such a case, these individuals were probably Omaha war dead, whose remains had been recovered for burial.

The final alternative disposal type observed has direct counterparts in the Larson cemetery. One individual was interred in a normal extended posture, but had been decapitated (the head placed at the individual's side). In addition,

the right arm was severed from the body and replaced in reverse anatomical order. Among the grave inclusions found with this individual was a large bifacially worked spearpoint.

Omaha social differentiation

The detailed ethnographic documentation of Omaha mortuary ritual provides a more accurate reconstruction of the principal social units of Omaha society than was possible from either the Pawnee or Arikara examples. Not only were details of social ranking visible, but also some elements symbolic of kinship units or horizontal differentiation were noted, as were a number of classes of alternative burial treatment (table 3.6).

Archaeological analysis, as in the Pawnee and Arikara cases, provided an accurate portrayal of social ranking among the Omaha, but was ambiguous in the identification of kin-based social subdivisions. Ethnohistorical and archaeological reconstructions of Omaha social ranking were in general agreement and, moreover, archaeological analysis was able to confirm ethnohistorical assertions concerning the manner in which specific types of social differentiation actually came to be symbolised in the mortuary treatment. The absence of a similar confirmation of horizontal elements of social differentiation will be discussed later.

Discussion

This study has focussed on the transformations which articulate the general theory of mortuary differentiation with the specific observations obtainable through archaeological analysis, and has concentrated on two specific relationships: the relative detectability of differing kinds of social distinction and the nature of temporal change. It is now possible to consider these in light of the results from the archaeological case study.

The first question was whether all types of social distinction have an equal chance of being observed through archaeological analysis. In light of the present case study, the answer to this question must be in the negative. In all three examples, elements of social ranking were clearly identified, while kin-based social subdivisions were not.

This difference between horizontal and vertical social subdivisions can be attributed to two related factors. The first is the manner in which differing types of social distinction are symbolised in the mortuary ritual. Binford (1971, p. 17) has argued that there is a systematic relationship between the type of social distinction recognised in death and the manner in which the distinction is symbolised, particularly rank differentiation and its dependence on the size and composition of the social group recognising status duties to the deceased. If such rank differences are communicated through wealth symbols and increased energy expenditure, then horizontal distinctions should be expressed through channels of 'neutral' value. Hence, 'unvaluable' tokens such as clothing, coiffure, symbolically distinctive artefacts, and elements of body posture and orientation, should be common indicators of

Table 3.6. *Ethnographic and archaeological observation of Omaha mortuary differentiation.*

Type of differentiation	Source of observations		
	Ethnographic		Archaeological
	Society	Mortuary practice	
Horizontal			
Moiety organisation	+		
Clan organisation	+	+	
Patrilineal residence/descent	+		
Societies	+	+	
Male/female	+	+	+
Adult/sub-adult	+	+	+
Vertical			
Chieftainship	+	+	+
Ranked males	+	+	+
Ranked females	+		+
Ranked sub-adults	+		+
Wealth	+	+	+
Deviancy	+	+	+
Alternative burial practice	+	+	+

horizontal differences. Unfortunately, such symbolic indicators are most likely either to be unpreserved or to be ambiguous to the archaeologist. The validity of this assertion can be illustrated by the manner in which social distinction was symbolised by the Omaha (table 3.7).

Most horizontal features were marked by the preparation of the body and other ritual which occurs prior to burial, and by the inclusion of totemic items within the grave, most of which were organic in nature. Social ranking, on the other hand, although also marked by pre-interment ritual, was distinguished by elaboration in the burial covering and by the nature and quantity of objects placed within the grave. In other words, vertical ranking tended to be symbolised in a manner which was readily identifiable, while horizontal differentiation tended to be shown through channels which at best were incompletely observable.

The second factor which may interfere with the accurate identification of horizontal distinction relates to the process of archaeological explanation. Elements of social rank can be distinguished by a hierarchical gradation in pervasiveness and energy expenditure, and by skewed demographic values (i.e., a particular rank level being restricted to adult males). Horizontal distinctions, however, are characterised by a normal distribution of age and sex classes and by varying levels of pervasiveness, depending on the type of social unit symbolised.

In other words, while rank distinction is easily recognised in archaeological terms, horizontal social units are often indistinguishable from a wholly random or idiosyncratic occurrence.

The recognition of such horizontal distinctions therefore rests solely on the detection of contrasting sets of discretely occurring attributes. In relatively simple cases, this may pose no particular problem, especially in instances where discrete burial areas are employed in the mortuary symbolism (as was the case at Galley Pond Mound: Binford 1964). Yet, such explanations are susceptible to considerable ambiguity, as illustrated in fig. 3.6. Suppose that a community is divided into three basic kin groups, each of which distinguishes its members by burial within a distinct portion of the community's cemetery and by including in the grave a distinct totemic symbol. These are represented by a star, a triangle, or a filled circle in fig. 3.6. In case A all three of these symbols are preserved for archaeological recovery, and the three-fold division of the burial population is obvious. In case B one of the three symbols is made of organic material and is not preserved (symbolised by an open circle). Here too three groups can be distinguished, two by distinctive symbols and the third by the absence of such an artefact. However in case C, where two of the symbols do not survive, it is no longer possible to establish unambiguously the existence of a tripartite kin structure. The pattern might be interpreted erroneously as a two-level rank

Table 3.7. *Omaha mortuary symbolism.*

	Horizontal differentiation		Vertical differentiation
Moiety	No distinctions documented	Chief or warrior	Increased community involvement in the mourning ritual (for individuals of especially high rank special rituals of community grief, culminating in scarification and reciprocal gifting)
Clan	Symbol of clan's taboo animal, frequently as an artefact made from the animal's skin Face painted in the distinctive pattern of the clan Burial with catlinite pipe if a member of the Hunga clans		Erection of special burial covering Public contribution of gifts to be interred with the deceased Sacrifice of deceased's best horse over the grave
Secret society	Pre-interment ritual directed by the society rather than the family of the deceased Removal of the deceased's society regalia and other symbols of membership Placing of the society's symbol on the grave after burial	Wealth	Greater quantities of artefacts interred with the deceased Special burial prerogative (this is particularly noted for the children of important individuals who, if dying while the tribe is on a hunting expedition, will be transported back to the village for burial, rather than receive the normative, scaffold burial)
Family	Pre-interment preparation of the body Payment of the grave-digger Prescribed mourning activities Maintenance of food and fire at the graveside for four days		
Individual	Personally owned items of value, chiefly ornaments in life, interred with the deceased		

structure, with limited access to the obvious sociotechnic artefacts, and with ranked and non-ranked burial zones. In the final case, none of the clan symbols are preserved and no conclusion can be drawn concerning the existence of any kin structure. If the separate burial areas were identifiable, the existence of the kin structure might be suggested, but there would be no further evidence to support such an assertion (as indeed was the case in the present archaeological study).

To summarise, social ranking can be observed readily from mortuary evidence. Such observations may even suggest detailed aspects of the ranking system which are not obvious in the society's ethnographically observed behaviour. The funerary expression of horizontal social distinctions, although occasionally identified (cf. Brown 1967), will not be recognised in many instances, and as such will not provide a reliable view of a society's horizontal structuring (although improvements in biological analysis may overcome this archaeological deficiency). It is important to stress that this is not because horizontal distinctions are less frequently recognised in mortuary ritual, but is rather the result of limitations in the archaeological recognition of such patterning.

The study was also concerned with the observation of regularity in the effects of time on mortuary differentiation. From the present study, it is clear that change can be expected both in the social distinctions given symbolic recognition and

in the means through which such distinction is achieved. This lack of temporal stability is significant both for the identification of ethnic groups, and also for the further specification of the relationship between the structure of living societies and their mortuary practices.

The late eighteenth and early nineteenth centuries were periods of intense change for the Plains villagers, as they came to terms with the altered physical and social environment produced by the coming of the Euro-Americans. All three tribal groups suffered from intense raiding and the effects of virulent epidemic diseases. Their social systems also experienced the destabilising effects produced by the merging of previously separate and semi-autonomous communities into larger, conglomerate villages (cf. Denig 1961, p. 41).

For the Arikara, who were intensely involved in the Euro-American trade as middlemen, change was rapid, leading to the effective disintegration of traditional Arikara social organisation (Deetz 1965, pp. 36–7). This situation is suggested by the change in Arikara mortuary treatment, which shifted from a highly organised ritual complex at Larson to a situation almost devoid of any community-wide structure in the mortuary practices at Leavenworth.

The Pawnee, because of their relative isolation from the main river-borne trade, had a longer period of time to effect counter-measures to the changing Plains environment, and responded by intensifying the internal structure of their society. So successful were the Pawnee that, in the face of starvation, murderous raiding from equestrian nomads, and finally their forced removal to Oklahoma, Pawnee social organisation remained intact (cf. Weltfish 1965, p. 3).

For the study of mortuary differentiation generally, these results suggest that changes in the organisation of a living society can be expected to produce changes in the pattern of mortuary symbolism. This supports Binford's assertion (1971,

Fig. 3.6. Ambiguity in the observation of horizontal social distinctions.

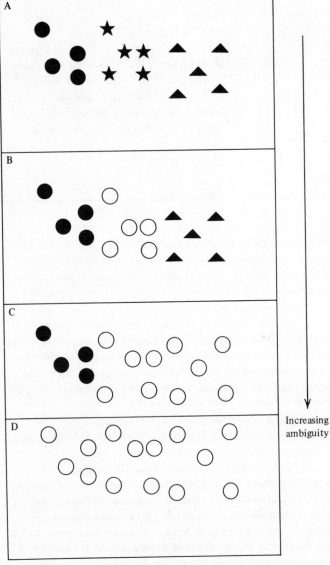

Increasing ambiguity

p. 23) that the mortuary practices of a society are patterned and circumscribed by the nature of the society at large. Yet this must also introduce a note of caution, since the very existence of a cemetery implies the passage of an often undetermined length of time. Just as a traditional analysis based on the occurrence of specific artefact types would distort the temporal and ethnic relationship of the five historic sites, so a structural analysis would come to grief if the possibility of significant temporal change were not considered for these sites, despite their close proximity in time. If accurate social inferences are to be drawn, mortuary practices must be viewed within their temporal context, and as reflective of adaptive changes occurring within the living society at large.

Conclusions

This study has considered the transformations which link a society's mortuary behaviour with the archaeological evidence for such behaviour, and has examined the possible existence of regularities in these relationships. The present investigation is only a case study and as such the results should not be over-generalised. This is particularly true since the specific samples considered do not represent a cross-section of human society, in terms either of their social complexity, or of their areal distribution. Furthermore, the examples employed represent societies in a state of flux and rapid change, which is hardly typical of the whole archaeological record. However, the results are of interest, both because they suggest that there are regularities in the formation processes affecting mortuary remains, and because they illustrate the successful use of mortuary analysis under highly unfavourable conditions and in a situation in which only very weak systems of social ranking existed.

The study emphasises the interdependence of a society's funerary practices with the other aspects of the total cultural system, and stresses that no aspect of the funerary behaviour exists in isolation from the adaptive priorities and necessities of the society at large. It is through this relationship that mortuary patterning can be used to study social change within its very broadest context. It also suggests that our perception of social organisation derived from the analysis of mortuary remains may be distorted, but distorted in a regular and predictable manner.

Acknowledgements

This paper has benefited from the comments of Colin Renfrew, James Brown and Paul Halstead, who read it in draft form. I have incorporated many of their ideas in the present paper, but must accept responsibility for any misapplication of these suggestions. I would also like to thank Sue O'Shea for valuable help and advice.

⬤
▲ } Observable symbolic tokens
★

◯ Symbolic token that has not survived for observation

Chapter 4

One-dimensional archaeology and multi-dimensional people: spatial organisation and mortuary analysis
Lynne Goldstein

Introduction

Spatial analysis has become very popular in archaeology today, but most of this work has centred on habitation sites and settlement patterning. As Clarke (1977, p. 9) has pointed out, however, sites selected for study should *not* be confined to settlements. Human activity, wherever represented, tends to be non-random, and spatial structure can be seen as the output of non-random human choice processes (Clarke 1977, p. 10). This paper addresses a somewhat neglected area of spatial analysis — the mortuary site.

Mortuary customs, mortuary sites and even isolated human burials have concerned archaeologists for many years. Until recently, however, there has been little attempt to deal with burials 'as a distinct class of variable phenomena' (Binford 1971, p. 6). Early trait-list approaches to burial customs assumed an intra-cultural uniformity that inhibited investigation of mortuary variation within and between societies. These approaches also implicitly assumed that formally similar objects and customs have fixed significance from one culture to the next. However, the same object may have different symbolic significance in different cultures, and in any given culture there may be many ways of symbolising the same concept (cf. Ucko 1969).

Recently, archaeologists have returned to the study of mortuary practices as a critical method for the determination of prehistoric social organisation. The validity of this approach is amply documented in the ethnographic literature (cf. Bendann 1930; Douglass 1969; Gluckmann 1937; Miles 1965; van Gennep 1960). 'Not only does death serve to activate the various levels of social organisation, but on each level it occasions the widest expression of such relationships . . . To a significant degree . . . it is through death that the social relationships of the living are defined and expressed' (Douglass 1969, p. 219). Archaeologists are now aware that in order to explain similarities and differences within and between sociocultural systems it is necessary to seek 'regularities in the *processes* that result in a set of mortuary practices rather than in the formal attributes of the practices themselves, each of which is necessarily unique' (Saxe 1970, p. 1). Past mortuary studies failed because they focussed on formal rather than processual regularities.

The ethnographic literature has been the source of several studies attempting to relate aspects of mortuary behaviour to the organisation of society (e.g. Binford 1971; Saxe 1970; Tainter 1975a; Goldstein 1976, 1980). Among other things, these studies have resulted in confirmation of two basic assumptions of current archaeological mortuary analysis: (1) the variables within a mortuary site cluster so that they partition the universe of mortuary practices, and these partitions represent different social statuses or classes; and (2) the principles which organise the sets of statuses are the same as the organising social relations in the general society (cf. Saxe 1970). To put it simply, a person treated differentially in death was probably also so treated in life; this differential treatment reflects the social structure of the society.

One of the basic concepts inherent in the study of mortuary practices is that of status and social identities. Indeed, most current mortuary analysis focusses on the identification and differentiation of social statuses. The concept of status is crucial, since burials afford archaeologists one of the best means of examining social interaction. The particular social relationships involving the deceased account for the specific disposal treatment. However, because different types of social organisation allow for different sets of social relationships, different organisations will also exhibit different disposal treatments. Mortuary analysis must link social relationships, social structure, and disposal treatment.

A review of current mortuary analyses

Recent mortuary analyses have taken several different paths. One of these can be termed the 'evolutionary classification' approach. Different levels of social organisational complexity should be reflected by different sets of disposal treatment. Fried (1960, 1967) and Service (1962) are frequently quoted in mortuary analyses because, as a part of their general evolutionary models, they have specifically defined several levels of socio-organisational complexity. These levels of complexity are differentiated primarily on the basis of form of organisation.

Binford (1962) first discussed the possibility of distinguishing archaeologically between Fried's egalitarian and ranked types of societies, offering predictions of the artefact assemblages which would be associated with each type of society. Specifically within the context of mortuary studies, Saxe (1968, 1970) has made similar observations. In his sample of ethnographic societies, burial mode was controlled by age, sex, and normal/deviant distinctions in egalitarian societies, while culturally defined social role and kinship positions controlled burial mode in ranked societies.

Focussing only on the artefactual dimension, King (1970) summarised archaeological definitions of egalitarian as opposed to ranked societies for mortuary sites. King's definitions or list of attributes deal exclusively with artefactual dimensions and resemble an updated trait-list approach for classification of societies. The definitions do not really examine interrelationships between dimensions.

The major problem with the evolutionary classification approach is that both Fried's and Service's schemes are relative, and translating the scheme into artefact dimensions results in an elaborate trait list. The analysis then becomes a process of pigeon-holing the particular culture as egalitarian, tribal, ranked, or a chiefdom. While useful in terms of partly standardising levels of sociocultural complexity and giving some idea of the general organisation of prehistoric societies, this procedure is not necessarily instructive as to the society's specific organisation and structure.

Renfrew (1972) has carried out perhaps the most elaborate application of evolutionary classification. Using Service (1962) and Sahlins (1968), Renfrew extracted twenty characterising features of a chiefdom and then compared his data with these features. The closeness of fit suggested that the data most resembled a chiefdom model. While this kind of scheme has the advantage of being easily reproducible, it is very rigid and only serves the function of identification or labelling, rather than explanation or interpretation (cf. Brown, this volume).

Saxe (1970), Peebles (1972), Tainter (1975a, 1975b) and others have attempted to circumvent some of these problems by stressing the advantages of information theory in the analysis of mortuary sites. Social organisation, burial organisation, and the relationships between them, have been examined from the standpoint of information and entropy (cf. Buchler and Selby 1968, pp. 279–317; Saxe 1970, pp. 102–18). It has been suggested that the information content of burial attributes and their combinations provides a measure and criterion for splitting a burial population into meaningful subpopulations.

Entropy has been suggested by Saxe (1970) and Tainter (1975a) as a measure of organisational complexity. Entropy is a measure of disorder within a system: high entropy has been interpreted to mean lack of organisation, and vice versa. Increasing organisation relates to increasing interaction between system components, and increasing entropy is related to decreasing interaction. Increasing entropy is also related to decreasing predictability of messages and decreasing constraints on behaviour.

Both Saxe and Tainter have applied entropy measures as an inverse measure of organisation. Saxe (1970, pp. 69–75) has hypothesised that the number of components in a disposal domain, the kinds of components, and the organisational complexity, are interrelated. The 'relative entropy and redundancy not only measures the degree of organisation among elements, but . . . also the number of different kinds of elements present in the domain' (Saxe 1970, p. 110). In other words, a decrease in entropy implies not only differences in the relationship between elements, but also the addition of more and more different kinds of elements.

A point which has been overlooked by Saxe and Tainter, but which needs clarification, is the problem of using entropy as a measure of organisation. Entropy may be less a measure of organisation *per se* than of differential classification. For example, if one has a ranked society which limits access to specific ranks, the ranking might be demonstrated as:

Rank A = 2 individuals
Rank B = 4 individuals
Rank C = 6 individuals

The measure of entropy for this system would be low. However, let us say there is another system in which there are also three distinctions, but organised as follows:

A = 4 individuals
B = 4 individuals
C = 4 individuals

The entropy measure for this system would be very high. Rather than implying *lack* of organisation, the measure implies *lack of differential access* to the classes within the system. Thus, entropy measures may measure organisational complexity, following the theory of Fried, Service and Sahlins, but there is no lack of organisation in a mortuary domain with a high entropy measure.

When one has a classification scheme based on a variety of types of data (nominal, ordinal, interval), entropy measures allow one to ask 'how differential is the classificatory scheme' and 'does this measure reflect what we know from other data'. This is the key advantage to the entropy approach.

In examining the degree of differentiation within a classificatory scheme, the measure of entropy used is not the actual entropy, since actual entropy reflects only the classification scheme itself, but rather *relative* entropy — the ratio between the actual entropy for the classification and the maximum entropy for that classification system. A measure of relative entropy approaching 1.0 suggests a lack of differentiation in the classificatory scheme of disposal types. A relative entropy measure approaching 0 would suggest much differentiation in the classificatory scheme.

This measure can also test how good a classificatory scheme is. A measure of 0.9, for example, for a disposal system which is believed to be ranked, could mean that the disposal types merely reflect a variety of acceptable disposal practices to which access is not restricted. However, 0.9 could also mean that the sample used is not representative. By re-examination of the data, one might be able to determine which

is the case. Examination of the classificatory scheme itself was implied in our earlier statement that entropy measures allow one to ask 'how differential is the classificatory scheme' and *'does this measure reflect what we know from other data'*.

Assuming that the measure of relative entropy or the differences in the measure of relative entropy between two systems is not a result of some form of sampling error, the extent to which the differences are the artefacts of the classificatory scheme must be examined. Simple numerical comparisons will not suffice, because, as stated earlier, a decrease in entropy also implies the addition of more and more different kinds of elements. For example, if one divides the same disposal system into two or four disposal types the relative entropy measures will be different. The four-division scheme will have a lower entropy measure. This lower measure is the result of addition of more elements, that is, a finer classification. Whether or not it is a *better* classification can only be determined by examination of the elements and their possible cultural significance.

In sum, the application of entropy measures in analysis of mortuary practices can be useful for examination of how differential a classificatory scheme is: is there limited access to certain disposal types? The problems of the approach, however, must also be accommodated.

In a similar context, Saxe (1970) and Tainter (1975*a*, 1975*b*) have discussed the usefulness of energy measures in the interpretation of mortuary practices. Tainter (1975*a*, 1975*b*) has suggested that the measure of energy expended on a burial be used as a means of ranking burials. Specifically, the amount of energy expended in inhumation will increase with the social status of the deceased. Thus, an alternative measure of social stratification might be the measure of the extent of 'unequal privilege' of energy expended.

As a test of the energy expenditure hypothesis, Tainter (1975*a*) has examined some of the ethnographic literature on mortuary practices. In 93 societies the energy expended bears a direct relationship to the social status of the deceased. Significantly, Tainter has found no societies which specifically contradicted the hypothesis. Theoretically, the amount of energy expended is not a culture-specific measure.

Unfortunately, there are some definite problems in the application and quantification of energy expenditure as a measure of social stratification.

The application of the energy hypothesis to a ranked society is based on a pyramidal model:

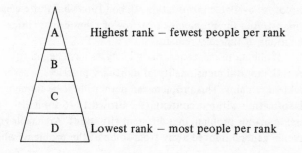

A   Highest rank — fewest people per rank
B
C
D   Lowest rank — most people per rank

The higher the rank, the more duty–status relationships owed, and conversely, the lower the rank, the fewer duty–status relationships owed by other ranks (cf. Goodenough 1965; Binford 1971).

While the notion of differential energy expenditure is certainly logical, one problem is the amount of noise generated by parallel status relationships. How much is owed to the people of a rank by others of the same rank? Is this reflected in the amount of energy expended? Further, how much noise does any within-rank ranking (however slight) contribute to the amount of energy expended? A less simplistic model is probably necessary. The noise created by status relationships of parallel-ranked individuals may increase the within-rank variance such that between-rank differences are less clear. Although the problem will probably not have a serious effect on rank differentiation, the extent of potential noise generated by parallel-ranked relationships (as these affect overall between-rank differences) should be examined.

Tainter (personal communication) has suggested that, to remove biases, measurable variables of energy expenditure be used, such as size of burial pit, volume of pit etc. How does one differentiate or measure energy when such data classes do not exist? How much energy does a secondary burial require, and more importantly, is it a consistent amount of energy? If measurable, how does the volume of rock on a grave compare with the volume of dirt taken from a pit? Relative measures of energy expenditure may be discussed, and a system of weights devised, but this too may inject biases into the sample. When different modes of energy expenditure are employed by the same society, the problems are greatest. Nonetheless, the use of energy expenditure, even as the basis for subjective divisions, does have advantages over some other schemes.

Measures of energy expenditure can provide a more objective method for the examination of variability in mortuary practices. The degree of quantification of energy-related variables, however, will vary with the type of data at each site. As Saxe (1970, p. 111) has noted, measures of energy may allow the archaeologist to determine not only forms of organisation, but also the degree of organisation of a society.

What is perhaps most critical in mortuary studies is not to limit the analysis to one dimension. Tainter (1975a) and Saxe (1970) have stressed energy expenditure because it is multidimensional and does not have the bias inherent in studies which, for example, stress artefacts alone (cf. Hatch 1974; Peebles 1974; Larson 1971). Because of the nature of archaeological data, it is imperative for the archaeologist to employ all available information. Ucko (1969) has quite clearly demonstrated the problems of narrow or ethnocentric interpretations of funerary remains.

While more recent mortuary analyses have begun to stress the multidimensionality of mortuary practices, a severe problem remains. This problem can perhaps best be termed 'classification without context' (see Brown 1976 for a discussion of this problem in a different situation). Archaeologists have, in general, moved away from some of the problems which were characteristic of past mortuary studies (see above). Unfortunately, rather than moving toward a system of study which helps elucidate the underlying social structure, we have created a more complex version of an old problem.

The focus of most mortuary studies in the last ten years has been the identification of status types or social groupings. Once the groupings have been determined, they are frequently placed within an evolutionary classification scheme or the information theory structure discussed earlier. While this type of analysis is useful, it is not complete. The result is a new classification or pigeon-holing. Burials are classified by internal differentiation, but the *context* of the classes is not taken into account. What does each group or status type mean? How do the groups relate to each other? What are the functions of each group, and what are the functional relationships between groups? While many of these questions may not be easily or reliably answered, current mortuary analysis does not even approach or attempt to *ask* these questions. Can we really say, particularly given the problems cited earlier, that a culture in which we have determined seven social groupings is more complex than one in which we find six groupings? Our current approach not only fails to examine function and relationships between groups; it ignores the possibility of sampling biases.

The term 'sampling bias' is used in this paper to refer to several possible conditions. Bias, in general, means something which sways or unduly influences a measurement or observation. In the archaeological analysis of mortuary sites, there are several sources of bias. First, there is the manner in which sites are selected for study. The tendency has been to focus on all mortuary sites either of a given type or in a given region or, because of the very complex nature of mortuary site analysis, to focus on the site or sites just excavated. Secondly, bias is introduced by the familiar problems of selective recovery and differential preservation. In working with mortuary site materials excavated, however carefully, by others, biases may be introduced by the historically different recovery objectives. Further, were this not enough, a subtle bias is introduced by the prehistoric funerary customs employed. Archaeologists must be very cautious in interpreting even the mortuary practices displayed over a series of sites. In the absence of other evidence, there is no reason to believe that one or another segment of the prehistoric population has not been systematically excluded from the sites examined. This is not to say that mortuary analysis *per se* is hopeless, merely that the investigator who deduces six social ranks should not be surprised to discover that other ranks exist and have been disposed of elsewhere. Likewise, if one culture has six ranks and another has five, the first is not necessarily more complex than the second — you may have missed the 'extra' rank in the second.

As any archaeologist is well aware, a mortuary site frequently represents considerable time depth. Further, the time depth must be regarded with respect to the rate of social change in the prehistoric society. What we may interpret as different ranks may in fact represent changes in funerary behaviour through time. This problem can also introduce a sampling bias. It is for this reason that context is crucial.

Quite simply, what does the presence of eight disposal types tell us about culture or social structure?

It is clear that one must look beyond grave associations to understand the structure of a mortuary site and the society which produced it. The archaeologist now knows that the treatment of the body, preparation of the disposal facility, burial context within the grave, and the population profile and biological dimensions must all be examined. In other words, *the mortuary system is a multidimensional system.*

The key to resolving the 'classification without context' problem is the recognition of all components of this multi-dimensional system. There must be a way to organise the various components so that co-variations and interrelationships become clear. It is argued here that the best way to examine these relationships is to use the spatial component of the mortuary system as the organisational framework.

Examination of the spatial component of the mortuary system

As Binford, *et al.* (1970, p. 1) have noted, 'the archaeological site should exhibit a complex formal-spatial structure in direct correspondence to the degree of differentiation of activities and social units performing the various activities'. Mortuary sites reflect both a differentiation of activities and a differentiation of the social units performing the activities; mortuary sites should thus also exhibit a complex formal-spatial structure.

Within anthropology, it has long been recognised that the spatial organisation of behaviour is culturally significant. For example, Eisenstadt (1949, p. 63) noted: 'The spatial and temporal orientation of social activities, their definite ordering and continuity are focused on the ultimate values of a given social structure.' Similarly, statements identifying the significance of space in funerary practices are common in the ethnographic literature (see especially Douglass 1969).

Because mortuary practices are reflections of inter-personal and inter- and intragroup relationships, as well as a reflection of the organisation of the society as a whole, examination of the spatial component can yield information on at least two broad levels: (1) the degree of structure and spatial separation and ordering of the disposal area itself may reflect organisational principles of the society as a whole; and (2) the spatial relationship to each other of the individuals within a disposal area can repr sent status differentiation, family groups, descent groups, or special classes, dependent upon the correlation of these spatial relationships with other dimensions of study.

Curiously, with one notable exception, archaeologists have ignored the spatial component. Frequently, in fact, a detailed map of the site showing the placement of burials is not even included in reports. The one important exception to this omission of spatial organisation is the mound or barrow. For mounds, one often refers to central features or tombs,

ramps, peripheral burials, and so on. Most researchers accept that some social significance is associated with the placement of a particular burial in a particular place within the mound. Further, archaeologists will make broad spatial distinctions, such as placement in a mound or in a village area. But within a village or within a cemetery or other non-mounded disposal area the same sorts of distinctions are not made. Yet it is clear that societies have sets of rules for disposal, including rules for which body goes where in a formal disposal area (i.e. mound, barrow, cemetery etc.). In other words, mortuary space in these situations has also been partitioned, and patterning should be discernible; the processes reflected are certainly not random.

In mortuary analysis, archaeologists (either explicitly or implicitly) accept that particular cultural elements of the social organisation form the basis for rules governing various material representations (e.g. grave furniture, disposition, etc.). Given this, these same cultural elements should form the basis for rules governing spatial organisation. Coincidence of spatial organisation and grave associations must imply coincidence of cultural elements. The lack of acknowledgement of this simple point is another way of saying 'classification without context'. The same cultural elements may be expressed redundantly, along many dimensions, and to understand those elements fully all dimensions must be examined. On habitation sites, we examine materials and make interpretations based on spatial positioning (e.g. activity areas), and it is logical to do the same for mortuary sites.

The task in mortuary analysis is to identify the rules a society used and the cultural elements (e.g. kinship, wealth, etc.) represented. The rules can be seen as functions which are used to map the domain of cultural elements on to the set of appropriate funerary behaviour. The appropriate funerary behaviour is only partially represented in an archaeological context. Because not all aspects of funerary behaviour are represented, it is critical to examine as many representations of behaviour as possible (and the co-variations among and between them) in order to increase the probability of proper inference of both the rules and the cultural elements.

While utilisation of space is clearly a component of the mortuary system, within the disposal domain space can be used in many ways and at different levels simultaneously. For example, space utilisation can refer to placement of grave associations in relation to an individual, placement of the individual in relation to others, placement of groups of individuals, and placement of the disposal area itself. Therefore, *the spatial component is also multidimensional.* The different dimensions may represent different cultural elements, and thus should be carefully sorted out and analysed.

The necessary distinctions to be made in a mortuary study which incorporates the spatial component are analogous to the geographer's problem in differentiating spatial languages. A spatial language provides a set of rules for the use of co-ordinate systems. One obvious example of a spatial language is longitude and latitude. Harvey (1969, pp. 215–16) discusses two basic types of spatial languages. The location of an object or event in space and time can be described by the four-dimensional co-ordinate system (x, y, z, t); this is a *space–time* language. The non-spatial co-ordinate system, which describes an object or event by measures on a set of properties or attributes $(p_1, p_2, \ldots p_n)$, is called a *substance* language. If two things are the same in a substance language, then they both have the same properties. If two things are the same in a space–time language, the implication is that they occupy the same physical position. The point being made here is that archaeologists have analysed mortuary sites almost exclusively in terms of substance languages, but should in fact be examining those sites within space–time languages as well. Further, it is necessary to examine the results of both in relation to each other. As Harvey (1969, p. 386) points out for geographers: 'Each simple language (space–time or substance) can have several dimensions, but in this case we are forming a complex language by bringing together two different languages into *one information system*' (emphasis added). Given this background, it is necessary to examine methods for investigating the spatial component in a mortuary site.

Clarke (1977) has outlined the various spatial models used by archaeologists, and has also noted many of their limitations. Archaeologists have, in particular, been drawn to geographic, economic, and ecological models. The problems noted by Clarke are applicable to mortuary sites, but mortuary sites create other problems as well. A key problem, for example, is that mortuary sites represent a large amount of information condensed into a relatively small space. Some of the major problems of applying models from other disciplines can be outlined as follows:

1. Many techniques and models are regionally orientated and assume regular interaction or interactive networks (e.g. central-place theory, gravity models, etc.).

2. The models, especially in geography, often tend to be deterministic and/or descriptive, having little explanatory power. This is really a limitation rather than a specific problem but these techniques do not allow the flexibility one would like for mortuary analysis.

3. Some techniques and measures can accommodate only one variable or set of variables at a time. Given the multidimensional nature of the mortuary system, restrictions of this type do not allow examination of the interrelationships among and between components.

4. Some methods used are difficult to apply to mortuary sites, simply because the techniques were designed for twentieth-century civilisation, or for plant distributions. The number of assumptions which one would have to violate for application to a mortuary site is frequently great.

5. Pattern tests frequently are designed to examine whether or not a distribution is random, but will not isolate the nature of the non-random distribution represented. Because a mortuary site, almost by definition, is non-random, these tests do not really tell us anything we do not already know.

6. Techniques such as nearest-neighbour analysis have severe problems near boundaries. The amount of space (border) left around the area being tested will in part determine whether or not the result is significant. A wide border will result in a 'clustered' pattern; if there is no border clustering may or may not be picked up, depending upon the number of points and their density. Since mortuary sites are frequently densely packed, the nearest-neighbour analysis will be either significant or confusing; it will seldom give us the information we need.

In sum, mortuary sites rarely meet the assumptions of most spatial-analytic techniques, and the techniques are rarely designed to ask the necessary questions of mortuary-site analysis.

At the risk of appearing blasphemous, I suggest that within a mortuary site, the spatial dimension is uniquely amenable to simple visual inspection for locational organising principles. It is reasonable to assume that the spatial principles used by a society will be fairly distinct and apparent. It is probable that rules for placement of individuals will have been followed consciously by the members of a society (especially in a cemetery, barrow or mound), and it is unlikely that these people had computers or random-number tables to assist them in developing a visually incomprehensible pattern. A modern example of obvious spatial structuring would be Arlington National Cemetery (the official armed services cemetery) in Washington, D.C., where burial is in a distinct grid-like system. Even early pioneer cemeteries were clearly organised in rows and/or family groupings or plots.

Given that many spatial-analytic models are not usually applicable to mortuary sites, although we would expect apparent ordering of space, simple visual inspection of the mortuary site is a logical first step of analysis. This idea is similar to Thomas's (1978) recent point about abuses of statistics: one need not prove with statistics that which is apparent. More appropriately, we are merely following Tukey's dictum: a thing that is not worth doing is not worth doing right.

The spatial pattern of a mortuary site may not always be completely clear or obvious. However, even when this is the case, visual examination should be undertaken as a means of hypothesis generation.

The spatial patterns themselves may not necessarily be complex, but because the spatial component itself is multidimensional, different kinds of spatial relationships (or societal relationships) should be represented. The archaeologist should analyse the different dimensions of space represented, e.g. grave goods around the body, the burial in relation to other burials, groups of burials, and the placement and structure of the entire disposal area. These studies using space–time languages must then be compared with those resulting from substance language studies, and the relationships between the two kinds of studies should give clues to the cultural elements represented. The archaeologist should then be able to identify the various rules of placement and the cultural elements.

Dimensions of study
It is apparent (as mentioned earlier) that the domain of

mortuary practices consists of a set of dimensions that are reflected in more than the archaeological expressions of the disposal of the dead. However, for the purposes of archaeology, the domain is limited by archaeological knowledge and by assumptions drawn from ethnographic sources. Binford (1971) summarised some of the dimensions of study, and these dimensions can be expanded by inserting those which specifically address the spatial component.

1. Treatment of the body itself
   a. degree of articulation of the skeleton
   b. disposition of the burial
   c. number of individuals per burial
   d. mutilations and anatomical modifications
2. Preparation of the disposal facility
   a. form of the facility (e.g. grave, tomb)
   b. orientation of the facility and the body within the facility
   c. location of the facility in relation to the community (e.g. within village, adjacent to village, in spatially differentiated location)
   d. location of the facility within the disposal area itself
   e. form of the disposal area (e.g. cemetery, mound, house-floor)
3. Burial context within grave
   a. arrangement within grave of specific bones with relation to grave furniture and grave facility
   b. form of the furniture
   c. quantity of goods
4. Population profile and biological dimensions
   a. age
   b. sex
   c. disease states and/or circumstances of death
   d. nutritional evidence and environmental stress
   e. genetic relationships.

Although the dimensions of population and biology are not part of the disposal domain in a formal sense, in that they are given and cannot be changed by funerary behaviour, the treatment of the categories included may be differential, and thus the culture at least controls the differential treatment of these categories.

Hypothesis generation using the spatial component

A set of examples should prove useful in clarifying these concepts. Recently I (Goldstein 1976, 1980) examined Mississippian social organisation by utilising information from two cemeteries in the lower Illinois River valley in West-central Illinois (fig. 4.1). Both sites date from around A.D. 1100–50. Schild is a large Mississippian cemetery of about 300 individuals and was excavated by Perino in 1962–3 for the Thomas Gilcrease Institute of American History and Art, Tulsa, Oklahoma (Perino 1971). Moss is a small cemetery of about fifty individuals which I excavated in 1971–2 under the sponsorship of the Northwestern University Archeological Program, Evanston, Illinois.

The first set of analyses concerned the nature and placement of the disposal area itself, i.e. it was done in terms of substance language. Both Moss and Schild were bounded disposal areas used exclusively for burial. Given this, an hypothesis proposed by Saxe (1970) seemed especially pertinent.

Saxe (1970) has made an important study using the ethnographic literature; he concentrated specifically on the archaeological analysis of mortuary practices. He attempted to construct a body of theory designed to bring the study of mortuary practices and their sociocultural determinants under the realm of scientific determination; i.e. his goal was 'to build and test models of how treatment of the dead is related to other elements of sociocultural systems' (Saxe 1970, p. 12). He accomplished this by formulating a set of eight hypotheses generated by anthropological models. These hypotheses were tested by using a very small, but diverse, ethnographic sample.

Saxe's Hypothesis 8 is of critical importance in analysing the spatial dimension of mortuary sites, if the hypothesis is supported. Because of its implications, this hypothesis was examined in detail and tested on a sample of ethnographic data (Goldstein 1976). Hypothesis 8 states: 'To the degree that corporate group rights to use and/or control crucial but restricted resources are attained and/or legitimised by means of lineal descent from the dead (i.e. lineal ties to ancestors), such groups will maintain formal disposal areas for the exclusive disposal of their dead, and conversely' (Saxe 1970, p. 119). By formal disposal area, Saxe means a permanent, specialised, bounded area such as a 'cemetery'. As any of the variables involved decreases, the formality of the disposal area should also decrease; i.e. the disposal area should be less restricted to burials.

Hypothesis 8 is based on another hypothesis and argument set forth by Meggitt (1965a). In working with the Mae-Enga, a New Guinea Highland society, Meggitt discovered that among horticulturalists increased pressure on available land resources is likely to result in a group which is structured in terms of agnatic descent and patrilocality; i.e. if land is both important and scarce, the group will be patrilineal and patrilocal. Specifically, the hypothesis states that, 'where the members of a homogeneous society of horticulturalists distinguish in any consistent fashion between agnates and other relatives, the degree to which social groups are structured in terms of agnatic descent and patrilocality varies with the pressure on available land resources' (Meggitt 1965a, p. 279). In another article, Meggitt expanded upon this hypothesis and explained the subsequent effect on ritual and religion: 'the people emphasise the importance of the continuity of solidary descent groups which can assert clear titles to the highly valued land. The popular religion is well designed to support these ends . . . rituals regularly reaffirm the . . . patrilineal group . . . the dogma in itself implies a title to land by relating living members of the group to a founding ancestor' (Meggitt 1965b, p. 131). Meggitt's hypothesis is specific in terms of land, patrilineality, patrilocality and horticulture. He developed and showed (1965a) the value of agnatic descent and patrilocality in terms of controlling scarce land. The force of his argument lay in the fact that, in order to cope with the scarce land resources, groups had to have patrilineality and patrilocality.

Meggitt cited examples of other horticultural groups with scarce land, and found the situation was the same. Essentially, Meggitt's hypothesis is based on a type of environmental stress.

Saxe (1970, p. 121) has carried Meggitt's formulation one more step. Since effective agnation is a response to an eco-logical variable, and since ancestor-centred dogma reinforces agnation, Saxe postulates a connection between ecosystem factors and treatment of the dead (i.e. ancestors) as reflected by cultural variables such as inheritance rules. In an attempt to make the hypothesis cross-culturally applicable, Saxe changed 'land' to 'vital resources' and 'agnation' to 'lineal descent'. Also, he added 'and conversely' to the hypothesis, which of course is more useful to the archaeologist.

I reviewed the ethnographic data employed by Saxe in formulating the hypothesis and subjected the hypothesis to further testing with a world-wide sample of societies (Gold-stein 1976). The test demonstrated that the hypothesis did not work in both directions: not all corporate groups that control

Fig. 4.1. Location of the Moss and Schild cemeteries.

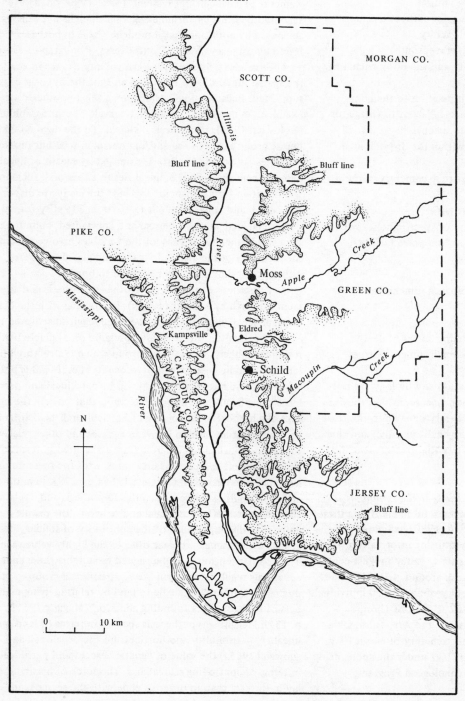

crucial and restricted resources through lineal descent will maintain formal, bounded disposal areas exclusively for their dead.

Hypothesis 8 can perhaps best be restated in three separate but related sub-hypotheses.

    A. To the degree that corporate group rights to use and/or control crucial but restricted resources are attained and/or legitimised by lineal descent from the dead (i.e. lineal ties to ancestors), such groups will, by the popular religion and its ritualisation, regularly reaffirm the lineal corporate group and its rights. *One* means of ritualisation is the maintenance of a permanent, specialised, bounded area for the exclusive disposal of their dead.

    B. If a permanent, specialised bounded area for the exclusive disposal of the group's dead exists, then it is likely that this represents a corporate group that has rights over the use and/or control of crucial but restricted resources. This corporate control is most likely to be attained and/or legitimised by means of lineal descent from the dead, either in terms of an actual lineage or in the form of a strong, established tradition of the critical resource passing from parent to offspring.

    C. The more structured and formal the disposal area, the fewer alternative explanations of social organisation apply, and conversely.

The major problem found in the application of Hypothesis 8 was the unintentional implication that cultures will ritualise a particular aspect of their social organisation in the same form, i.e. by maintaining formal specialised disposal areas when corporate group rights to restricted resources are legitimised by lineal descent. Considering the wide range of variability in cultures, there is a low probability that certain groups, even when in similar economic and environmental conditions, will symbolise and ritualise aspects of their organisation in precisely the same way.

The implications of the revised hypothesis for examination of the spatial dimensions of mortuary practices are most significant. It appears that if a particular situation is discovered archaeologically, then statements can be made about social structure as well as the nature of the resource utilised by the society.

The evidence supporting the hypothesis suggests that if there is a formal bounded disposal area, used *exclusively* for the dead, then the culture is probably one which has a corporate group structure in the form of a lineal descent system. The more organised and formal the disposal area is, the more conclusive this interpretation.

When an archaeologist excavates a mortuary site, the work is seldom done in a cultural void: usually the site is assignable to a particular cultural period. Often, habitation sites of this same period have been excavated and there is already some idea of the subsistence base of the society and its organisation *vis-à-vis* settlement pattern and type. Thus,

using this hypothesis in conjunction with what is already known, the culture's organisation can be discussed with a greater degree of certainty, and the critical resources can perhaps be determined in the case of a formal disposal system.

The re-analysis of Hypothesis 8, as well as the original formulation of Hypothesis 8, is an example of substance language as specifically applied to the spatial component. The unit of study is the mortuary disposal area, and the property examined is the degree to which and the circumstances under which a disposal area is formal and bounded.

An example of mortuary site analysis using the spatial component

Before proceeding with the example, a short introduction to the cultural context is in order.

The term 'Mississippian' refers to cultural systems in the eastern United States which date, roughly, A.D. 900–1400 (see also Brown, this volume). Attributes of Mississippian society are generally considered to include shell-tempered pottery, ceremonial centres, pyramidal mounds, palisaded towns, various 'ceremonial' artefacts and symbolic motifs, and agriculture.

Site location is usually along major rivers and streams. Large ceremonial structures on many sites and thick village middens suggest long and continuous occupations. Sites which have been termed Mississippian have been found from Wisconsin to the Gulf Coastal Plain, and from Texas to the Atlantic Coast, although the original centre of Mississippian development is believed to have been the central Mississippi valley area. Population density was high, and Mississippian sites were often quite large. The presence of domesticated plants on Mississippian sites, the occurrence of these sites on fertile, easily worked soils, and the discovery of ridged agricultural fields (cf. Fowler 1969; Morrell 1965; Kelly 1938), suggest that agriculture was an important aspect of Mississippian subsistence. Maize, beans, squash, pumpkins, sunflowers, and other minor crops were cultivated, although hunting and fishing were still major components in the subsistence economy. Griffin (1967) hypothesises that increased dependence on agriculture resulted in population increase, specialisation of labour, markets, and elaborate religious ceremonies.

As one might expect in a complex society, Mississippian settlements were organised in a graded or hierarchical manner: there may have been a large urban centre with the characteristic truncated temple mounds arranged around a plaza; around this centre were several smaller towns, with perhaps one or two temple mounds and a plaza; and surrounding these towns were smaller villages, hamlets, and farmsteads which had much smaller populations and no elaborate structures.

In sum, Mississippian can be seen as a cultural system which is represented by increased complexity in the technological, social and organisational realms from the preceding late Woodland period. Mississippian people had not only agriculture, but specialisation of labour, trade, and social ranking

— it was a cultural system in which it was necessary to proliferate a diversity of material forms and social positions.

As mentioned earlier, Moss and Schild cemeteries are two Mississippian sites located in the lower Illinois River valley (fig. 4.1). The sites are approximately fifty miles north of Cahokia, the large Mississippian centre in the central Mississippi valley. Both Schild and Moss are located on South-facing slopes of secondary valleys adjacent to the eastern edge of the Illinois valley floodplain. Both sites are located within one mile of Mississippian habitation sites. Schild (Perino 1971) is divided into two parts: Knoll A is a natural knoll which abuts against the late Woodland Mound 9 (fig. 4.2) and is located at the highest point at the end of the bluff. Knoll B (fig. 4.2) is a terrace extending from the lower part of Knoll A. Knoll A is slightly earlier than Knoll B.

It was clear that both Moss and Schild cemeteries fit the pattern of formal, organised disposal areas. This would mean that some form of corporate group was probably operating to control access to limited resources. Given this, the next step was to analyse the structure present and identify the various groups represented.

A substance-type multidimensional approach was used to isolate disposal types within each site. The approach was similar to that employed by Peebles (1972, 1974) for the Mississippian Moundville phase, although variables in addition to grave associations were included in this analysis. A monothetic-divisive cluster analysis using the information statistic was the initial technique employed for division of burials, but the resultant groupings were then examined and, where necessary, recast into groupings which made better archaeological sense. The groups were then ordered according to: (1) general knowledge of Mississippian; (2) information gained from the preliminary data analysis (univariate listings and two-way tabulations); and (3) the application of Saxe's Hypothesis 3 (1970, pp. 69–71), which states that personae of lesser social importance or significance will be defined by fewer positive components (in binary distinctions), and conversely.

Peebles (1972, 1974) and Tainter (1975*a*, 1975*b*) have discussed the value of the monothetic-divisive clustering procedure using the information statistic. The information statistic is seen as being particularly useful since it is not

Fig. 4.2. Schematic drawing of the Schild cemetery. Source: Perino 1971.

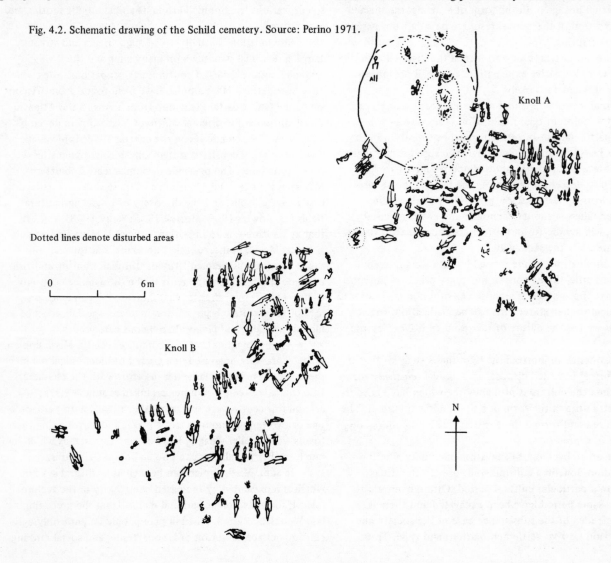

Knoll A

Dotted lines denote disturbed areas

0   6m

Knoll B

N

sensitive to skewness, and since (as discussed earlier) social organisation and mortuary practices can be seen from the perspective of information and entropy (cf. Peebles 1972, p. 4). Further, this kind of classification was particularly suited to this data set because of the results obtained by Peebles for the Moundville data.

Before continuing with this example, it is necessary to make a point about cluster analysis. Cluster analysis can be seen as a 'number cruncher', or an inductive search routine. As Hodson (1970) has noted, multivariate techniques are an 'arbitrary summary of data'. The researcher must determine whether or not the results have cultural significance. The results of a cluster analysis should not be an end, but a means to an end.

Formal analysis (cf. Saxe 1970, Brown 1971a), however, is a deductive technique, one of whose problems is cumbersome calculation and juggling of variables. One might think that the results of a cluster analysis, particularly the monothetic-divisive procedure, might be used to set up the necessary information for a formal analysis of burials. Unfortunately, this is not necessarily possible. The required ordering in a formal analysis key (from most to least restrictive type) may not be possible with a cluster-analysis dendrogram. The reordering may not preserve the dendrogram structure. Also, reordering is based on burial *attributes* rather than on burial *treatments*. Further, the reordered key is one for *clusters* rather than for *individuals*. For these reasons, a formal analysis was not done, although clusters were reordered into disposal types, then interpreted.

The structure of the disposal domain, as seen from a formal-analysis key diagram, can range from a perfect paradigm to a perfect tree (Saxe 1970). The structure of a cluster-analysis dendrogram can be similarly viewed (cf. Tainter 1975a; Peebles 1972, 1974). A perfect paradigm is characteristic of an egalitarian society; a perfect tree is characteristic of a highly structured stratified society. Saxe has discussed the differences in detail, and while the concept is briefly summarised here, the reader is referred to his original discussion (Saxe 1970, pp. 38–63, 75–9).

The structure of the disposal domain is a perfect paradigm if the definition of each and every disposal type contains one positive component from each and every dimension. In a key diagram, each column would contain only one dimension and a dimension occurs in only one column. Perfect paradigms are maximally non-redundant; dimensions are independent. A change in a single component changes the type into a definition of another disposal type. The organisation is more random with more alternative dimensions.

A perfect tree is a maximally redundant structure. In the key diagram, except for the root feature and the first column, all other columns contain more than one dimension which can occur only in that column. Trees are examples of complete non-randomness. Many more dimensions are required to define a given number of disposal types.

Peebles (1972) found two primary dimensions of vari-

ability in his Moundville data. The clusters on the basis of vessel form suggested an egalitarian-type distribution, with no indication of ascription of status. Conversely, clusters generated on items of dress and office cross-cut age and sex and were independent of vessel form, suggesting status ascription. Peebles postulated a situation analogous, perhaps, to the Ashanti as analysed by Saxe (1970). The two major social strata within the Ashanti showed qualitative differences in burial dimensions; the 'royals' exhibited ascribed dimensions, and the 'non-royals' exhibited achieved dimensions, as in an egalitarian society.

When cluster analysis and consequent reordering were done on the artefact associations at Moss and Schild, burials were differentiated first on the basis of presence of vessels, next on vessel form, and finally on additional artefact associations. The key diagrams for the cluster analysis were clearly paradigmatic, thus analogous to Peebles's results. This does *not* mean that there is no differentiation of treatment, nor does it mean that Mississippian society is egalitarian, or that there are only chiefs and indians. Formally, it does mean that a change in any single component changes the disposal type. Also suggested is that the differences between the 'elite' and 'non-elite' are far greater than the variability within either group. Although Moss and Schild can be seen as representing the 'non-elite' in Mississippian society, many disposal types are represented, and several definitely appear to have restricted access. Some groups were differentiated on the basis of age and sex.

Another set of cluster analyses was done for Schild Knoll A, Knoll B, and Moss. This set incorporated burial positioning, fragments of individuals buried with other individuals, and orientation as well as artefact associations. The key diagrams were once again paradigmatic, but the disposal types were defined on the basis of different dimensions. The types differed not only in definition, but also in number of burials per type, and in individual composition of each type. This second variety of analyses divided the population first on the basis of arm positioning, then on vessel form and orientation.

In both sets of analyses, burials of the most restrictive group were the same; these individuals probably represented the 'high status' groups within each cemetery area. Beyond these groups, however, many variations were evident. The subsequent space–time studies described below revealed that the two sets of analyses reflected, in part, two different aspects of social organisation.

The next stage of work involved a space–time approach to determine cemetery structure. The resultant structure allows a framework for close examination of the disposal types and their interrelationships.

At Moss (fig. 4.3) a row structure was delineated. Four rows running south-west to north-east were discernible. Plotting the disposal types on the map revealed that a series of kin units was probably represented. All four groups or rows were probably linked in terms of some overall corporate group structure, because the disposal types were differentially distributed with the most restrictive types occurring in the northernmost row.

Initially, rows were also noted in both knolls at Schild. With the exception of a semi-circular row around Mound 9 in Knoll A (see fig. 4.4), the rows seemed to run roughly west-south-west to east-north-east, especially in Knoll B (fig. 4.5). A set of definitions for what constituted a 'row' was compiled. The basic definition used was: the set of all burials which lie between an arbitrary pair of parallel lines set one and a half body lengths apart; this set must include complete burials, at least five in number, arranged so that five have parallel axes. Specific conventions used in connection with the definition addressed proximity, orientation, and position of the body in relation to its neighbour.

Using the definitions, these 'rows' were outlined, then tested by employing a regression model. Each burial was assigned an X and Y co-ordinate, which was the map location of the pelvis or, roughly, the body midpoint. A simple bivariate regression was done for each hypothesised row. Of course, while the regressions on the individual rows were statistically significant, such significance is meaningless. Rather, the important question is how effective is a model of rows for a cemetery? To test the model of row structuring or effectiveness an analysis of co-variance model was used. At a better

than 0.01 significance level, there was a preference for a row model over a random placement model. More significantly, another analysis of co-variance model, using the slopes of the regression lines, showed that the rows within the cemetery areas were generally parallel.

Although the row model fitted nicely at Moss, there seemed to be a patterning in the residuals of the Schild Knoll A and Knoll B analyses. The residual burials tended to occur in pairs generally orientated East−West, or perpendicular, to the rows; this was especially true in Knoll B.

An attempt was made to test whether the distribution of East−West burials at Schild was dependent or independent of the individuals orientated North−South in rows. Were the densities dependent, or did they fit a Poisson distribution, as one might otherwise expect? The problem fits the form of a discrete-time Markov chain model or density-independent cell count model. The East−West burials in the test were treated separately; i.e. rather than each state of the model representing time, each state represents orientation (East−West v. North−South). If an individual is added to a distribution without regard to who is already there, one has a density independent situation, of the Poisson variety. If the opposite is true, the process is more likely to be density dependent.

While this analysis supported the density dependent

Fig. 4.3. Schematic drawing of the Moss cemetery.

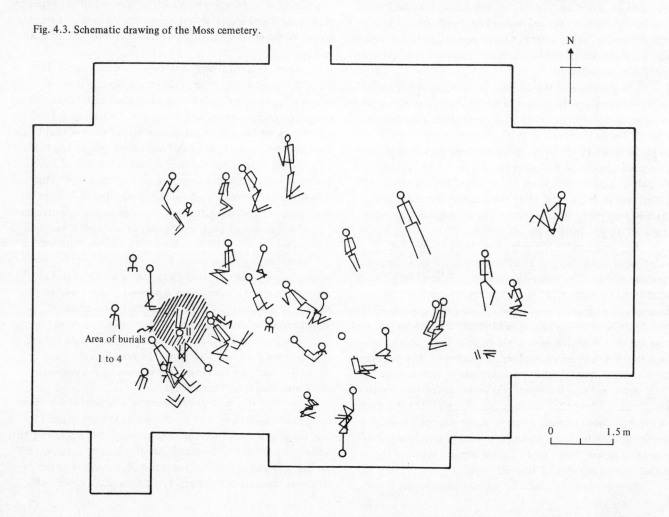

N

Area of burials

1 to 4

0   1.5 m

model, confirmed the semi-circular row in Knoll B, and further confirmed that rows were a reasonable model for the Schild structure, the results were still insufficient for the explanation of the structure. There seemed to be a lot of noise, or unexplained variance. Clearly, rows worked for Moss and parts of Schild, but something else also appeared to be operating at Schild. The analytic approaches taken were all variants on a row structure – perhaps rows were important, but examining only variants of them would not address the question of what else was happening.

The easiest way to approach the problem appeared to be through a series of distribution maps for each of the two knolls. Each map was a simple plot of all burials possessing particular variables or attributes of variables. Maps of the distribution of each disposal type for both sets of disposal-type analyses (artefacts only and artefacts and positioning) were also prepared. As a result, the distributions of charred bone, fragmentary remains, large pieces of limestone and fully extended burials defined what can be termed an empty space in the east-south-

east portion of Knoll A and in the northern portion of Knoll B. In both cases, this area is roughly rectangular and contains some disarticulated and incomplete burials (figs. 4.6 and 4.7). At the northern end of each area was a row or set of extended burials representing the most restrictive disposal types.

On both knolls, there apparently existed at one time a charnel structure which was later burned. On Knoll A, there is evidence that this area was capped by a low mound or thin earth cover (fig. 4.8). On Knoll B, there seem to have been two groups operating (see fig. 4.7), one related to the charnel sequence and one apparently independent of it. The groups are discernible only from a spatial perspective; the row orientations vary slightly, and in each group the most restrictive disposal types occur in the northernmost row. This illustrates the power of simple visual techniques. The existence of the key structures of the sites was deduced solely by visual examination.

The differences between the two different sets of cluster analyses become clear at this point. The artefact-only analysis

Fig. 4.4. Schild Knoll A burials. Source: Perino 1971.

isolated individualised treatments, often divided on the basis of age and sex. The artefact-and-positioning groupings isolated the same most highly restrictive groupings, but the remaining types in fact delineated the charnel areas, and reflected group membership over and above individualised treatments. These types are larger and less restrictive; they are not differentiated by age and sex, but represent group or perhaps kin affiliation.

Perino, the original investigator of the Schild cemetery, noted some evidence which suggested the structure (e.g. the additional topsoil over part of Knoll A; differential distributions of fragmentary, burned and broken artefacts and bones) and he looked for evidence of postmolds in both knolls (Perino 1971). He did not, however, pool his information and examine the data spatially; because of this, he failed to see the structures present.

In summary, there were two knolls with burials at Schild, and these probably represented differences in time. The row structure was present in each knoll, as at Moss, but had been elaborated upon by the addition of the charnel unit. Schild clearly represented a greater number of individuals included in

the burial programme. The most restrictive disposal types in each knoll were at the northern end of the charnel structures, with 'lesser' family or kin units represented by other rows or groups. Knoll B had two simultaneous groups operating, one related to the charnel structure sequence and one independent of it. The Knoll B situation suggests that the organisation increased in size and scope and perhaps incorporated outlying groups who qualified for burial, but not for the charnel sequence.

The spatial and social group patterns were tested on a number of other Mississippian mortuary sites, and confirmed the basic pattern of increased elaboration on the row and charnel principles. Putting the information together, it is suggested that Mississippian society is organised on the basis of corporate or lineal descent groups which control access to critical resources (quite possibly agricultural land). The hierarchy of Mississippian mortuary sites may well reflect the progressive elaboration and incorporation of small corporate groups. The degree of communal emphasis increased with site size and the number of groups represented. Larger and more

Fig. 4.5. Schild Knoll B burials. Source: Perino 1971.

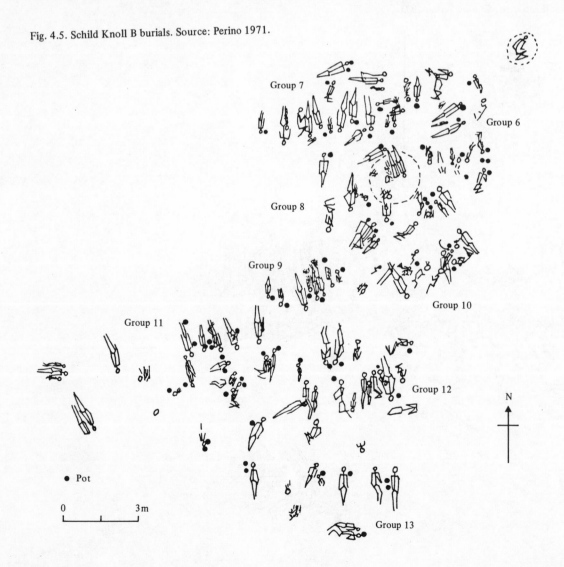

Group 7

Group 6

Group 8

Group 9

Group 10

Group 11

Group 12

N

● Pot

0   3m

Group 13

complex disposal areas reflect this higher degree of pooled resource utilisation.

This set of examples demonstrates the value of simple visual inspection and the importance of linking substance and space—time approaches. It has also shown some of the dangers in accepting too quickly results which are statistically significant. One must examine the residuals and noise in the model. Further, the statistical models used in spatial analyses should test for the presence of a specific type of pattern, and not fall into the problematic categories addressed in the earlier discussion of spatial-analytic techniques.

Conclusions

Although the examples used are necessarily brief and sketchy, it should be clear that a multidimensional approach which includes the spatial component is critical in mortuary studies. Specifically:

1. The mortuary system is a multidimensional system which includes the spatial component.

2. The spatial component is also multidimensional, and may reflect different levels of relationships and interactions.

3. The most profitable way to begin an analysis of the spatial component is to employ simple visual techniques.

4. The spatial component, when used as a *framework* for examining the results of 'substance language' approaches, can yield an understanding of the meaning and interrelationships of the groups or statuses represented.

5. It is the *interplay* between the 'substance' and spatial components which provides the maximum information about the cultural elements represented in a mortuary site.

Acknowledgements

Parts of this paper are based on my dissertation research. Funds for the dissertation research came from the Northwestern University Archeological Program, the Northwestern University Office of Research and Sponsored Projects, and the National Science Foundation Doctoral Dissertation Aid Program (GS-44431).

Fig. 4.6. Schild Knoll A burials showing semi-circular row and charnel structure.

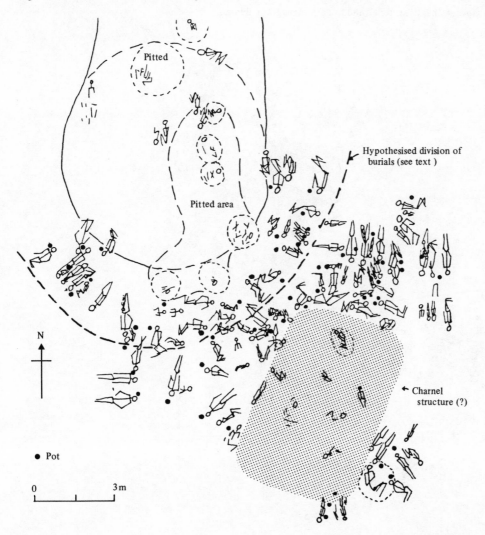

I would like to thank Gordon Hilton and John Hudson
for their assistance on statistical aspects of this study, and
James A. Brown and Jonathan Schneider for their criticisms
and support of various parts of this work. I am very grateful to
Gregory Perino for his co-operation and generosity with the
Schild data. Della Cook provided osteological information on
the Schild burials; George Milner did osteological work on the
Moss burials. The figures were prepared by Steven Ahler.

Finally, I would like to state my gratitude to the late
Donald Moss, on whose land Moss cemetery was located. Without his co-operation and assistance, Moss could not have been
excavated and this project could not have been completed.

Fig. 4.7. Schild Knoll B burials showing charnel structure and hypothesised group division.

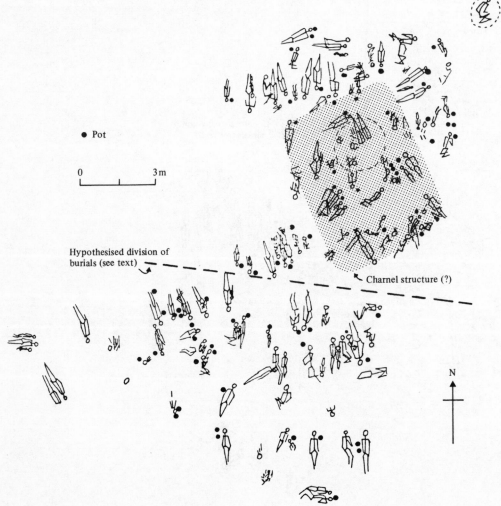

Fig. 4.8. Schild Knoll A burials showing charnel structure and probable location of mound.

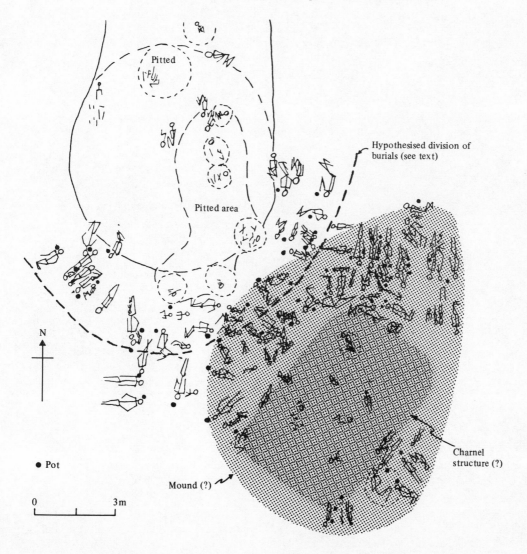

Chapter 5

The emergence of formal disposal areas and the 'problem' of megalithic tombs in prehistoric Europe
Robert Chapman

Introduction

Since the days of post-Renaissance antiquarian archaeology the megalithic tombs of western Europe have been a conspicuous focus of attention for those interested in the prehistoric past. By their size and construction they reveal an often impressive expenditure of energy involving the mobilisation of corporate labour. In distribution they occur from southern Scandinavia and the British Isles in the North to the Mediterranean in the South. In the fourth and third millennia bc they are the most frequently occurring field monuments in W. Europe and they far outnumber the known contemporary settlements. From Denmark and southern Sweden there are over 5000 known examples and from France there are at least 6000 (Daniel 1963).

The scale of their construction and distribution, as well as general similarities in form, communal burial and their continued usage over many generations, have all encouraged archaeologists to study megaliths as part of a unitary phenomenon — an intrusive, coherent burial rite spreading into Europe by a combination of invasion and acculturation. The main questions asked of the data were 'who were the megalith builders and where did they come from?' (Daniel 1970, p. 267). The most frequent answer to the second question was 'the eastern Mediterranean'. Methods of study were typological, aiming at the definition of broad standard types, such as 'passage-graves' and 'gallery-graves', which could then be plotted on distribution maps and their diffusion tracing according to progressive changes in the form and dimensions of individual tombs. As for the 'megalith builders' themselves, they were imbued with religious fervour:

> It is not, I think, inapposite to consider these monuments in the same terms as one would the churches of Christendom or the mosques of Islam, had the religions to which these afford architectural witness wholly vanished from our knowledge. The collective chambered tombs of . . . western Europe are in their way monuments to a lost faith, the adoption or propagation of which must have preceded the construction of the monuments themselves.   (Piggott 1965, p. 60)

Childe referred to 'megalithic missionaries' (1957) and Almagro and Arribas compared the spread of megaliths from the eastern Mediterranean with the conquest of Mesoamerica by the Conquistadores (1963). More recently Mackie has adopted the highly contentious views of Darlington (1968) to propose the spread of theocrats from urban Mesopotamia to western Europe:

> The appearance of efficient professional priesthoods — their members selected for their skill in dominating the peasant population intellectually and emotionally and in extracting tribute and wealth from them — might . . . have set in motion the steady outward spread of people wanting to practise this new and comparatively civilised way of life. The whole phenomenon of the European collective tombs could well be explicable in terms of the movement of such professional theocrats.
>   (1977, p. 196)

In general terms we may view these contributions to the 'problem' of the megalithic tombs as examples of the historical-distributional approach to the study of culture. Different 'cultures' are assumed to have had distinct and internally homogenous traits and customs, including methods for the disposal of the dead. As Binford has succinctly expressed it, it is assumed that 'the degree of formal similarity observed among independent socio-cultural units is a direct measure of the degree of genetic or affiliational cultural relationship among the units being compared' (1971, p. 9). Thus in western Europe the individual inhumation practices of early Neolithic farmers were succeeded by collective monumental burial, for which formal similarities can be observed in other cultures distributed over a wide area of the Mediterranean. The differences in disposal rite imply differences of culture and population and the spread of this intrusive rite was measured by the methods mentioned above.

But what if we adopt alternative assumptions? What happens if we assume that similarities and differences between cultures are not necessarily directly related to the degree of contact between them? What happens if we assume that variation in mortuary practices is not necessarily related directly to religion? What if we go behind the purely *formal* study of mortuary practices (e.g. numbers of individuals, inhumation

as opposed to cremation, individual as opposed to collective burial) and look at the *processes* that might have given rise to these forms? Can different forms be related to each other as part of a common developmental process? It is proposed in this paper to pursue an anthropological approach to Neolithic mortuary practices, which, it should be noted, Mackie claimed was essential (1977, p. 8), but which he failed to do. I assume that absolute dating methods will not present us with a solution to the megalithic 'problem', any more than they will for the other major problems of European prehistory (Chapman 1976). I would argue that there are many problems associated with Neolithic mortuary practices and that we should approach their study within a multidimensional framework (cf. Goldstein, this volume). In this paper I am concerned with the relationship between these practices (both individual inhumation and collective megalithic burial), aspects of social organisation and the availability and control of critical resources by human communities. The wider implications of this study are also discussed.

Megaliths, territoriality and formal disposal areas — the theory

The most important recent attempt to interpret the appearance of megalithic tombs in a local European context has been made by Colin Renfrew. He argues:

> The initial step . . . is to see in these monuments an expression of territorial behaviour in small-scale segmentary societies. The second step is to suggest that such forms of territorial behaviour may be particularly frequent in small-scale segmentary societies of this kind in circumstances of population stress. And finally it has to be shown that there are grounds for thinking that such population stress was in fact experienced along the Atlantic/North Sea seaboard, but was not felt among approximately contemporary communities in central or eastern Europe.   (1976, p. 200)

He defines segmentary societies as lacking the centralised, hierarchical structure of a chiefdom or state and consisting of cellular and modular autonomous units. For such societies megaliths and other types of monument functioned as territorial markers, by which, as he puts it, 'the territorial division of the terrain is given symbolic expression' (1976, p. 206). The population stress which stimulated this emphasis on territoriality resulted from the expansion of Neolithic farming communities into the Atlantic area of western Europe where, he argues, there was already a substantial population based upon the exploitation of marine resources. In addition he points out that this area was, apart from the British Isles, the end of the line for communities expanding ultimately from south-east Europe. Finally Renfrew draws three implications from this discussion: first that there would be several generations between the adoption of farming and the development of the population stress which stimulated greater territoriality; secondly that the stress would occur over a large area and consequently we should expect the tombs to appear simultaneously over similar-sized areas; and thirdly that the forms of the tombs in each area would be dependent on local factors.

Now this is a useful contribution. But I would argue that there is a sufficient body of anthropological research to enable a more incisive analysis of the relationship between the development of megalithic tombs and changes in the broader sociocultural system. We need to broaden our conceptual framework and relate changes in population, resources, society and mortuary practices. Furthermore we also need to broaden our temporal perspectives: instead of considering megalithic tombs apart from other disposal practices which occurred in western Europe from the Mesolithic into the Neolithic, I suggest that we view them in a longer-term perspective. How do the social and economic changes that took place from the Mesolithic into the Neolithic interrelate with changes in mortuary practices?

Let us start by considering differences between hunter-gatherer and agricultural societies. According to Claude Meillassoux (1972, 1973), in the former, land is 'the subject of labour': population size and density are related to the seasonal distribution of resources, there is no investment of labour in the landscape, no continued membership of the same social groups, no concept of a fixed, exclusive territory. 'The shortness and the sporadic repetition of activities lead to a way of life which is tied *to the present* without any duration or continuity . . . The preoccupations of hunters and foragers are directed towards day-to-day production far more than towards reproduction' (1973, p. 194). Hence there are no durable ties joining the younger members of society to the elder members, a genealogical memory extending back only one to two generations, no funerals, no cult of the dead and no celebrations relating the living to the dead ancestors. In contrast, for agriculturalists land is 'the instrument of labour', there is a longer and more continuous production, a deferred output, greater labour investment and more continuous and longer cooperation.

In such societies, where duration, expectation and cyclical repetition — that is time — are paramount, the future becomes a concern and, along with it, the problem of reproduction: reproduction of the total strength of the productive unit, both in number and quality, in order to ensure continued supplies for its members; reproduction of the structures of the unit in order to preserve the hierarchy which ensures its functioning. Descent — which provides for group membership and renews the relations of production — and marriage — which renews the hierarchical structures — become major concerns. (1973, p. 198)

This is the context in which we find ancestor cults, developed genealogies etc.

Thus a link is established between subsistence, social groupings, territoriality and ancestor cults. This is a useful starting point, but Meillassoux's approach is not truly dynamic, since he is contrasting static and idealised subsistence types.

Of more value, and taking us into the realm of mortuary practices, is Maurice Bloch's work in Madagascar (1971, 1975). The Zafimaniry are swidden agriculturalists living in the tropical forests of western Madagascar. In discussing them, Bloch writes:

> In swidden agriculture, almost by definition, land is not ancestral property, since there is a sense in which . . . labour creates land, that is by clearing the forest. Secondly although an initial capital investment can be said to be made by the original clearing it is an investment for only a very short time, completely unlike the kind of investment involved in making rice terraces, which is of value for perhaps a century or more. In such a system labour is the bottleneck in the productive system, the limiting factor on the amount of production.
>
> (1975, p. 212)

The mobility associated with swidden agriculture is facilitated by exogamous marriage. There are no territorially based descent groups, no ancestor cults, and burials tend to be located away from the settlements under rocks in the forest. In contrast, on the central plateau of Madagascar the Merina practise irrigated rice agriculture. Cultivation is limited to narrow valleys between areas of poor quality plateau land. Land is scarce and terracing requires a higher capital outlay and embodies the labour of previous generations. There are territorially based descent groups (*demes*), which are linked to the ancestors, endogamous marriage helps to keep scarce land within the community and burial occurs in monumental tombs within individual *deme* territories. Bloch sums up the position of the tombs as follows:

> Tombs are the symbols of continuity of the group not only because they are the containers of the ancestors but because they are the containers of the ancestors fixed in a particular place. The basic representation of the deme is the permanent link of people to land, the land of the ancestors . . . The importance of the tombs is that they create the permanent relationship of people to land by placing them there. The deme is therefore represented as a group owning land. Deme membership in Merina ideology is seen as a relationship not between people but between people and land.   (1975, p. 208)

As a final point it is interesting to note that where population pressure on land has led some Zafimaniry to adopt rice irrigation, they have been distinguished by a move to more endogamous marriage, although unfortunately there is no information on any changes in mortuary practices (but see below for an example from another context).

Here then is an example of clear relationships between resources, social groups and mortuary practices. Formalised mechanisms for the transfer of property are associated with changes in the availability and distribution of critical resources and are symbolised in the appearance of the formal disposal of the dead. As far as property transfer and resources are concerned, Harner's study of the Jivaro Indians of the Amazon

Basin leads to the following conclusion:

> elaborate and formalised descent and alliance structures
> for assuring the supply of . . . labour . . . only evolve
> when there is an increasing scarcity of land to support
> them. The formalised structures, which are hereditary,
> cannot exist and persist without a stable and valued
> material base to support them. Thus we find that the
> Jivaro, without land scarcity, have no formal kin or
> descent units, despite their often desperate need for
> labour for defence and household production. The need
> for labour is not enough in itself for the development of
> elaborate kinship networks in precapitalistic societies;
> such systems occur when the supply of land is not
> adequate to the demand and kinship structures must be
> seen first and foremost as units for holding natural
> resources.   (1975, pp. 129–30)

The role of descent groups in the control and transmission of
restricted localised resources has been emphasised many times
in anthropology (e.g. Fortes 1953; Sahlins 1961; Meggitt
1965a). Richards (1950) attributed the lack of lineage organisation among the Bemba to the absence of inheritable rights to
land or livestock. Whether or not such descent groups are
restricted (unilineal) or unrestricted (cognatic) is an interesting
problem: it has been suggested that cognatic groups have an
advantage in distributing land in the face of periodic fluctuations in the size of kin groups and in the event of acute
resource shortage (Goodenough 1955; Ember 1962; Lloyd
1966), although this is not always the case (Caplan 1969). The
part played by endogamy in resource control has also been
discussed elsewhere (e.g. Hammel 1964; Goody 1976).

The linkage between corporate groups, resources and
formal disposal of the dead (e.g. in a cemetery or similar well-
defined area) was first made by Saxe (1970, 1971). We have
already seen that more formal burial occurred in Madagascar in
association with territorially based descent groups and restricted resources, but these were synchronic rather than diachronic
observations. However Saxe and Gall (1977) have recently
observed these correlated changes among the Temuan of
Malaysia. Prior to the second world war land was owned com-
munally by villages, there was no shortage of such land nor any
restricted resources and no formal disposal of the dead in
cemeteries. Since that time a number of important changes
have occurred: land has become increasingly scarce (mainly as
a result of government intervention), there have been shortages
of critical resources (e.g. forest), population has increased and
wet rice cultivation has been introduced on limited areas of
suitable land. As a result there have emerged supra-household
'proto-lineages' and the formal disposal of the dead in
cemeteries.

Goldstein (1976, this volume) has also conducted a
cross-cultural ethnographic survey of thirty societies to test
Saxe's initial work (1970). She comes to two major conclusions.
First, if we find evidence of permanent, spatially defined burial
areas such as cemeteries, then:

> it is likely that this represents a corporate group which

has rights over the use and/or control of crucial but
restricted resources. This corporate control is most likely
attained and/or legitimised by means of lineal descent
from the dead, either in terms of an actual lineage or in
the form of a strong, established tradition of the critical
resource passing from parent to offspring.   (p. 61)

No ethnographic case contradicted this conclusion. Secondly it
is quite likely, but not necessarily the case, that the absence of
such formal disposal areas reflects the absence of such corporate groups. In these cases it may be that lineal descent from
the dead ancestors is expressed by symbolic or ritual practices
other than the use of cemeteries.

These kinds of links between resources, social groups and
mortuary practices have been illuminating in anthropology and
I suggest, along with Saxe, Goldstein and others, that they are
also of value to archaeology. In the case of the megalithic
'problem' the critical point is to regard such monuments, along
with others of stone and/or earth construction in Neolithic
western Europe, as examples of formal disposal areas which
may succeed cemeteries or may occur in their absence. In either
case we may relate them to the conceptual framework outlined
above and view them in the longer-term perspective of changes
in resources, society and mortuary practices during the postglacial period. The following sections of this paper consider
the evidence for Mesolithic, early Neolithic and later megalithic mortuary practices in Western Europe as part of this
long-term perspective. It should be stressed that the term
'resources' incorporates foods, water and land necessary for
subsistence, as well as other materials not related solely to
human consumption. Such resources may vary spatially and
temporally and within any one human group particular
resources may be especially critical and territorially defined,
while others are not so viewed (Dyson-Hudson and Alden
Smith 1978, pp. 33–4).

Formal disposal areas in the Mesolithic

With the possible exception of the Neanderthal burials in
the cave of La Ferrassie in the Dordogne (Vandermeersch
1976) and the late Palaeolithic 'nests' of skulls at Ofnet in S.
Germany (Clark 1967, pp. 117–19), the earliest evidence for
formal disposal areas in western Europe occurs in the late
Mesolithic during the Atlantic period. From the shell middens
of Moita do Sebastãio, Cabeço de Armoreira and Cabeço da
Arruda in the Tagus estuary in Portugal come a large number
of individual inhumations (about 250 – see Roche 1966).
Middens containing burials are also known from the sites of
Téviec and Hoëdic in southern Brittany. At Téviec ten graves,
with up to six individuals in each, were placed in stone-lined
pits and some were covered with cairns (Péquart M. and S.-J.,
Boule and Vallois 1937). At Hoëdic a similar range of grave
goods (e.g. red-deer antler, shells, flint tools) was associated
with burials in nine tombs (Péquart M. and S.-J. 1954). Radiocarbon dating indicates occupation in the mid-fifth millennium bc. But the biggest surprise in recent years has been the

discovery of a cemetery of flat inhumations at Vedbaek, near Copenhagen in Denmark (Albrethsen and Brinch Petersen 1976). At the Bøgebakken site earlier excavations had concentrated upon the prehistoric beach area, where stratigraphy and good preservation of organic materials were guaranteed. More recently excavations were extended further back onto drier land and revealed seventeen graves, which were contemporary with Mesolithic occupation in the second half of the fifth millennium bc. It seems likely that further graves were destroyed during clearance of the site and during the construction of a road further to the west. The graves were arranged in rows, mostly orientated East–West and each containing one individual. Grave goods included flint and stone tools, red-deer antler, animal-tooth pendants and perforated snail shells.

For other areas of southern Scandinavia and indeed for Europe as a whole, Mesolithic burials are only known from isolated finds and not from cemeteries (Albrethsen and Brinch Petersen 1976). However it must be admitted that the Vedbaek site encourages the view that, in northern Europe at least, sampling strategies may be partly to blame. Outside western Europe note should be taken of the site of Lepenski Vir in the Iron Gate part of the Danube valley (Srejovic 1972). In the trapezoidal houses of this hunter-fisher-gatherer village (dated c. 5400–4600 bc) are burial areas in front of or behind the hearths, containing on average two or three inhumations without associated grave goods. This appears to represent a move towards disposal of the dead in more formal areas and is not present in earlier periods of occupation on the site.

Admittedly our knowledge of formal disposal in the Mesolithic is at present based upon a small sample of sites, but can they be related to the theoretical framework outlined in the first part of this paper? Meiklejohn (1978) has recently discussed population growth in late glacial and early postglacial north-west Europe. He argues that the late glacial period was characterised by 'a pattern of population decline and rebound' related to resource fluctuations. The postglacial shift to a more broadly based subsistence produced a more dependable food supply and reduced seasonal mobility. He relates these changes to population growth since, among other things, changes in the amounts of body fats in females affect the onset of menarche and the frequency of ovulatory cycles (cf. Binford and Chasko 1976 for discussion of population growth in relation to sedentism). Given these factors Meiklejohn argues that population would have grown, initially slowed down by the vegetational succession taking place in north-west Europe, but rising more rapidly during the climax Atlantic period c. 6000–3000 bc. These arguments find some support in the numbers of Mesolithic sites in the Low Countries and Denmark, where population growth was slow in the Pre-Boreal and Boreal periods, non-existent during the early Atlantic and renewed in the later Atlantic (Brinch Petersen 1973; Newell 1973). The same increase in numbers of late Mesolithic sites has been noted in Britain (Jacobi 1973).

If the emergence of formal disposal areas was related to an increasing territorial behaviour and 'the use and/or control of crucial but restricted resources', then we must turn our attention to those resources. Now a popular model for the later Mesolithic in western Europe is that of the appearance of sedentary occupation on coastal sites, dependent upon the exploitation of marine resources. Recent research has been critical of this model. Bailey (1978) has neatly devalued any claims that shell-fish were a staple diet, by pointing out their inferiority in protein and calorie yields compared with terrestrial mammals and the higher energy expenditure involved in their exploitation. Osborn (1977) has argued that marine food resources in general are inferior to land resources in terms of human labour investment and protein yields: for example the ratio of net primary productivity of land to marine environments is 4.7:1 and it has been calculated that sea mammals overall have around 50% of the protein of terrestrial mammals. As Osborn writes: 'subsistence strategies involving such resources are selected only in those contexts in which alternative *low* investment, *high* return foods are inadequate for human populations' (1977, p. 164).

Given arguments such as these, palaeoeconomists have asserted the overall importance of land mammals in later Mesolithic diet (though note the evidence of the carbon 13 content in the bones of the inhabitants of the Vedbaek site for 'a heavy marine diet' – see Albrethsen and Brinch Petersen 1976, p. 26) and have stressed the evidence for the seasonal occupation of sites both on the coast and in the interior. Evidence for seasonality in Denmark has been produced, for example, from the Ertebølle shell middens (Clark 1975) and from the contemporary inland site at Ringkloster (Andersen 1973–4). But the crucial question is 'What was the *size* of the annual territory exploited by each group of hunter-fisher-gatherers?' The changes in population in north-west Europe during the Mesolithic must be related partly to economic and dietary changes, and partly to pressures caused by the rise in sea level, which inundated many recently colonised areas (e.g. the North Sea basin). Pressures can also be seen in the spread of climax temperate forest. In line with Osborn's arguments we can see the late Atlantic extension of subsistence strategies to include more marine resources as a density dependent response to these pressures. At the same time it must be noted that greater residential stability was also becoming possible in a number of locations and annual territories decreased in size. The potential of ecotones for greater residential stability has been mentioned by Harris (1977) and Osborn (1977) and the significance of the forest edge–water margin ecotone in Denmark has been raised by Bay-Petersen (1978). For the Meilgaard shell midden of the Ertebølle culture, Bailey discusses seasonal occupation but points out that: 'the data do not, however, exclude the possibility of a continuous human presence on the middens, and a mobile-cum-sedentary economy, with a high degree of residential stability on the coast and occasional movements by some if not all of the coastal population to other sites, is compatible with the archaeological data' (1978, p. 51). In western Norway Indrelid (1978) has argued that there were small annual territories and increased residential stability during the Mesolithic. On the Västerbotten coast of Sweden, the area within ten kilometres of the Lundfors site incorporated coastal and marine resources, along with springs and quartz sources, and gave access to a major river estuary to the North and a lake and stream system to the South (Broadbent 1978, especially fig. 5, p. 192). In addition the periods of occupation on the coastline correlate with transgression phases when more saline water favoured marine resources. Broadbent has argued that the Mesolithic occupation reflects 'a degree of stability beyond that of migratory hunting' (1978, p. 194). For the British Mesolithic Bradley (1978a) has related subsistence changes, including reduced annual mobility, to increased population and the spread of climax temperate forest.

From studies such as these it is clear that, while the notion of permanent coastal dwellers based upon a marine diet is no longer adequate for the interpretation of late Mesolithic economies, there were still some areas in which increased residential stability and year-round settlement were possible. This has been argued cogently by Paludan-Müller (1979) in his analysis of the late Mesolithic occupation of northwestern Zealand. In this area he distinguishes seven 'resource spaces' (estuaries, freshwater systems, outer peninsulas, narrow straits, open coasts, islands and closed forest), which are ranked in terms of their productivity, diversity, seasonality and overall stability. What is abundantly demonstrated is the ecological potential for stable residence of estuaries, peninsulas—straits and straits—islands (1979, pp. 135—7). The emergence of sedentary Mesolithic communities in these particular resource spaces would have had predictable consequences for population levels (Binford and Chasko 1976). With the changes in the natural environment (rising sea levels, climax forest), this is the context in which we argue that density-dependent selection and territorial behaviour (related to the level of 'economic defendability' − Dyson-Hudson and Alden Smith 1978) operated. The part played by the exploitation of anadromous fish and the development of associated storage techniques in particular European latitudes and parts of rivers (see Schalk 1977) may also be of relevance (e.g. the northern Irish salmon and eel runs, though evidence of increased residential stability in the Mesolithic is still not secure − Woodman, pers. comm.).

According to the theoretical framework of this paper, the interaction of these factors should provide the context for the emergence of formal disposal areas for the dead. What is fascinating here is that, of the known burial areas in western Europe, Vedbaek is located on a former inlet which extends two kilometres inland from the coast, the Portuguese middens are upstream from the Tagus estuary at the limit of warm salt water and the Breton middens are located in an area of coastline where several estuaries (e.g. the Loire, Vilaine and Morbihan), peninsulas, islands and straits were closely juxtaposed during the later Mesolithic (fig. 5.1).

Increased residential stability associated with economic

changes has also been observed in pre-agricultural populations elsewhere in the world and its occurrence with formal disposal of the dead in cemeteries is encouraging for the theoretical perspective adopted in this paper. Examples can be quoted from the Old World in Africa (Saxe 1971; Wendorf 1968; Sampson 1974), Russia (Sulimirski 1970) and the Far East (Chard 1974) and from the New World in the eastern United States (e.g. Tuck 1971; Dragoo 1976; Brown 1977) and California (King 1978). A cross-cultural study of these contexts would be informative.

Formal disposal areas in the early Neolithic

The next period during which one would predict the emergence of cemeteries is the European Neolithic, beginning in the south-east at c. 6000 bc and in the north-west by c. 4500—4000 bc. Given the theoretical basis of this paper, this is not simply a change from a hunter-fisher-gatherer to an agricultural subsistence base, as argued by Meillassoux, but of the relationship between society and critical resources. But first let us review the burial evidence for the early Neolithic, considering the earliest known cemeteries of flat inhumations, mainly in West and central Europe.

There are no known cemeteries belonging to early Neolithic agricultural communities in south-east Europe: where found, burials are scattered in refuse pits within settlement sites (Tringham 1971). Indeed it appears to be at least a millennium before such cemeteries appear. When one moves into central Europe, and into the distribution of the Linear Pottery 'culture' (LPC − c. 4500—4000 bc), there are examples of cemeteries which have been claimed to date from the beginnings of agricultural colonisation (e.g. Sonder-

Fig. 5.1. The location of the late Mesolithic shell middens at Téviec and Hoëdic in southern Brittany. The solid line represents the modern coastline; the dotted line is at −10 m and represents the coastline in the late fifth millennium bc, when the middens were occupied. Source: Péquart, M. and S.-J., 1954.

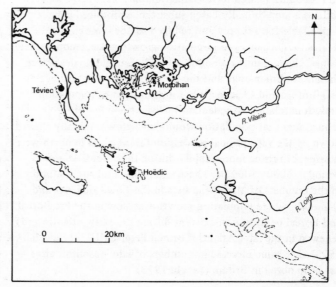

shausen, Sengkofen), whilst others do not occur until the later phases of the LPC (e.g. Nitra in Czechoslovakia – Pavuk 1972). But in the Rhine valley not a single cemetery of undisputed early LPC date has been noted. In the upper Rhine there are settlement traces of the early LPC, but no associated cemeteries, and the earliest examples of the latter (e.g. Hoenheim, Rixheim, Quatzenheim) date to the later LPC (Gallay 1970). In the middle Rhine the earliest cemetery is at Flomborn, but the majority (e.g. Monsheim, Worms-Rheingewann) belong to the Hinkelstein group, which is a development of the later LPC, dated to *c.* 4000 bc (Meier-Arendt 1975). In the lower Rhine again there are no early cemeteries: at Niedermerz (Czarnetzki and Czarnetzki 1971) a cemetery of over one hundred graves begins at the end of the early LPC (according to the chronology of Dohrn-Ihmig), while at Elsloo the associated cemetery belongs to the later phases of the site's occupation (Modderman 1970). At the same time there are also cases of continuing isolated burial, as at the later LPC settlement of Müddersheim (Schietzel 1965). Lastly in the Paris basin, where many late LPC sites appear in the first half of the fourth millennium bc, many burials are isolated, but cemeteries are mentioned at Champceuil, Varennes and Vinneuf, although their precise chronological position in the local LPC is not made clear (Whittle 1977).

According to our theory, we would expect the appearance of cemeteries to be linked with corporate groups and the use and transmission of critical resources. In the context of agricultural communities we might expect that the socio-economic changes associated with the appearance of formal disposal areas would not be visible until several generations after initial colonisation. Corporate groups for controlling critical resources are not known for the Zafimaniry of Madagascar (see above), nor for such other contemporary colonising groups as the Iban of Borneo (Freeman 1972). In addition to the examples in the work of Bloch and Saxe and Gall mentioned above, it is also worth noting that similar processes of change involving greater territorial localisation and the emergence of lineages *subsequent* to forest clearance have been discussed by Wilks (1977) for West Africa. At the same time it is clear that these changes may occur in areas of agricultural colonisation, in which population density is low but critical resources are spatially restricted, as for example among the Nakanai of New Britain Island in Melanesia, where lineages control the clearings in the virgin rain forest (Frake 1956).

How does the LPC evidence relate to this framework? Clearly there do appear to be cemeteries belonging to the earliest phases of colonisation, whether or not one believes that shifting cultivation was practised. But as we have seen, in the Rhine valley there appears to be a gap of some generations between the appearance of the earliest farming communities and the first cemeteries, the point made by Renfrew at the end of his paper, in relation to the building of megalithic tombs (1976). Now of course it can be argued that we are dependent upon inadequate sampling strategies for our knowledge of LPC cemeteries. Milisauskas has pointed to the location of LPC

cemeteries from 100–500 m from their contemporary settlements, as for example in eastern Bavaria (1978, pp. 113–14 and fig. 5.16) and at Elsloo in Dutch Limburg. Do locational factors impede the discovery of LPC cemeteries? On the other hand extensive clearance of the Aldenhoven plateau near Cologne has so far yielded only the one cemetery at Niedermerz, compared with the large numbers of settlement sites.

I think the important question here is whether we can find support for the interpretation of LPC cemeteries outlined here in other types of evidence. For example how does the evidence for settlement and settlement patterns correlate with the burial evidence? In particular, what about the infilling of the landscape after initial colonisation and the emergence of enclosed settlement? Is there evidence for increased territoriality which might be reflected in the appearance of more formal disposal areas for the dead? A survey suggests a tentative correlation between infilling and enclosed settlement, although their relationship with mortuary practices is more problematical. In the middle and lower Rhine area comparison of the numbers and location of sites suggests that primary colonisation concentrated on loess soils in the major valleys and plateaux. Numbers of sites in areas like the Untermaingebiet increased during the course of the LPC from *c.* 4500–4000 bc. In the middle Neckar valley Sielmann (1972) gives the following figures for the same period:

Phase	Numbers of sites	Sq. km per site
1	7	1028.5
2	62	116.1
3	122	59.0
4	59	122.0

From *c.* 4000–3500 bc settlement takes in the higher sides of the valleys (especially the upper Rhine) and the lower terraces and alluvial areas (lower Rhine) and in the Aldenhoven area there is evidence for more nucleated settlement. At the same time we possess increasing evidence for sites enclosed by palisades, ditches and banks in the later LPC and Roessen 'culture'. Although, as Whittle has recently emphasised (1977), these enclosures have a variety of forms and possible everyday functions, on a symbolic level I find it difficult to believe that their appearance along with evidence for infilling of the landscape was entirely coincidental. The burial evidence reviewed above shows the presence of cemeteries in the later LPC, around the turn of the fifth and fourth millennia bc. For the period *c.* 4000–3500 bc there is at present a marked absence of cemetery evidence from the middle and lower Rhine, but examples are known from the upper Rhine (e.g. Erstein, Lingolsheim – Gallay 1970).

In the Paris basin we see again evidence for initial colonisation on the light well-drained valley soils by LPC groups and the subsequent extension of settlement on to the edges of the plateaux and upland areas between the valleys. This process continued through the second half of the fourth and the first half of the third millennium bc. Enclosed sites are known from *c.* 3200–3100 bc, although an unconfirmed example at Barbuise-Courtavant may go back to c. 3500 bc (Whittle 1977). Thus there is again a correlation between the later stages of colonisation and the appearance of enclosed sites, with an increasingly marked presence of the latter on plateaux edges and the alluvial floors of valleys such as the Seine (e.g. Mordant and Mordant 1977, p. 232, fig. 4) and the Aisne, on to which Neolithic settlement had expanded from the initially occupied lighter soils. The known cemeteries of the LPC must be dated earlier than c. 3500 bc. For the period from 3500–2700 bc, when the first megalithic tombs appear, I know of no definite cemeteries in this area. Given that our knowledge of Neolithic settlement in the Paris basin has increased immensely in the last decade, and that the known LPC cemeteries have been comparatively recent discoveries, it may be that this gap will soon be filled. Alternatively can we envisage the enclosed sites taking over and extending the symbolic territorial role previously filled by cemeteries?

In the light of this evidence I would suggest that the current degree of correlation between the evidence for LPC settlement (both form and distribution) and mortuary practices in north-west Europe indicates that the theoretical framework adopted in this paper may take us in profitable directions. Further examination of colonisation and settlement patterns, and their relationship to resources and the disposal of the dead will help to test this framework.

The appearance of megalithic tombs

The types and distribution of megalithic tombs in western Europe have been summarised by Daniel (1963) and the evidence for their absolute chronology has been presented by Renfrew (1973, 1976). Problems of definition are immediately apparent, since by labelling a series of tomb types 'megalithic', we create a unitary class for which it is tempting to search for a single source. This point has been made by Renfrew, who wonders why 'somewhere along the line the tombs of Sardinia and the Balearic Islands were . . . dropped from the discussion, and for reasons not entirely clear are considered less megalithic than the passage-graves of Brittany or Iberia, many of which were built of small stones' (1976, p. 199). How exclusive or inclusive should we be in defining 'megalithic' tombs? Certainly it is clear that there is a large and largely unexplained amount of variation in the forms and dimensions of these tombs. Many archaeologists have even preferred to avoid such variability and use the presence of communal as opposed to individual burial as the distinguishing characteristic. But even here there is quite clear variability in the size and exclusiveness of social groups accorded interment within these tombs. For the purposes of the present discussion I wish to emphasise their monumentality, with all that this characteristic implies in terms of visibility and symbolism. It is their monumental nature which marks them off from earlier cemeteries of flat inhumations. Indeed if we use this characteristic there is no reason why we should not include discussion of the monumental stone tombs of the Aegean Bronze Age or the earthen long barrows of northern Europe and Britain. I will return to these topics later.

We have seen that territorial behaviour and its symbolism in mortuary practices were not exclusively associated with megalithic tombs as implied by Renfrew. Evidence to support this has been presented from the late Mesolithic and the early Neolithic. Indeed I suggest that the inhumation cemeteries and monumental tombs were different types of formal disposal areas which replaced isolated disposal of the dead in different parts of Europe. In some areas monumental tombs, whether of stone construction (i.e. truly 'megalithic') or not, succeeded cemeteries and in others they represented the first formal disposal areas. In the traditional megalithic area of Atlantic Europe inhumation cemeteries (whether of Mesolithic or Neolithic date) preceded monumental tombs in the Paris basin, Denmark and Brittany. In much of France megalithic tombs appear to have been the first formal disposal areas, although they did not all appear at the same date, nor in a pattern that would suggest diffusion. It seems more profitable to relate their appearance to wider changes in subsistence, settlement and society.

In southern France megalithic tombs did not appear until the mid-third millennium bc, some three thousand years after the beginning of the Neolithic. However it should be noted that until the later fourth millennium bc agriculture probably did not play a dominant role in local subsistence. Certainly the distribution maps of Neolithic settlement in this area show population as being confined essentially to Mediterranean France until the third millennium bc (Bender and Phillips 1972). The sudden expansion of settlement which was then associated with the Chassey 'culture', taking in much of the Rhône and Saône valleys, as well as higher areas on the Massif Central, fits well with the evidence for population growth consequent upon the more intensive adoption of agriculture. Recent research by Nigel Mills (pers. comm.) shows how megalithic tombs were constructed on the marginal *garrigue* and *causses* country, into which settlement expanded during periods of population stress. In the *garrigue*, settlements and tombs were widely distributed, but on the even more marginal *causses*, which were exploited by transhumance, the tombs occurred in small clusters associated with restricted patches of favourable pasture. This is a direct association between monumental tombs and critical resources. What is more, this occurred at precisely the period when the first enclosed settlements appeared (e.g. Boussargues – Roudil, 1978, pp. 678–9).

In the Iberian peninsula current thought supports a development of megalithic tombs both in the south-east and the south-west in the fourth millennium bc, although the lure of eastern Mediterranean parallels still attracts many Iberian scholars (e.g. Savory 1968, 1977). In neither area are there earlier flat inhumation cemeteries. Furthermore both areas reveal the development of larger and/or more complex tomb forms over a period of at least a thousand, and probably nearer two thousand, years. At the same time a more marked differentiation in grave goods, the adoption of copper metallurgy and the construction of stone-built fortified settlements witness the emergence of a more complex social structure. In south-east Spain these changes occurred in an area which was, and still is, the driest in the whole of Europe and in which, it is argued, water supply was the most critical resource, making irrigation essential (Chapman 1975, 1978). Not only do we find formal disposal areas in the form of megalithic tombs, but also well-defined groups or cemeteries of such tombs, the most famous being that associated with the settlement of Los Millares (Chapman 1977, 1980).

The critical resources associated with social groups practising formal disposal of the dead in either flat or monumental graves will, of course, vary in both time and space. In southern Sweden, for example, Clark (1977) has noted two different areas of megalithic tombs: in Scania and further to the North, megaliths are concentrated in areas of lime-rich soils which form the focus of modern farming, while in Bohuslan the tombs occur in the poorest agricultural zone of the province and are closely related to the coast, on which Sweden's modern fish canning and conservation factories are concentrated. Local settlements dated immediately before and after the megalithic construction period show evidence for considerable emphasis on coastal and marine resources in the Bohuslan area. Thus in one area the critical resources for subsistence relate to agricultural land, while in the other they relate to the coastal and marine environment.

The relationship of megalithic tombs to colonisation and settlement is also of relevance when looking at the middle Neolithic period in Holland. On the aeolian sands of the eastern province of Drenthe occur the locally known 'hunebedden' with their rectangular stone chambers and long mounds. Some eighty examples are known. Their construction fell within the ceramically defined Drouwen and early Havelte periods of the local Trichterbecher 'culture' (broadly dated 2700–2200 bc), although there are still many problems to be solved concerning the absolute dating of these periods and the exact length of time during which construction took place. What is interesting is that while there is evidence for clearance phases in pollen diagrams going back to 3000 bc (e.g. Bargeroosterveld – van Zeist 1967), cereal cultivation may have been practised as early as c. 3500 bc in eastern Holland (Polak 1959; van Geel 1978). The pollen evidence here is in accord with the presence of cultivated cereals in the sedimentary basin of western Holland at Swifterbant (van der Waals 1977; Casparie *et al.* 1977) and Hazendonk (Louwe Kooijmans 1974, 1976) by c. 3300 bc. Thus there appears to have been a gap of a few hundred years between the earliest evidence for cultivation and the earliest possible construction of megalithic tombs. The territorial perspective of this paper would appear to be relevant in this context. Cultivable and indeed inhabitable areas within eastern Holland are restricted by the dissected topography to higher, drier areas, as in adjacent parts of north-west Germany. Such

a confinement leading often to lineal strips of settlement, is an alternative to the view that all tombs in this area mark prehistoric routes (Bakker 1976).

Further to the North, in Denmark, the same chronological gap between the earliest possible evidence for cultivation and the appearance of monumental tombs cannot be detected. Recent research within Jutland has demonstrated that the earliest definite Neolithic material of the TRB 'culture' appeared c. 3100 bc and that with it were low earthen long barrows, constructed for between one to five individuals. Such barrows were constructed in the main from c. 3100–2800 bc, although examples going on to c. 2650 bc are known (Madsen 1979). Towards the end of this period (c. 2700–2600 bc) the first truly megalithic tombs appeared, in the form of stone-built chambers surrounded by circular to rectangular stone settings, the so-called 'dolmens'. This does not, however, represent a complete change in mortuary practices, since elements of formal and constructional continuity are becoming more visible (Madsen 1979 and pers. comm.). Furthermore, similar numbers of individuals were accorded interment in the dolmens as in the earthen barrows. A further development from the dolmen type of tomb then appeared in the form of a stone chamber, a covering mound and a passage affording access to the chamber from the outside, the so-called 'passage-graves'. The majority of these passage-graves were constructed and used within the period c. 2600–2450 bc (middle Neolithic periods 1–2 – see Kaelas 1967; Kjaerum 1967). Indeed stylistic analysis of the pottery suggests the period of construction may have been even more tightly confined in the middle Neolithic 1b period (Kjaerum 1967). Once again the initial use of these tombs was for a small select number of individuals, although re-use of them later in the middle Neolithic was for large numbers of people in eastern Jutland and Zealand.

Thus during the course of the Danish early and middle Neolithic periods there appears to have been formal and constructional continuity in a series of three major types of monumental tomb, in which selected individuals were accorded interment. On the other hand, although there was this continuity, there was not necessarily an even rate of construction: the bulk of the earthen barrows appear to have been erected within about three hundred years, while the dolmens and passage-graves seem to have been constructed within an even shorter period. What these short, discrete rates of constructional activity mean in terms of population and territoriality are interesting questions. A lead here was given by Randsborg (1975a) who correlated the dolmens with local areas of high population density and clustering. A further step may be taken when it is noted that the period which saw the appearance of dolmens and then passage-graves (c. 2700–2500 bc) also witnessed the first evidence for sites enclosed by palisades and interrupted ditches at Toftum (Madsen 1977), Sarup (Andersen 1975) and further to the South in Schleswig-Holstein at Büdelsdorf (Hingst 1971). Can we see their appearance, along with the burial evidence, in terms of increased territoriality, with in this case the critical resource being land? But in the light of the discussion at the beginning of this paper, we would also have to see the earlier appearance of earthen barrows as an example of formal disposal areas associated with pressure on critical resources and lineage organisation. As we have already noted, such tombs appeared right at the beginning of the Neolithic, so we cannot argue for a simple model of agricultural clearance leading to more territorial behaviour, lineages and the formal disposal of the dead.

A stimulating way out of this difficulty is provided by consideration of the Mesolithic communities that inhabited Denmark. Earlier discussion has indicated the potential of certain resource spaces (e.g. estuaries) for more stable, and ultimately permanent residence by hunter-fisher-gatherer groups. Given the arguments presented here and the work of others (e.g. Paludan-Müller 1979), it is possible to predict the future discovery of further Ertebølle cemeteries. What is more, current research is revealing increasing evidence for more economic and technological continuity from Ertebølle to early Neolithic TRB communities, to the extent that one should question the view that all the changes that did occur were the result of agricultural colonisation and population change (Madsen pers. comm.). The changes that occurred *c.* 3200–3100 bc can now be seen more in terms of longer-term local pressures that had built up within Mesolithic hunter-fisher-gatherer communities. The adoption of cereal agriculture continued and then intensified those pressures and the changing mortuary practices were associated with, and symbolised, the locally developing social structure. Within the coastal and river valley area in which Mesolithic and Neolithic settlement occurred, successive formal disposal areas can be seen as a response to recurrent imbalance between population, resources and society.

Conclusions and discussion

This paper has focussed attention upon the social and economic factors associated with the disposal of the dead in formal, defined areas and has attempted to relate this theoretical framework to the emergence of monumental burial in the Neolithic of western Europe. From an anthropological basis I have argued that interment in cemeteries or monuments will emerge in periods of imbalance between society and critical resources. Such imbalance may arise in many ways, but in all cases society perceives the spatial and/or temporal variation in important resources to have approached a critical level and devises new mechanisms to regulate access to these resources. The emergence of territorially based descent groups, whether restricted or unrestricted, exogamous or endogamous, is a response to this process and the new social order may be symbolised to the community at large by the use of formal disposal areas, through which a permanent claim to the use and control of critical resources is established by the presence of the ancestors. The evidence for formal disposal in flat inhumation cemeteries in the later Mesolithic and early Neolithic and the later megalithic tombs has been discussed in relation

to these ideas, with particular emphasis being placed upon the balance between society and critical resources. The nature of these resources has been shown to vary in both time and space: for example the resources viewed as critical to a hunter-fisher-gatherer community living on a river estuary will be different in composition to those of an agricultural village in the middle of a loess plain.

As far as the 'problem' of the megalithic tombs is concerned, it has been argued that the historical-distributional approach, with the search for origins based upon formal similarities, is insufficient to explain the processes which lay behind the erection of a wide range of monumental tombs at different times in a range of cultural contexts in western Europe. In fact it is not just insufficient: it makes no attempt to explain these processes and subsumes their study under the umbrella of a single problem. The approach adopted in this paper has been to argue that all forms of disposal of the dead must be understood in their sociocultural context (e.g. Binford 1971) and that similar processes may have been operative in the appearance of both flat cemeteries and monumental tombs. In this way the megaliths may be viewed not as a separate, intrusive phenomenon, but as part of a continuing tradition of mortuary practices. Now I do not mean to imply that this approach answers all our questions (see Kinnes, this volume) or that the processes behind the erection of megaliths were identical to those associated with disposal in flat cemeteries. There were quite clear changes in energy expenditure, durability, visibility and perhaps the degree of inclusion of the whole community in the formal disposal area which set the megaliths apart from the earlier flat cemeteries (in areas where they occurred). On a local level there is much to explain in such variation as the spatial patterning of tombs in the landscape, their patterns of clustering or dispersal, their elevation and orientation and their relationship to settlements and subsistence resources (Chapman 1977, 1980). But if we isolate the general areas of the sociocultural system which relate to the disposal of the dead in formal areas, rather than scattered over the landscape, then it should be possible to approach the differences between cemetery and monumental burial in a new light. For example, in areas where megaliths succeeded cemeteries, one might argue that the reasons for the change were the greater pressure upon the critical resources and greater strains within the social system, necessitating a formal disposal area that symbolised control of these resources in a more impressive, visible manner. But on the other hand one is still left with the problem of areas in which megaliths were the earliest formal disposal areas: why were they built in preference to interment in cemeteries? These are important questions which deserve close scrutiny.

Clearly a wider perspective is also useful. I have frequently stressed the monumental nature of megalithic tombs in this paper. In fact monumental tombs occur throughout European prehistory and at different levels of social complexity. Surely there is much to learn from comparison of the forms and particularly the contexts of these tombs? Within the Neolithic we have already discussed the earthen long barrows of Denmark, and similar constructions in Britain and Poland also deserve consideration. Equally the stone-built monumental tombs of the Aegean Bronze Age can be related to the kinds of social and economic processes discussed in this paper, as has been well demonstrated by Bintliff (1977*a*, pp. 145–8). He has noted the association of tombs with restricted areas of good cultivable soil, with the best example coming from the Agiofarango gorge in southern Crete (1977*b*). Indeed the presence of the ancestors which establishes the claim of individual families and villages to the restricted areas of fertile soils is noted still at the present day: in rural areas of Melos and Mykonos, for example, chapels and cemeteries are associated with the lands of individual families and support their claims to these lands, serving as focal points in a landscape which is dominated by a dispersed settlement pattern (1977*a*).

Finally we must turn our attention towards the more general implications of this discussion for the study of mortuary practices, which has been dominated in the last decade by research based upon the seminal work of Binford (1971) and Saxe (1970, 1971). The value of their approach has been the construction and partial testing of hypotheses linking social structure and mortuary practices within anthropological contexts. As O'Shea notes elsewhere in this volume, archaeological analysis has contributed little to this process and there has been little attempt to investigate how the formation processes of the archaeological record affect the preservation of mortuary remains. The theory relating social structure and critical resources to formal disposal areas was put in the form of a hypothesis by Saxe (1970) and tested in three ethnographic contexts, while subsequent research by Goldstein (1976, this volume) has extended this testing to thirty societies. But as far as I am aware there have been no attempts to test this hypothesis in an archaeological context. With the enormous time depth of the archaeological record we can consider many problems and changes which are not observable in the ethnographic present. Changes in the degree of formality in the disposal area can be related to social change. The spatial and temporal variation of critical resources (once these are defined) can be measured within the context of variation in economy and society and then related to the frequency of formal disposal of the dead (cf. Bradley, this volume). Do periods without evidence for cemeteries or monumental tombs reflect resource stability and social stability or are they the results of our poor knowledge of the archaeological record? Alternatively, what other ritual or symbolic practices may express lineal descent from the dead ancestors apart from formal disposal areas? How do changes in the social system (e.g. increased complexity) affect the ways in which its claim to control certain resources is symbolised? In this paper I have attempted to extend the work of Saxe and Goldstein into an archaeological context, using some of the rich burial record of prehistoric Europe. Their theoretical discussion has been extended and the definition of formal disposal areas expanded to include individual monumental tombs as well as cemeteries

of flat graves (contrary to two previous papers in which I have considered cemeteries of monumental tombs as formal disposal areas – Chapman 1977, 1980). I do not claim to have tested any hypotheses, rather I have attempted to offer broad correlations between the mortuary evidence and particular changes in its social and economic contexts. Hopefully the potential of this approach to the archaeological evidence will stimulate constructive comment and productive research.

Acknowledgements

A draft of this paper was presented at the Prehistoric Society's conference on 'The Archaeology of Death' in London in April 1979. I am grateful for comments received on that occasion and for information provided for me by John Bintliff, Nigel Mills, John O'Shea and Peter Woodman. Jim Brown must be thanked for sending me a copy of the paper by Arthur Saxe and Patricia Gall. The Research Board of the University of Reading supported my visit to Denmark in the summer of 1979 and I am extremely grateful to Torsten Madsen for his hospitality and stimulating discussions. Lastly the paper has been read by Richard Bradley, Lynne Brydon and Colin Renfrew, to all of whom thanks are due.

Chapter 6

Dialogues with death
Ian Kinnes

The past is a foreign country: they do things differently there.
L.P. Hartley, *The Go-Between* (1953)

Food, reproduction and death are the common factors of humanity, and the greatest of these is death. Human societies are moulded by their dialogue with death: frameworks, by which individuals and communities establish their own world-picture, are stretched and then defined by the need to comprehend and incorporate mortality.

The choice of Neolithic chambered tombs to illustrate this is fraught with the problems of European prehistory: sites robbed, ruined or destroyed, most often badly excavated and ill recorded, too often serving as vehicles for theories based on conviction rather than research. These sites are visible accounts of motives and stimuli otherwise lost. Without excavation these accounts are, at best, partial and very few sites have been well-excavated. Given these qualifications, the following discussion will be restricted by the nature of the evidence, and indulgence is asked for necessary generalisations in an attempt at reconstruction of the dynamics of mortuary practice.

The construction and effective use of chambered tombs covered some two millennia. In one form or another they occur from Kujavia to County Sligo, from Almeria to Scania. They were primarily a post-colonisation feature, related to fourth-millennium cultures involved in massive progressive land uptake after initial corridor expansion (Chapman, this volume). They were built of available materials within the limits of a lithic technology and pre-state system. Architecturally and conceptually they share one feature: the provision of an enclosed space, simple but functionally distinct from the grave. The idea of a chamber is inextricably linked to prolonged activities, expressing and even invoking practices geared to continuing and continuous use. Functional extensions of this focal component follow naturally: structures such as forecourts, enclosures and mortuary houses, and activities reflecting sequential or cumulative processes. Much of this is obscured by a rigid taxonomy of chamber shapes, all too readily transferred to typology and thence to sub-Darwinian lineage systems. Although it is true that particular traditions in the physical organisation of the mortuary space can be recognised, a preoccupation with variations from perceived 'standard' or 'basic' forms can militate against realisation of the quintessential functional analysis.

The critical developments of the last generation of research have stemmed entirely from new approaches to excavation. At Ascott-under-Wychwood Benson has shown the importance of meticulous recording and analysis of mortuary deposits (paper to the Prehistoric Society Spring Conference, April 1979). Elsewhere other large-scale projects have revealed the complexity of structures when both mound and chamber are dissected. The *ci-devant* 'multiperiod' sites are now becoming a commonplace, and in both Britain and Europe a realisation of the true extent and importance of the non-megalithic component begins to cohere (Daniel 1967; Savory 1977; Madsen 1979).

We are still far from establishing the structural variability induced by the need to accommodate received ideas to available resources. It is possible, however, to break through the barriers of strict typology and affirm the fundamental importance of functional identity. In example, early megalithic and non-megalithic chamber forms in Britain can be distinguished only by architectural materials and not by style or function (fig. 6.1). By extension, the postulation of potential time trajec-

tories for both social and ritual factors permits further rejection of typology as a means of explanation. In Britain broad regional developments can be shown which can be rationalised within a modular system (Kinnes 1975, fig. 7). A particular differentiation is the northern trend to linear extension and the southern to agglomeration and dispersal. Thus the chronological differentiation set against likely socioeconomic development and elaboration of ritual is sufficient to explain the observable sequence at Wayland's Smithy (fig. 6.2). Here an initial non-megalithic chamber was replaced by a transepted slab-built structure, occasionally held to be evidence for an otherwise invisible direct contact between the Morbihan and southern England (the Pornic-Notgrove type – Piggott 1962). At present the true relationship of non-megalithic and megalithic techniques cannot be assessed and it is certainly premature to claim universal precedence for the former. At least two sites, Lochhill and Ballymacaldrack (Masters 1973; Collins 1976), show both within a single structure.

The concept of multiperiod structures, often explained by induced changes in local sequences, must give way to overriding functional explanations and attempts to trace processes rather than events. All chambers were 'multiperiod' in use and duration: only in some instances was this visibly expressed by structural modifications.

The very provision of an open chamber in itself dictates or reflects continuing use. Whatever the true function of such structures they were clearly focal points within the conceptual landscapes of local communities. The provision of forecourts and facades seems an obvious extension of this focal component, and it is conceivable that these assumed specialised roles within the complex of mortuary observances. The extreme example of the full-court variant within the Irish series (de Valera 1960, plate 1) suggests that such roles can assume greater importance than that of the avowed critical factor, the chamber proper. Comparable specialisation, incidentally demonstrating the balanced interplay of the struc-

Fig. 6.1. Megalithic and non-megalithic chambers: A. Cairnholy 1; B. Wayland's Smithy.

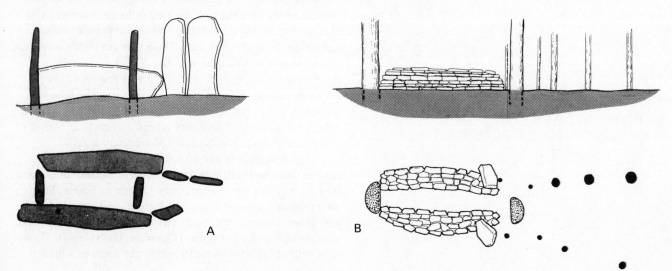

A   B

tural repertoire, can be seen at Dyffryn Ardudwy where the initial monument involved a low platform cairn, the prime function of which was the declaration of a defined area around the chamber and the provision of a setting for a simple forecourt (fig. 6.3). The chamber itself was empty (perhaps, though not certainly, robbed) but activities in the forecourt had involved the deposition of sherds of several vessels (Powell 1973).

The reservation of a zone around the chamber may have been variously expressed, but, of course, can only be distinguished where structurally defined. In the non-megalithic series rectangular palisade enclosures are common, and are strongly reminiscent of the long-houses basic to West European Neolithic tradition (fig. 6.4). Known variations include ring-ditches (fig. 6.5), perhaps echoing another recurrent aspect of Western practice – the causewayed enclosures. Other ancillary structures provide further versions of basic themes. The focussing aspect of forecourts is re-expressed by devices such as the post-avenue at Kilham (fig. 6.6), or can assume new proportions in substantial buildings as seen at Nutbane (fig. 6.7). The continuity and durability of social tradition could involve the incorporation of ancestral, or even outmoded, architectural devices within a new monument. The false portals of lateral-chambered cairns in the Severn–Cotswold group are a specific reproduction of the frontal aspect of portal dolmens (fig. 6.8). Again, the long cairn at Ty Isaf concealed, but was structurally integral with, a round cairn enclosing one of the chambers (fig. 6.9), so that a unitary construction recapitulates the cumulative remodelling seen at sites such as Dyffryn Ardudwy.

Clearly, further resolution of these processes must depend on increased understanding of likely social trends. It is possible to discern a movement towards specialisation of the mortuary areas through changes in size or spatial organisation (linear extension, agglomeration or dispersal, on the modular system). Unless these represent no more than the need to house a greater number of dead from increased populations or an extension of the burial privilege down the hierarchy, it seems likely that these spatial developments reflect greater social complexity. The little evidence available is inconclusive but there is some reason to postulate the reservation of particular areas for sex- or age-linked groups (fig. 6.10). It should be remembered that these chambers were not, *sensu stricto*, burial places, but provided storage or temporary housing for the dead, removal being as common as deposition. The actual number of individuals recorded from any context is certainly no guide to population size. Whatever the determining factors of the decision to terminate chamber use by formal blocking, still perhaps the major unanswered question for the study, the presence of bodies seems not to be critical. Disregarding the inevitable cenotaph explanation, this can be seen in 'empty' chambers such as that at Thickthorn Down (Drew and Piggott 1936).

Fig. 6.2. Wayland's Smithy: the structural sequence. Source: Atkinson 1965.

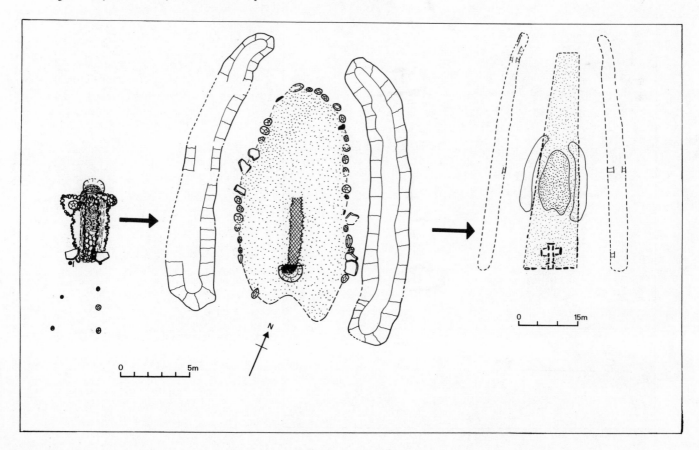

The final version of many sites was a sealed monument, long or round mounds immediately visible in the landscape (figs. 6.7 and 6.9). It is not yet possible to quantify the proportion not so marked although an increasing number of Continental sites suggests that these were common (Daniel 1967). A central place for any social group might be a mortuary site: equally it could be any other structure, boulder or tree. Since most would be unrecognisable archaeologically, depending upon social agreements unknowable to prehistorians, this aspect cannot be profitably pursued. In Britain the Neolithic pattern seems to have been one of spaced small farmsteads, and the communal monuments not therefore a product of enlarged residence groups. If each unit had its own mortuary site this should be susceptible to territorial analysis

(Renfrew 1976). Certainly the frequency of massive mounds, constructed after the end of mortuary use, suggests a need for durable reminders to communities and their descendants. Where stratified levels exist in their vicinity, notably in the open quarry-ditches of earthen mounds, non-domestic activities extending into the second millennium bc are attested by artefact deposits (as at Thickthorn Down and Skendleby 1 — Phillips 1936). Equally, the provision of interim mounds (figs. 6.5 and 6.6) stresses their conceptual identification with mortuary sites. The existence of monumental forms which do not commemorate such original use (Smith and Evans 1968) argues for a situation in which the mound (and perhaps the labour of its construction) was recognised as conferring territorial or social rights on its proprietors.

Fig. 6.3. Dyffryn Ardudwy: the structural sequence. Source: Powell 1973.

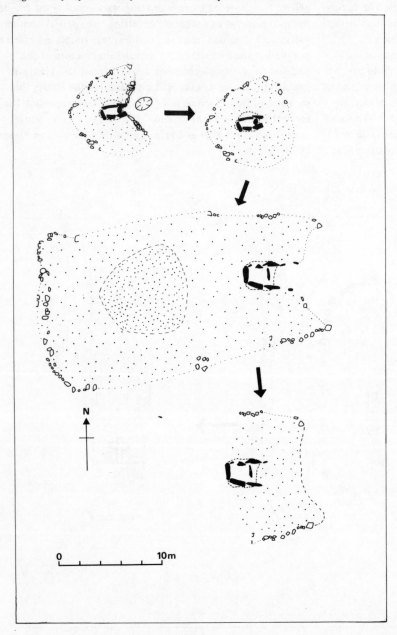

N

0   10m

The simple use of dividers to postulate such territories is insufficient (*pace* Renfrew 1976). As yet there are no areas in which sufficient excavation has been undertaken to quantify the chronological factor, and all monuments within any given zone cannot be assumed to be contemporary in construction or use. Unknown rates of selective destruction since the Neolithic and the likely existence of invisible sites (those not marked by a monumental cover) render existing distributions unsuitable for such analytical techniques. Further complications are introduced by economic factors, such as the possibility that upland and lowland tombs might be paired in a transhumance cycle, or by the relocation of sites within a given territory over time. Even with these reservations, it is necessary to go further and recall the potential existence of social, religious and conceptual territories which need bear no observable relationship to political or economic tenures, as Bloch (1971) has shown for Madagascar.

Clearly much will depend on the next generation of studies. Increased information from full excavations is critical, and much will depend on the context provided by new understanding of the nature and extent of domestic activities. At present the overwhelming proportion of information derives from earlier work which was not geared to answer the questions now being posed. Despite the cautious pessimism of much of the foregoing, it is nevertheless clear that the situation can only improve.

Note

In certain instances the structural sequences delineated here, although based on the published reports, do not coincide with the excavators' own interpretations. Readers are advised to consult the originals and form their own opinions.

Fig. 6.4. Fussell's Lodge: the structural sequence. Source: Ashbee 1966.

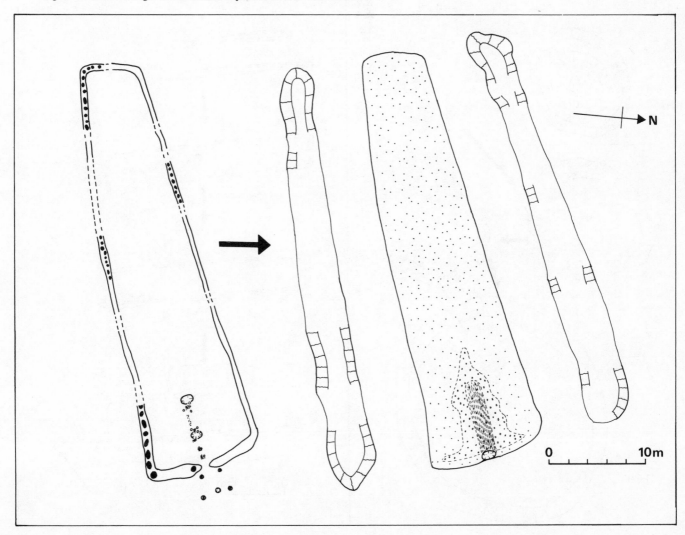

Fig. 6.5. Aldwincle: the structural sequence. Source: Jackson 1976.

Fig. 6.6. Kilham: the structural sequence. Source: Manby 1976.

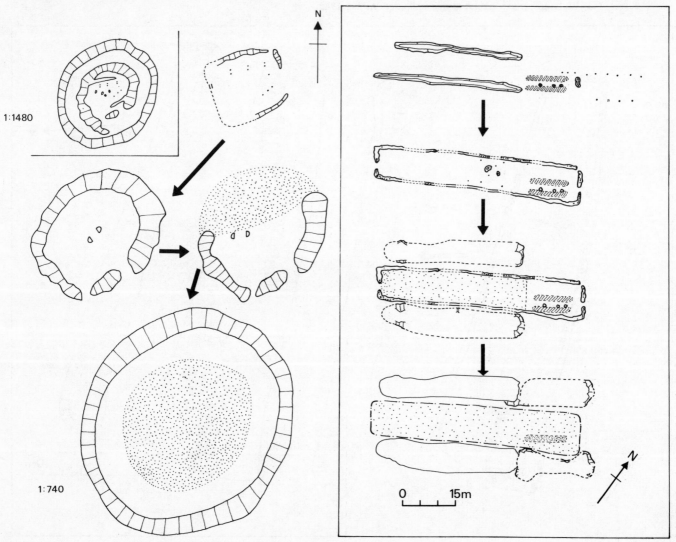

1:1480

1:740

0   15m

Fig. 6.7. Nutbane: the structural sequence. Source: Morgan 1959.

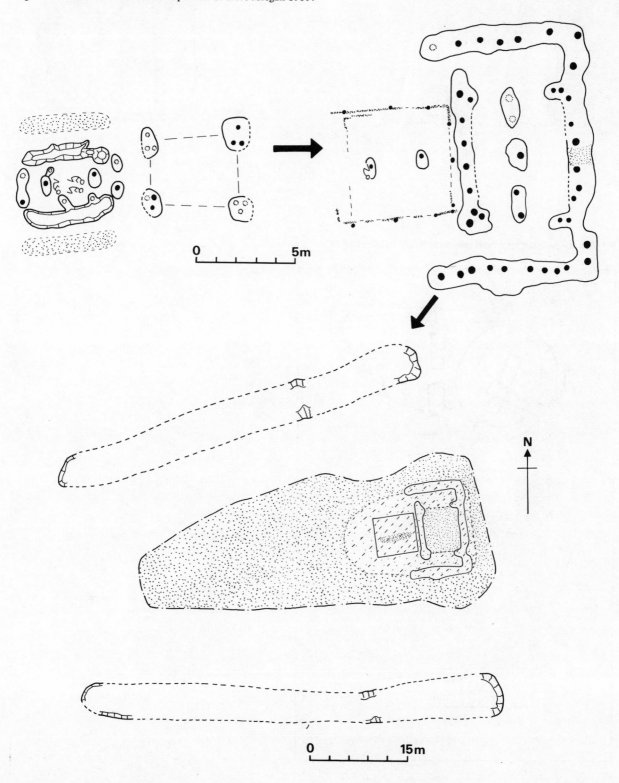

Fig. 6.8. A. Belas Knap: the false portal; B. Drumanone: elevation of portal (not to scale).

A

B

Fig. 6.9. Ty Isaf: the structural sequence. Source: Grimes 1939.

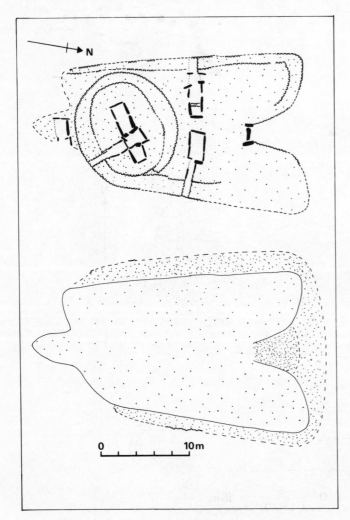

Fig. 6.10. Distribution of mortuary deposits by age and sex: A. West Kennet; B. Fussell's Lodge; C. Lugbury.

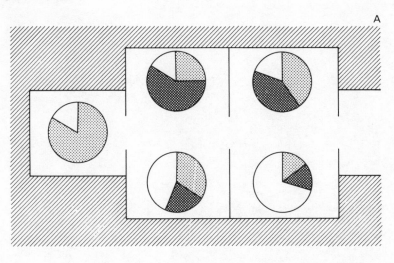

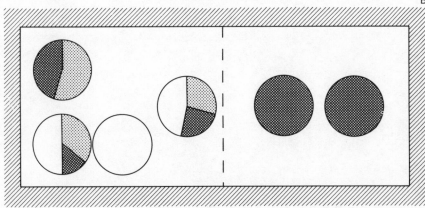

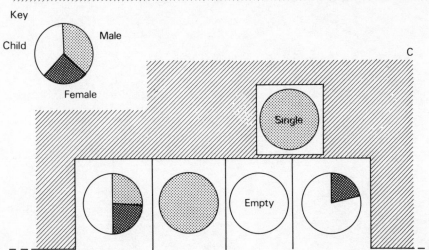

Chapter 7

'Various styles of urn' —
cemeteries and settlement
in southern England
c. 1400–1000 bc
Richard Bradley

I have our brochure here setting out our service. Were you
thinking of interment or incineration? . . . I have some photographs here of various styles of urn.

Evelyn Waugh, *The Loved One* (1948)

Introduction

Renfrew has recently suggested that the burial evidence
in prehistoric Europe conforms to two successive modes:
'group orientated chiefdoms', represented by communal burials,
and 'individualising chiefdoms', marked by the 'single grave'
tradition (1974). There is, however, a third widespread pattern
which he does not consider, and this is the subject of the
present paper. As many writers have noted, the rich burials of
the second millennium bc, the time of Renfrew's 'individualising chiefdoms', are followed by another phase of communal
cemeteries. The contrast is best expressed in the central
European terminology, in which the Tumulus culture is
succeeded by the Urnfield culture (Coles and Harding 1979,
pp. 335ff.). Each group has been regarded as a distinct population. This paper considers one facet of this change, within a
socioeconomic framework.

Southern England shows rather the same pattern as the
European mainland, although the British Isles occupy an
extremely peripheral position. This is compensated for by a
wealth of settlement evidence which has few counterparts in
the core areas of Urnfield Europe. For this reason Britain
offers the prospect of relating the changes in the burial record

to changes in subsistence and settlement. This does not imply that the model presented here should be transferred to these other areas, but this paper may help to show that such a change in the burial record *can* be explained by the workings of the social system more simply than by population change.

Terminology and chronology

It is necessary to say a little about terminology and chronology, although the detailed evidence is discussed more appropriately elsewhere (Barrett 1976, 1980). The whole subject has been bedevilled by the 'various styles of urn' deposited with the dead, and the rigid seriation of these vessels has produced a spurious sequence. In this sequence graves with settlement pottery have been dated to a later period than those with burial urns. This has meant that the British evidence has been viewed as a simple sequence from a Wessex culture, characterised by rich barrow burials, to a Deverel Rimbury culture, which is represented by smaller burial mounds and by cremation cemeteries. No allowance has been made for the distribution of different urns among separate sections of the burial population, and instead a chronological structure has

been imposed on the evidence. The basic division falls at about 1200 bc. The Wessex culture was defined by several specialised classes of urn and by a series of prestigious bronze artefacts. The Deverel Rimbury culture was characterised by burials with coarser pottery of varieties which also occurred in settlements.

These views now seem too simple. Radiocarbon dates show that the Wessex culture burials had a longer currency than was originally envisaged, whilst there is growing evidence that Deverel Rimbury settlement patterns extended back towards 1400 bc. It follows that this paper is concerned, not with a clear-cut sequence, but with two overlapping and contrasting *structures*.

The nature of the evidence

The Wessex culture burials are found on the chalk downland of central southern England (Piggott 1938). Most of the richer graves are from a series of burial mounds which tend to cluster around the major ceremonial centres, including Stonehenge and Mount Pleasant (fig. 7.1). These regions will be referred to as 'core areas'. The mounds in these areas are

Fig. 7.1. The distribution of major 'Wessex' cultural barrow groups in relation to Deverel Rimbury cremation cemeteries with ten or more individuals. The arc picks out cemeteries within 40 km of the major coastal harbour at Christchurch.

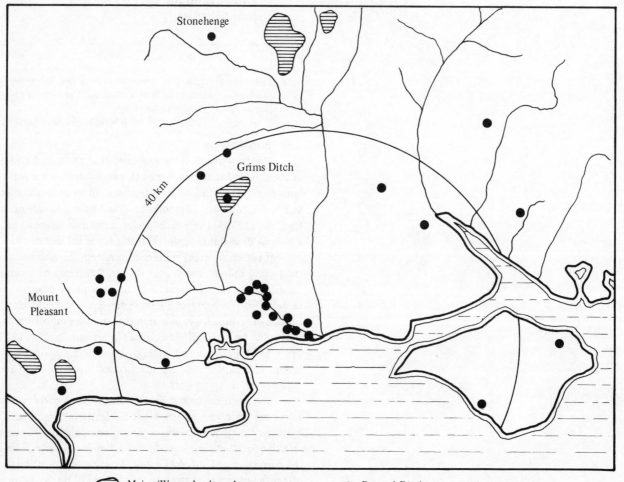

⬭ Major 'Wessex' culture barrow groups   ● Deverel Rimbury cremation cemeteries

significantly larger than those elsewhere on the chalk and include the highest proportion of specialised barrow types, notably bell barrows, which seem to be associated with male burials, and disc barrows, which cover female graves (fig. 7.2) (Fleming 1971). The chronology of the Wessex culture can be subdivided, but in each phase the range of male associations seems to be about five times as wide as that of female grave goods. It is possible that the earlier female graves were the richer ones (Gerloff 1975). It is misleading to describe all the Wessex graves as 'single' burials since a number of the mounds show a complex sequence of extension and continued use, but many burials do possess individual grave goods, whereas some of the mounds — and even the graves themselves — have been reused several times (Petersen 1972). It is clear that only part of the population received formal burial (Atkinson 1972).

The burials with domestic pottery are the poorest of all the furnished graves and occupy a rather marginal position. They may be inserted into existing mounds or may occur in newly constructed barrows around the edges of the core areas (fig. 7.3) (Ellison 1980*a*). They rarely contain other grave goods and might be considered as the burials of lower-ranking individuals, rather than those of a separate community, although some notably late Deverel Rimbury cemeteries are known. The spatial separation of low-status burials is considered by James Brown elsewhere in this volume.

The classic Deverel Rimbury culture is defined by the styles of pottery found in a series of cremation cemeteries on the lower ground towards the coast (Calkin 1962). Although many barrows are known in this area, few of these are of specialised types (fig. 7.2). The mounds are significantly smaller than those on the chalk, and there are no outstanding clusters of barrows, just as there are no ceremonial centres. A few of the mounds include classic Wessex culture material, but these are very sparsely furnished. Although these barrows contain the types of burial urn found on the chalk, the majority of the cremations in this area are with types of pottery which

Fig. 7.2. The distribution of bell and disc barrows in relation to the chalk (stippled).

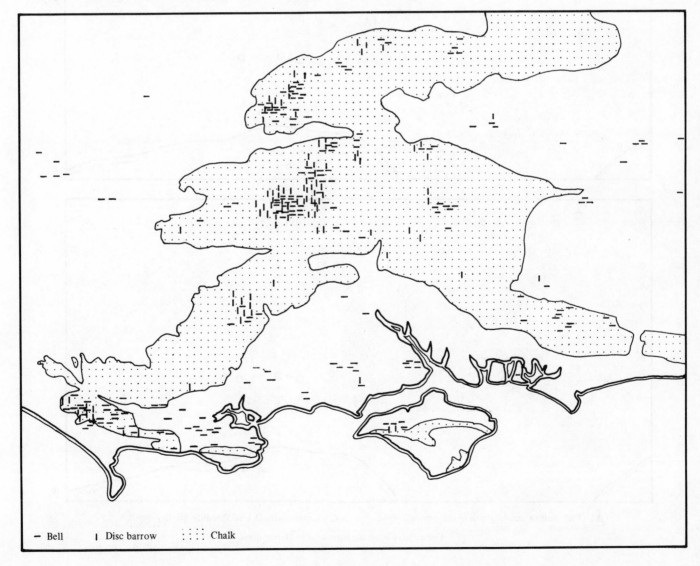

— Bell   I Disc barrow   ⠿ Chalk

also occur in settlements. Such vessels are normally the only grave goods in the coastal area, and a common pattern is for cremation cemeteries to develop within or alongside the barrows. Flat cemeteries are also known (Ellison 1980*a*).

The distribution of the main Wessex barrow groups complements that of Deverel Rimbury urnfields, the majority of which occur within 40 km of the most sheltered harbours on the coast (fig. 7.1). From this it appears that the centres of gravity of both cultures are quite distinct. The evidence for a

more flexible chronology also means that neither group can be studied in isolation. For this reason the two areas will now be referred to simply as the 'downland' and the 'coastal' regions. A similar geographical relationship appears between the rich burials of the upper Thames and the cremation cemeteries around the river estuary.

Burial structure
The monuments of the downland present most of the

Fig. 7.3. Bronze Age burials on the chalk of the Dorset Ridgeway (unstippled area). Source: Royal Commission on Historical Monuments 1970.

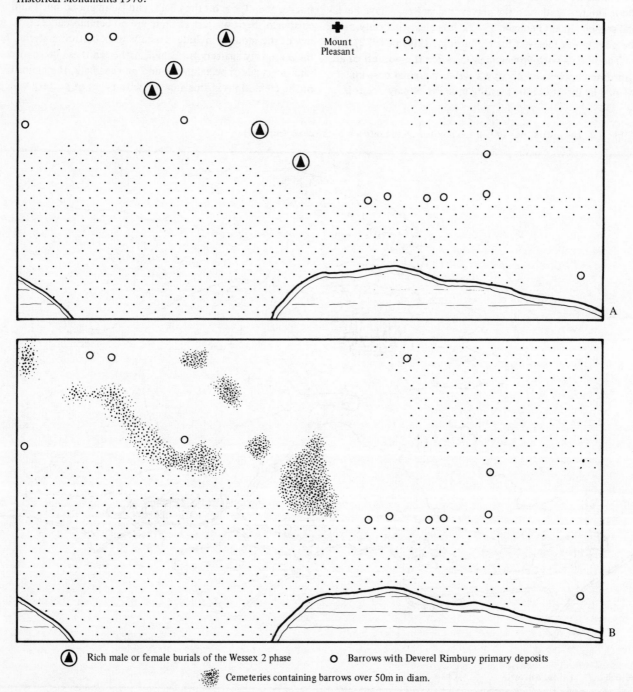

▲ Rich male or female burials of the Wessex 2 phase ○ Barrows with Deverel Rimbury primary deposits

Cemeteries containing barrows over 50m in diam.

characteristics of a ranked society, and the Wessex culture has already been claimed as a chiefdom. The archaeological evidence conforms quite well with the five criteria laid down by Peebles and Kus (1977). The weakest aspect of the burial record is the actual skeletal material, since most of this was recorded in very early excavations. Whilst many artefact associations have been preserved, few age and sex data are available and there is a danger of circularity in estimating these parameters from the grave goods. Even so, richly furnished male, female and infant burials seem to be represented (Fleming 1973). For more secure information it is necessary to turn to the skeletal evidence from the Yorkshire Wolds, another chalkland area where substantial burial mounds occur together with ceremonial centres. There is a far larger sample of skeletons of known age and sex from this area. These have recently been studied by Pierpoint, whose results show both of the patterns described by Peebles and Kus — evidence for increasing wealth with the adult burials, cross-cut by some signs of ascribed status. The evidence for ascribed status only appears after a phase of rich adult burials, suggesting a 'big man' social structure. Although female burials do include distinctive artefacts, these remain poorer than the male graves (I am grateful to Dr Pierpoint for allowing me to refer to his as yet unpublished work). The same broad divisions appear to be present in Wessex.

The second characteristic of a ranked society is the presence of a 'hierarchy of settlement types and sizes'. The evidence from the Wessex downland has already been considered by Peebles and Kus, although most of their information refers to a series of ritual and ceremonial sites (1977), and the dating of *settlements* on the chalk still needs to be refined. The associated earthwork enclosures certainly show differences of size and labour investment (Startin, pers. comm.). Peebles and Kus also suggest that chiefdoms should show 'a high degree of local subsistence self sufficiency' and refer to the restricted ecological variety on the Wessex chalk. This point will be considered in more detail in this paper. Ellison has found a linear relationship between the size of late-second-millennium bc enclosures and the quality of the surrounding land (1980c). This recalls Peebles and Kus's case study at Moundville.

Peebles and Kus suggest two other correlates of ranked societies, both of which can apparently be recognised in this area. There is clear evidence of craft specialisation, most of all in the goldwork, which may be the product of one individual or his school (Coles and Taylor 1971). There is some evidence for centralised pottery production (Barrett, Bradley, Cleal and Pike 1978) and the rich graves contain a variety of items of exotic origin and inspiration (Gerloff 1975). Many of these employ raw materials not present in this region. There is some evidence for basic mathematical and astronomical expertise, and Renfrew has pointed out that very large work forces would need to be organised in order to create the ceremonial centres (1973). There is less evidence for the control of interregional trade as a means of insuring against environmental strain and this factor may have contributed to the collapse of Wessex

society (see below). However, Ellison's research has shown how major enclosures in the late second millennium bc tend to be sited at the edges of ceramic style zones and towards the centre of local groups of metalwork. The amount of metalwork falls off with distance from these sites, and this implies that such enclosures may have played some part in regional exchange (Ellison 1980b).

The burials in the coastal region suggest a rather different pattern. Although burials with special types of urn are known, these graves rarely contain other items, and there is only a small range of barrow types. The graves are hard to classify and show little sign of the hierarchical arrangement in evidence on the chalk (Ellison 1980a). Only one barrow contains much metalwork, and individual burials are usually no richer than those in the cremation cemeteries. Analysis of the burial data has shown three very important characteristics. First, there is a wide variety of slightly different burial types: barrows were still being built; earlier mounds might be reused; and cremation cemeteries also occur, either in isolation or with existing mounds. At the same time, whole groups were being buried together in these cemeteries, with few, if any, grave goods and no real indications of relative rank. Lastly these cemeteries show a series of distinct spatial clusters, the mean size of which is about ten cremations. The skeletal evidence indicates that all age and sex groups were present in normal proportions and it is tempting to regard these cemeteries as the burials of families or other small settlement units (Ellison 1980a and c). An extended family structure has also been inferred from contemporary settlements (Drewett 1980).

These cemeteries present a series of contrasts with the richer burials on the chalk: group burials rather than individual burials; the burial of whole families rather than of selected individuals; a distinct lack of social ranking displayed in the funerary rite; and a difference in the proportion of domestic pottery among the burials. The presence of both male and female cremations suggests one more contrast with the pattern on the chalk, where the disc barrows with their female burials are confined to the main barrow clusters. Although small bell barrows are recorded close to the coast, the urnfields perhaps provide evidence for greater female status. These contrasts are summarised in table 7.1.

Settlement history

For most of the period considered in this paper, the coastal and downland regions must have complemented one another (Barrett and Bradley 1980). The natural environments of the two areas differ almost completely. The chalk downland has a limited range of soils and is less agriculturally productive than the coastal area (fig. 7.4). Indeed, in later periods much of the downland was regarded as marginal land. The best arable is confined to the river valleys, whilst the uplands would have been more suitable as pasture. It was here that the major barrow cemeteries were located. The coastal region contrasts with this pattern and includes restricted areas of excellent agricultural land. The contrasts between the resources in these two zones recall the traditional symbiosis of arable and pastoral farmers.

It is just as important to stress their differing access to other resources. The Wessex culture was very dependent on a supply of artefacts and raw materials imported from other areas. The majority of this material will have been filtered through the coastal area, a region which assumed a comparable importance for inland trade in the Iron Age (Cunliffe 1978). It was through a regular influx of prestige artefacts that social status could be displayed and social transactions controlled

Table 7.1. *Contrasts between downland Wessex culture barrows and coastal Deverel Rimbury culture burials 1400—1000 bc.*

	Downland	Coastal region
Range of barrow types	Wider in the 'core areas'	Limited
Size of mounds	Larger in the 'core areas'	Predominantly small
Ceremonial centres	Present in the 'core areas'	Absent
Evidence of ranking	Widespread	Limited
Predominant mode of burial	Individual	Communal
Evidence of female status	High-status burials mainly in 'core areas'	Equal female status in urnfields?
Burial population	Selected individuals or lineages	Whole families or settlement groups?
Specialised types of urn	Predominant	Uncommon
Metalwork in graves	Common	Exceptional

Fig. 7.4. The major topographical zones discussed in the text.

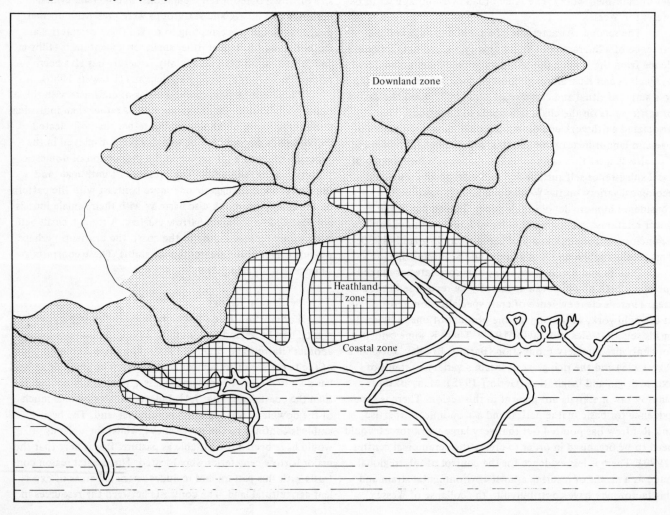

Downland zone

Heathland zone

Coastal zone

(Bradley 1980). In this respect the population of the land-locked area had to rely on the coastal communities, through which these items would pass. The downland region might also have depended on the coastal zone for a reliable grain supply, at least at times of major communal undertakings like the building of Stonehenge. More doubtfully, the coastal region could have lacked sufficient upland grazing, especially for sheep.

This relationship recalls Rathje's interpretation of Classic Lowland Maya settlement patterns (1972, 1973). He distinguishes between a rigidly stratified 'core area' and a 'buffer zone' with a more fluid social structure. The core area was entirely land-locked and without a range of essential materials, whilst the buffer zone commanded the sea and river routes by which these commodities were obtained. These items were distributed within the core area through a network of ceremonial centres that did not extend into the buffer zone. He sees the control of ceremonial activity as an artificial 'resource' of the core area.

Such a balance was not particularly static. In southern England neither zone could accommodate much expansion, although the need to mobilise and feed a communal labour force may perhaps have encouraged greater production, even from a stable population. At the same time there may be evidence for environmental change. In the coastal zone economic growth could occur only through more intensive land use or by the simpler option of colonising unstable soils in the surrounding area. On the chalk, where the best land was less resilient, secondary colonisation may have appeared the only solution. The widening distributions of artefacts and monuments show clearly that the second millennium was a period of sustained expansion, but it also seems very likely that this expansion was followed by a phase of contraction (Barrett and Bradley 1980).

This cycle is seen in both regions considered here, and much of the surrounding heathland seems to have developed in the second millennium as a result of improvident land use. This was the easiest area to settle from both regions, but it could hardly sustain a long period of settlement, and many of the barrows were built on degraded soils. The effect of such rapid wastage might have been that communities were unable to fulfil their obligations to the elite, whose authority was threatened (Bradley 1980). Control over food production became ever more important.

These difficulties may have increased in two ways. First, it seems possible that the supply of bronze objects was failing, or was being diverted from Wessex into the Thames valley (Bradley 1980). This would affect both communities, but in very different ways. The coastal group had prospered partly by controlling the supply of prestige items to the core areas. The downland community probably controlled the distribution of the same material within the social hierarchy. Thus the power structure came under pressure from outside at a time when the internal economy was failing. Faced with this dilemma, the elite tried to substitute greater control over their land for their

diminishing power over trade. Since further expansion into marginal areas was blocked, a second alternative had to be taken, and there are signs that by the later second millennium bc regular field systems were being planned throughout southern England. On the chalk in particular, areas of land were reorganised for arable use. The field systems now assume a prominence previously reserved for cemeteries and ceremonial centres (Bradley 1978*a*, pp. 116ff.).

It is at this point that the contrasts between settlement in different parts of the study area become really important. In the heathlands, further settlement would have been short lived because of the poor quality of the soil. Similarly, on the downland, the chalk soil could not support very intensive farming and some of the settlements were quite short lived. Only the coastal zone continued to receive prestigious artefacts, and it is noticeable that, as the Wessex culture declined, the distinctive burial patterns of this region trespassed on the southern edge of the downland (Barrett and Bradley 1980). As one group faltered, then, the other may have expanded. By 1000 bc their common boundary was marked by a major linear earthwork, the Grims Ditch (fig. 7.1).

These processes are summarised in table 7.2.

In summary, the decline of the Wessex culture corresponds with a gradual change in the character of wealth in society. Until the end of the second millennium bc, there was remarkably little relationship between the areas with much portable wealth and those with the greatest agricultural potential. For example, the daggers which feature so prominently in the burial record are rarely found on high-quality land, and there seems little doubt that power and authority were based less upon direct control of the best agricultural resources than on control of the use and distribution of prestigious artefacts among different elements in society (Bradley 1980). Wealth might be exchanged for tribute and labour, and the frequent relationship between the locations of rich burials and of ceremonial centres can hardly be an accident. But with the changes outlined above there is not only a renewal of farming techniques but also an urgent concern with agricultural production as an alternative form of wealth and, perhaps, as another path to power. Wider European changes in the scope and orientation of exchange may have as much relevance here as any changes in the natural environment (cf. Rowlands 1980). The essential characteristic of late-second-millennium bc Wessex is the way in which control of land was substituted for control over trade and for a while may have acted as the critical force in society.

The location of cemeteries

It is against this background that the siting of burials can be considered. It is again worth following the distinction between individual and communal burial considered earlier in this paper. On the chalk the barrows and barrow cemeteries do not show a completely consistent siting, although they tend to occupy upland positions which give them a particular prominence. In some cases they were clearly meant to be seen from

Table 7.2. *Contrasts in settlement in the heathland, downland and coastal regions of southern England, 1400–1000 bc.*

	Coast	Downland	Heathland
Initial stage	Quite widely settled	Widely settled	Little settled
Main resources	Good arable land; control of inland trade	Pastoral land; control of ceremonial	Woodland; rough pasture; hunting
Deficiencies	Limited areas of good land; ?shortage of upland grazing	Lack of extensive arable; rather unstable soils; lack of raw materials	Very unstable soils
Developed stage	?Expansion into heathlands	?Expansion into heathlands	Secondary colonisation
Deficiencies	Degradation of colonised areas; decline in bronze supply	Degradation of colonised areas; decline in bronze supply	Rapid land wastage
Possibilities of local intensification	Adequate	Quite restricted	Very limited
Final stage	General continuity of settlement	Collapse of elite; competition for land; partial continuity	Gradual desertion

considerable distances, and in the great Dorset Ridgeway cemetery intervisibility may have been a very important factor (Royal Commission on Historical Monuments 1970, pp. 425–9). The barrows are normally situated among fairly unproductive soils, and there is growing evidence that they were built on pasture or, less often, abandoned arable land (Fleming 1971). At present there is very little evidence that these burial sites were close to contemporary settlements, which may in fact have been on lower ground. The siting of the rich barrow burials has been well summed up by Barrett: 'Many barrow cemeteries would have been of considerable visual significance within an increasingly cleared landscape. It is perhaps fitting that the dead should lie not simply on the edge of one world but at the meeting place of many' (1980, p. 81). In the coastal zone and on the heathland the evidence is less extensive but there is nothing to contradict these general statements.

The location of the cremation cemeteries in the buffer zone and its fringes in fact presents a vital contrast. It was only in 1971, almost two decades after the near-by settlement had been excavated, that a cemetery was discovered at Itford Hill in Sussex (Holden 1972). The size of this cemetery was appropriate to one phase of the near-by settlement, and this link was decisively confirmed by the recovery of two parts of the same pot, one in the cemetery barrow and the other in the living area. At that time the discovery attracted considerable interest and it is still quoted as the one instance of a connection between a cemetery and a domestic site in the British Bronze Age. It is becoming increasingly apparent that this relationship in fact occurred quite widely, a view which finds support in recent fieldwork. A series of outline plans is presented in fig.

7.5 and a detailed summary of the evidence from this region is now available (Barrett and Bradley 1980). Three patterns seem to emerge from this evidence. First, cremation cemeteries seem to be found with contemporary settlements more frequently than individual burials with domestic pottery. Second, there is a consistent range of distances between settlement and cemetery locations, extending to a maximum of 700 m, but with its peak between 50 and 300 m. The full range of distances is the same as that noted by Dutch scholars working with broadly contemporary evidence (Hulst 1969). Lastly, the few well-recorded sites seem to suggest that the burial areas were located 'behind' the settlements and avoided the axes both of the individual houses and of the parent enclosures (fig. 7.5).

The variety of burials with settlement pottery (and not just in the coastal area) does pose a number of problems. Why the range of burial rites and why so many barrows with only one primary cremation? It is perhaps relevant that a similar contrast can be found in the landscape. Sites like Crichel Down, Dorset (fig. 7.6) seem to suggest a contrast between small scattered mounds with individual deposits and nucleated cemeteries which often developed around a single barrow (Piggott and Piggott 1944). This contrast between nucleation and dispersal is also found in the settlements. Re-examination of some of the classic sites on the chalk has shown that very few of these were directly integrated with field systems. Instead many of the best-known enclosures were superimposed on the fields, even when these fields were of no great antiquity. There is some reason to suppose that settlement within these systems was initially more dispersed and that houses were scattered about the cultivated area (Barrett and Bradley 1980).

If so, the change to more nucleated settlement might mirror the changes in the burial record. This perhaps occurs at Handley Hill in Dorset, where the Angle Ditch enclosure was clearly secondary to the surrounding field system, just as the nearby urnfield was secondary to one small Deverel Rimbury barrow (Royal Commission on Historical Monuments 1975; Toms 1925; Pitt Rivers 1898, p. 147).

Only one area has enough data for this contrast to be

pursued much further. This is the area of the Avon and Stour valleys, together with the surrounding heathland of south-east Dorset. It lies at the heart of the coastal region. Here the large cemeteries are very well known, but single barrow burials also occur, and contain identical pottery (Calkin 1962). Their relative locations suggest part of the solution: it is clear that in this area at any rate nucleated cemeteries are closer to good agricultural land than the single burials, whether these were

Fig. 7.5. Four Deverel Rimbury settlements and their associated cemeteries.

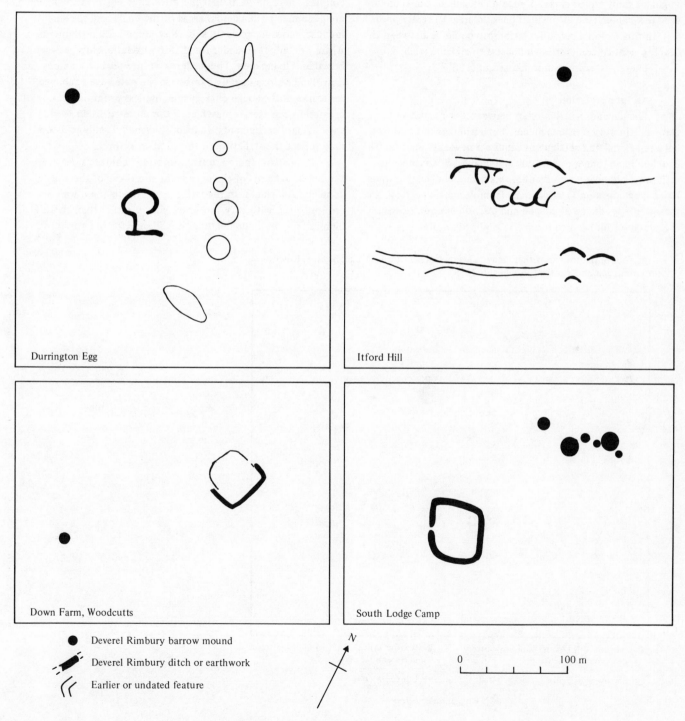

Durrington Egg

Itford Hill

Down Farm, Woodcutts

South Lodge Camp

●   Deverel Rimbury barrow mound

◖●   Deverel Rimbury ditch or earthwork

⌒⌒   Earlier or undated feature

N

0   100 m

placed in specially constructed barrows or just inserted in earlier monuments (fig. 7.7). This can hardly be a valid index of population. At times there may be more people buried near the best land, but the scattered barrows of the heathland would have demanded more labour. Also, if early accounts are to be believed, they were distributed quite widely across the landscape. Indeed, a scatter of separate barrows could contain more burials than one small cemetery. Put at its simplest, any move towards nucleated settlement or communal burial may have been influenced by the quality of the land. Some barrows might be built on, or close to, high-quality land, but there are very few cemeteries, even small ones, in areas of really poor soil. In this region a second relationship could be between the development of cemeteries and access to riverine trade.

These patterns are summarised in table 7.3.

An interpretation

The chronological overlap between the Wessex and Deverel Rimbury cultures means that a number of contrasts between burial and settlement require a new explanation. The problem is no longer one of cultural change, but rather the differences between two contemporary and contrasting *structures*. The common factors, apart from domestic pottery, are the interdependence of coastal and inland communities and the pressures on both to intensify food production.

In a sense earlier students have been right in distinguishing two 'cultures' in the study area. But, if cultural behaviour is viewed as a type of 'language', some of the contrasts which they have considered take on a special meaning beyond their relationship to subsistence agriculture. As Lévi-Strauss has remarked, 'the image a society evolves of the relationship between the living and the dead is, in the final analysis, an attempt, on the level of religious thought, to conceal, embellish or justify the actual relationships which prevail among the living' (1976, p. 320). A number of contrasts deserve greater emphasis here, in particular the difference between the prominent mounds visible across areas of the chalk and the small inconspicuous barrows tucked away behind the settlements. Again one might consider the different relationship between burial and living area. The patterns of intervisibility among the downland barrows surely symbolise the extensive exchange networks of the social elite, just as the less prominent siting of cremation cemeteries may match the more enclosed world of the ordinary settlements. Indeed, the small 'family' clusters may reflect the structure of the rural workforce.

This apart, there are five important contrasts between the burial patterns of the core areas and those of the coastal zone and its fringes. In the latter area there is the burial of groups, often with very few grave goods, rather than that of high-ranking individuals; there is evidence for the burial of

Fig. 7.6. Burial sites and other monuments on Crichel Down, Dorset. Source: Royal Commission on Historical Monuments 1975.

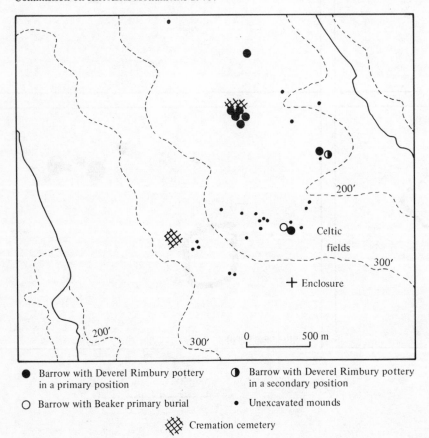

● Barrow with Deverel Rimbury pottery in a primary position

◑ Barrow with Deverel Rimbury pottery in a secondary position

○ Barrow with Beaker primary burial

• Unexcavated mounds

▨ Cremation cemetery

Table 7.3. *Contrasts in locational relationships of individual barrow burials and urnfields, 1400–1000 bc.*

	Individual barrow burials	Urnfields (with or without barrows)
Siting in the landscape	Siting often conspicuous	Siting rarely conspicuous
Evidence of intervisibility	Well known	Not known
Relationship to settlements	No conclusive evidence but mounds are visible from a distance	Quite common. Siting sometimes 'behind' the settlement
Relationship to resources	Siting often on marginal land	Association with good agricultural land

whole families or communities rather than that of one part of society; there is evidence that women might have enjoyed roughly the same status as men; there is sometimes evidence for a close relationship between the siting of settlements and that of cemeteries; and there are some indications that the cemetery principle was at its most developed around the best land.

Chapman (this volume) has suggested that cemeteries are most likely to be found in areas and periods in which there is an imbalance between society and critical resources. In this instance the major resource was land, although Rowlands (1980) has argued that some settlements would have been located close to the river system to take advantage of external trading links. The close relationship between cemeteries and settlements considered here is found in other periods of agricultural expansion (Chapman, this volume), and the decision to adopt a form of communal burial must have been closely tied to the economic prospects of the land farmed by particular communities. Such a pattern has been seen in fig. 7.7. Nucleation of settlement may be another sign of intensified subsistence. Hodder has recently suggested that the distributions of certain of the domestic artefacts could be expressions of local identity in relation to outside groups (1979; Bradley and Hodder 1979); there is a linear relationship between settlement size and land potential, suggesting an attempt to maximise production (Ellison 1980c); and the building of early land boundaries could be equally relevant (Bradley 1978a, p. 117).

But if land was a more important resource, do these cemeteries represent any more than a symbolic change of control? The placing of cemeteries so near to individual settlements may be important here, especially when there is evidence that they were in use over a long period. Goody has argued that changes in attitude towards the ancestors may be linked with changes in the ways in which property is inherited (1962). It is likely that the fragmentation of the landscape into small production units, like the basic process of enclosure, is related to changes in outside contacts. In place of the long-distance contacts of the Wessex culture, there is a sense of isolation and withdrawal, symbolised in the changing location of burial monuments. For a while competition may have been for land rather than for portable artefacts.

Any changes in the status of women may be particularly important here, and in the Danish early Bronze Age Randsborg has discovered a comparable relationship between higher female status and the use of more productive soils (1974). This is a feature which Goody has linked with the presence of intensive, plough-based agriculture (1976). Other elements in this relationship are an emphasis on endogamy, rather than exogamy, the passing of property rights to both males and females, a closer communal identity and greater control over the choice of marriage partner. Women become more important members of the community once they are no longer exchanged between groups and can inherit land. Such features, in Goody's view, control the alienation of land at death and ensure that property will remain within the community. Land becomes more important because of the greater effort invested

Fig. 7.7. The location of Deverel Rimbury barrows and urnfield cemeteries in south-east Dorset and the Hampshire Basin. This diagram plots the distance of both classes of site from the nearest good agricultural land. The contrast is under-emphasised here since some of the cemeteries are in urban areas where the original extent of good land is conjectural. Based on Agricultural Land Classification of Great Britain.

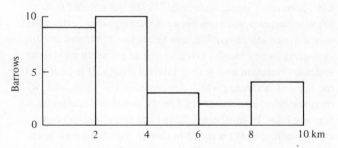

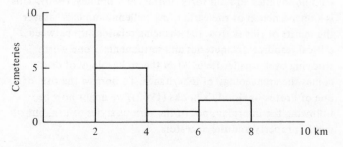

in farming it. 'The scarcer productive resources become and the more intensively they are used, then the greater the tendency towards the retention of these resources within the basic productive and reproductive unit, which in the large majority of cases is the *nuclear family*' (1976, p. 20; my emphasis).

These arguments may have a bearing on the way in which the adoption of cemeteries in the study area appears to be related to the quality of the land. They also shed light on the detailed structure of the urnfields, with their discrete 'family' clusters. To some extent this pattern recalls the land allotment characteristic of this phase. Work in northern Europe has suggested that Iron Age field systems may have been laid out employing a series of uniform area and size modules (Lindquist 1974; Bradley 1978*b*). There is some reason to suspect that this happened in Britain in the Bronze Age. It is usually supposed that these units were determined by the organisation of work, or by a season's food requirement, but another possibility is that they are connected instead with the appearance of individual property rights. This was the view taken by Hatt (1955) in his pioneering studies of Celtic field systems. The parallel with Europe may go further. In the later Bronze Age, it is noticeable that the adoption of communal cemeteries may again correspond in time to a phase of more intensive farming. The settlement and burial evidence from the Knoviz culture of north-west Bohemia is perhaps the best illustration of this point (Bouzek, Koutecký and Neustupný 1966; Bradley, in preparation). And in the Iron Age a similar relationship may be found between the collapse of the bronze trade in northern Europe and the widespread adoption of Celtic fields (Bradley 1978*b*; Kristiansen 1979). On the island of Gotland, where these field systems have been studied in great detail, rich individual burials are again replaced by cemeteries with less evidence of social distinctions (Lindquist 1974; Nylén 1974).

The changes discussed in the present paper are likely to have been short lived. As Goody (1976) has pointed out, exogamy creates wide ties between communities — ties which may serve to lessen conflict and to contain competition. But endogamy, a too careful safeguarding of property rights, can engender isolation and with it internal strains. It is clear that the type of landscape which developed in the study area, with its cemeteries, settlements and fields, could not remain intact for very long. In southern England the end of formal cemeteries corresponds remarkably closely with the breakdown of these simple patterns and the increasing development of land boundaries and hill forts (Barrett and Bradley 1980). This is a phenomenon of the earlier first millennium bc. Whatever the merits of this sketch, the changing relationship between critical resources, cemeteries and settlements is one worth studying over a wider field. After the archaeology of death comes the archaeology of inheritance. To borrow the title of one of Professor Goody's books (1962), we might now be following the interplay, not of the various styles of urn, but of death, property and the ancestors.

Acknowledgements

I am grateful to John Barrett, Ann Ellison and Stephen Pierpoint for allowing me to refer to their work in progress; to Barry Cunliffe for the use of his notes on the Hengistbury area; to Vince Gaffney and Barry Mead for their help in fieldwork, and to Jo Bacon for the original illustrations. This paper can only have been improved by discussion with John Barrett, Bob Chapman and contributors to the conference on 'The Archaeology of Death' in London in April 1979.

Chapter 8

**Burial, succession and
early state formation
in Denmark**
Klavs Randsborg

Introduction

Archaeological studies of the burial practices of state
societies are few outside the areas of ancient civilisations and
the Classical world. In addition, these studies only very rarely
relate changes in burial rites to the socio-economic structure of
states. The same is quite true for studies of undeveloped
societies in the past. However, an increasing body of anthropo-
archaeological literature has managed to relate burial data to
the structure and function of prehistoric societies in various
parts of the world. Unfortunately such investigations are
extremely rare for more developed societies where, apart from
a few studies of the Mayas and other American civilisations,
we are left merely with descriptions of the burials and their
contents.

We shall try here to relate the data on death in the
Viking Age in Denmark (approximately A.D. 800—1000, the
end of the prehistoric period in Denmark) to the decisive
social changes taking place during these centuries in southern
Scandinavia (Randsborg 1980). At the beginning of the period
Denmark was still settled by simple traditional societies, but
during the tenth century A.D. a West Danish state gradually
integrated the whole of the area and even succeeded in establishing a short-lived empire around the North Sea comprising,
at the beginning of the eleventh century, Denmark and
England and, at times, Norway and parts of Sweden too. We
are dealing with a so-called 'secondary' state-formation taking

place outside the ancient primary centres of development. Furthermore, Denmark was never under the rule of the Roman Empire and thus constitutes a remarkable example of a state being formed by a combination of an inner process and the impact of trade and warfare with neighbouring states in western Europe. The burial data clearly reflect this development. We have, though, a further methodological problem, which is also an interesting ideological and social aspect of the Viking Age: the introduction of Christianity. This means that grave goods from the late tenth century onwards are extremely rare, though the 'wrapping' of the body may be very elaborate, as is evident from a stroll through one of the ancient cathedrals. In fact, states, Christian or not, show many examples of conspicuous coffins, burials, chapels, mausoleums etc., from the Pyramids to Halicarnassus and Westminster Abbey. Memorials with inscriptions are especially common. In the Danish Viking Age they are represented by the runestones. The latter are in some cases connected with graves but, although they are memorials for dead persons, most stand in isolated positions, for example beside roads. They supply us with crucial information on succession to social rights and land.

Economy and society

Before turning to the economic and social background — for which the data on death are illuminating — we should take a look at the map (fig. 8.1). The geographical area we are dealing with is larger than present-day Denmark. It is the Denmark of the seventeenth century, before the Swedes conquered most of the eastern provinces (including the fertile and populous Scania) and before the Germans, in the last century, took the southernmost part of Jutland in the West. This larger Denmark, which we name 'Denmark' in the following, is a

Fig. 8.1. Danish provinces and Viking Age localities.

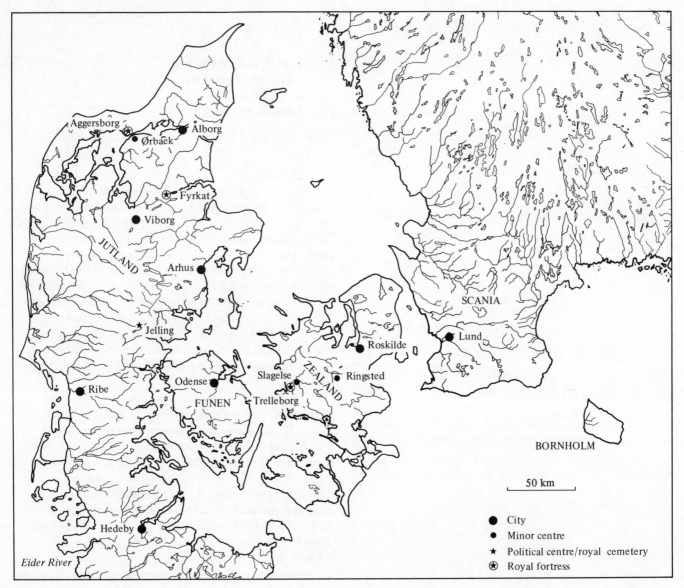

geographically well-defined province of Europe, surrounded by the sea except for the narrow land-corridor to Germany and on the densely forested Swedish border. Most of the area is fairly homogenous in terms of soil and good agricultural land. To the West in Jutland and to the North and East in the provinces (now part of Sweden) we do have more marginal lands, which are still rather sparsely populated today. Throughout prehistory cultural patterns within 'Denmark' were similar, but at no point in time before about A.D. 1000 was the country truly united under a single political system. To judge from burials, various parts of the country were more developed politically in some periods than in others but, in general, during the Bronze and early Iron Ages (up to the middle of the first millennium A.D.), we are dealing with rather small and autonomous societies, with leaders who were above the level of community-headmen and were engaged in external trade and warfare.

The map also shows a number of Viking Age towns and other centres. We note, for instance, the cities of the state of Denmark in the early eleventh century. Among these are Hedeby and Ribe in the south-west, already founded by the late eighth century as ports of trade linking the country with the Frankish Empire and with other parts of western Europe. At these two sites missionary churches were built in the middle of the ninth century. The towns of Århus in Jutland and Odense on Funen were founded in the early tenth century. In the later parts of the same century the towns of Hedeby, Ribe, Århus and Odense held bishoprics. The rest of the cities on the map were founded after about A.D. 1000. We also note the well-known fortresses of Trelleborg type (Aggersborg, Fyrkat (plate 8.4) and Trelleborg) from the mid-tenth century, which, along with the Danevirke ramparts at Hedeby, protected the West Danish state of the same period. The fortifications lie in a semicircle around the area which holds the early towns and its very centre is the royal farmstead and burial ground at Jelling. Jelling is also situated on the North–South highroad through Jutland, which a few miles to the South of the royal centre crossed a river valley on a two-lane bridge 1 km long, constructed of oak, another magnificent enterprise by the lords of this first state centred in the West of Denmark.

In contrast to the developments of the tenth century the society of the late eighth and the ninth centuries was much more firmly rooted in the traditional societies of the late Iron Age in Denmark. The structure of the landed settlements was much the same as in the Iron Age (Randsborg 1980, pp. 45ff.). The villages were made up of single farmsteads of varying size, but each comprising a large long-house with several functions (e.g. habitation, stable etc.) in addition to a number of minor buildings. In the late tenth and in the eleventh centuries some of these villages were regulated, seemingly according to central directives, and furthermore, a new type of farmstead emerged, the magnate farm. These had very large fenced crofts in the middle of which was a single hall for occupation (the type of building found on the royal fortresses). Along the fence were

other constructions, such as stables, storehouses and other living quarters. The importance of these finds can hardly be underestimated. They demonstrate a difference in conditions of living and in access to land and resources among the primary producers which is not seen in earlier periods.

These changes in the landed economy took place during a climatic optimum phase (A.D. 700–1200) in which the population was growing strongly. Pollen diagrams reflecting the Viking Age environments show that fields and pastures were expanding at the expense of forest. In addition the diagrams demonstrate a new stress on cereal growing. In the early Iron Age animal protein was the dominant source of nutrition, but the growing population could not be fed without a change to plant protein: cereal-growing is more labour intensive, but requires less land than stock-rearing. We must see the changes in Viking Age settlement in the light of these observations.

We are poorly informed about the social structure and the political events of the period, but a few facts are clear (Randsborg 1980, pp. 11ff.). In the years around A.D. 800 the Danes witnessed the engulfing of their neighbours to the south-west, the Saxons, into the Frankish Empire under Charlemagne. Shortly afterwards the Franks attacked the Danes, who rallied under King Godfred and succeeded in keeping the Franks at bay by setting up a defensive wall along the southern border of Jutland. After the failure of their military attacks, the Franks took to intervention in Danish dynastic politics. By the middle of the ninth century the German church succeeded in getting permission to set up churches at the emporia of Hedeby and Ribe. Indeed, the period of Frankish attacks correlated with a period of intensive international trade. King Godfred also had Hedeby regulated and registered. The decline of international trade in the late ninth century corresponds with the period of the fierce Danish raids on western Europe, which were probably a result of diminishing income from trade with a variety of consequences for the traditional society. Seemingly the political establishments of Denmark in the ninth century were very fragile: none continued into the tenth century and there are few indications of a socio-economic milieu different from that of the late Iron Age. The only novel aspects were the ports of trade in the south-west and the military organisation set up to protect the area against the Franks and to carry out warfare and raids against other neighbours.

The tenth century started with another phase of close international trade contacts, which for a short period around the middle of the century were severed. The break resulted in a shortage of surplus silver in the country, but the crisis was solved internally and no attempts at raiding followed this decline (Randsborg 1980, pp. 136ff.). The social structure was obviously different from that in the ninth century, and it was no accident that the tenth century saw the coming of the magnate farm and other reflections of the private ownership of land. In fact, grants of land became more common and may have substituted for cash payments during the crisis. The manorial system of land tenure was well able to secure the provision of food-stuffs, raw materials etc. for the towns and for the many enterprises of the tenth-century state, which at first centred in the West but by the year A.D. 1000 covered both the western and the eastern provinces of Denmark.

Around A.D. 960 the Danish king of the Jelling dynasty, Harald 'Bluetooth', accepted Christianity as the state religion. Seemingly it happened as a voluntary act, although the tenth century also saw much German pressure and occasional attacks on the southern border. Moreover, the German emperor in the tenth century nominated bishops for Denmark. King Harald sought to turn his realm into a modern West European state, partly with the help of an establishment of warrior vassals (see below). This army, incidentally, made up the instrument of power that allowed the conquest of England in the early eleventh century by Harald's son and grandson — Kings Sven and Knud.

Succession and runestones

We meet the name of King Harald on a large, richly decorated runestone at the royal centre of Jelling (fig. 8.2). The stone was raised by Harald for his parents Gorm and Thyra, 'that Harald' — as the stone says — 'who won for himself all of Denmark and Norway, and made the Danes Christian'. The claim about Norway was not real and it is dubious to what extent King Harald exercised power over East Denmark about A.D. 960, the time of the erection of the stone. Another runestone from Jelling was set by King Gorm, the father of Harald, over Thyra, his wife and the mother of Harald. Indeed, almost all the runestones of the period around A.D. 950 are found in Mid and North Jutland (fig. 8.3) (Randsborg 1980, pp. 24ff.). They are all of the formula '*x* raised this stone after *y*'. In general the persons involved were men, but some monuments were set over very high-ranking women. Almost all the stones set over women are from Mid Jutland, the central area of the state and possible homeland of the dynasty (a number of stones from here refer to the royal lineage). The explanation of this concentration of stones set over women, which is second to no other area or period, might be that the first kings and their followers of the Jelling dynasty married high-ranking women from Mid Jutland to obtain land and position.

In a few cases the runestones refer directly to landed property rights. Furthermore the persons involved were nearly all closely related to each other, a son, for instance, erecting a monument for his father. Thus it seems clear that the stones mark the transfer of social and economic rights and duties. In addition to the '*x* raised this stone after *y*' formula the inscriptions contain information on titles, historical events, geographical localities etc.

Looking at the chronology and distribution of all the runestones a significant pattern emerges. The earliest stones are from the period around A.D. 800 and the ninth century in general. They are found in the central parts of the country (fig. 8.4). With a few exceptions the stones of the tenth cen-

tury are from Mid and North Jutland (fig. 8.3). The monuments from the decades around A.D. 1000, however, are found in two clusters, one in North Jutland and the other in Scania (fig. 8.5). Later stones are extremely rare, apart from a distinct late eleventh-century group from the island of Bornholm in the Baltic.

The traditional societies of the early and late Iron Age did not erect runestones over the dead, although the runic alphabet already existed in A.D. 200. Seemingly the rules of inheritance of position and property rested firmly within the precepts of the local communities and no monument was needed to underline the rights of the local potentates. The social transformation of the Viking Age included not only conflicts and the dissolution of traditional societies, but also the coming of new types of settlements and more personal types of rights. All of this would call for a special means of communicating the takeover of, for example, a village by a new social group. The moment this family was firmly established, the situation was brought back to normal and no further monument was needed. This would explain the 'jumping' distribution of the stones.

The early (ninth-century) stones cluster in the internal conflict zones of the country, the population medians or the central parts (fig. 8.4). We have indications that the political centre of gravity of the ninth century was in the same areas. At this stage the central parts were the most regulated and integrated, while the more marginal provinces were more unsettled. Consequently it is no surprise to find the stones of the tenth century (almost all in Mid and North Jutland) reflecting the organisation of some of the marginal areas (fig. 8.3). The last stones, at A.D. 1000, in smaller clusters, reflect special types of settlements within the integrated state of Denmark (fig. 8.5).

Only some of the earliest stones (of the ninth century) carry the formula '*x* raised this stone after *y*', most bearing just a single name. The function of the stones with regard to rights to land may, however, have been the same. Apart from the titles of office known from foreign written sources, like count of a town, military commander etc., these early stones record priests of local areas. This is a strong indication of the persistence of the traditional society. The priests ('good ones') were also magnates and on a stone from around A.D. 900 (Glavendrup) a 'good one' is mentioned as a high-ranking 'thane' too. The thanes or 'thegns' were royal vassals and became numerous in the tenth century.

We have already dealt with some of the characteristics of the tenth-century stones, but it should be added that we encounter a number of new titles. Some refer to land, like landman (a major vassal) and bailiff, and we meet more thegns and also drengs (literally 'boys'), junior vassals who, as we shall see in the following, probably had certain warrior obligations which could not be inherited by very young or old persons. Other titles are 'skipper' (in the service of a magnate) and, of course, king and queen, lord etc. The term 'fælle' is quite interesting; the word includes the element 'fæ', property, and

Fig. 8.2. King Harald's stone *c.* A.D. 960: three views. Source: Jacobsen and Moltke 1941–2, no. 42.

is used to denote 'fellows' inheriting somebody else's property, usually another 'dreng's'.

In short, these clear texts of inheritance also reveal the complexity of tenth-century West Danish society, in contrast with ninth-century Denmark. In addition to references to private property rights we note a number of civil titles. There is a clear difference in social milieu between the ninth-century stones, with few titles and references to 'tribal' areas and to magnates with priestly functions, and the complex civil society with towns of King Harald's time. Also it is clear that it was very important — and it was consistently done — to name both the deceased and the successor or heir in the text, by following the formula 'x raised this stone after y'.

The texts from around A.D. 1000 follow this formula strictly. All the monuments except one were raised over men and in terms of social milieu and information on titles etc.

they are similar to the stones from the tenth century. In addition to those titles already mentioned we meet land agents and so-called 'farmers' (magnates), 'residing men' (probably vassals), high-ranking craftsmen, captains of warships and housecarls, plus various other lords and even important freed slaves. It is also noteworthy that the number of 'fellow'-relationships sharply increases at the expense of the normal family ties. This reflects another step away from the traditional society built on kinship, with few or no property relations between non-relatives.

It is significant that the 'fellow'-stones cluster around the towns. In the catchment areas of the cities of Århus in Jutland and of Lund in Scania, the towns central to the two main groups of these late stones, the number of non-family relations is the greatest. In addition we have a similar stone from the city of Hedeby in southernmost Jutland. In the same

Fig. 8.3. Runestones of the tenth century A.D. Source: Randsborg 1980.

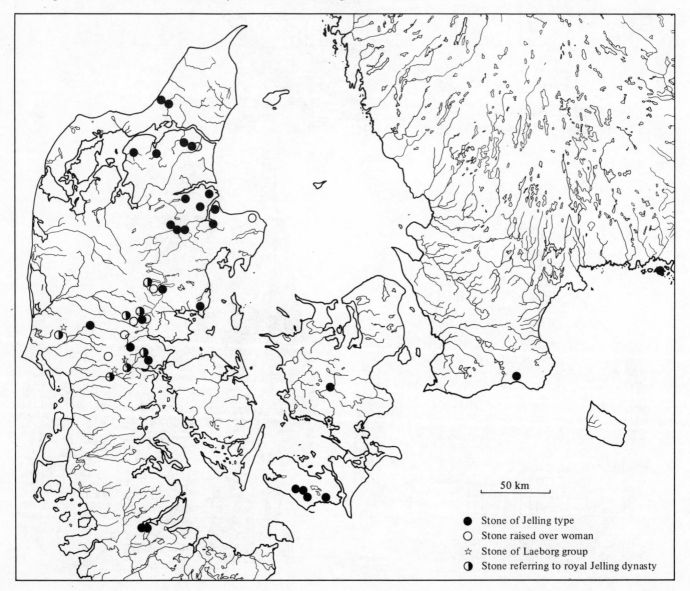

● Stone of Jelling type
○ Stone raised over woman
☆ Stone of Laeborg group
◑ Stone referring to royal Jelling dynasty

50 km

three city zones, and only here, we also meet references to violent deaths, often abroad. The Hedeby stone informs us that the junior vassals, the 'drengs', apart from being fellows, could or would serve as captains on the king's warships. Similar relations seem to be reflected in the distribution of the contemporary stones in South Scania (fig. 8.6.). The main cluster of Scanian monuments is divided geographically into a sub-cluster around the town of Lund and another along the South coast. In the eastern part of the southern sub-cluster we have monuments for dead fathers (and husbands), and senior vassals like thegns. In the West, however, we note a strange group of stones for young persons, basically for brothers who are also drengs. The complete absence of monuments raised by a junior over an elder person can only mean that succession here was dependent on certain obligations, probably to take an active part in the navy and army operations (the military

apparatus was organised in 'ships'). This reveals the establishment, though probably for only a short period of time, of 'age-sets', as we might call them, with special purposes, for instance the conquest of England and the control of the North Sea empire of Kings Sven and Knud (Canute). Also, the Scanian military settlement may have originated in response to the integration of East Denmark under the rule of the Jelling kings.

In terms of religious observance the early stones are definitely pagan, not infrequently referring to Thor, the god of strength.

The stone of King Harald, from about A.D. 960, is the first Christian one, carrying also a representation of Christ (fig. 8.2). Christian allusions are most common among the latest stones (from around A.D. 1000). When dealing with the burials we note the Christian influence in exactly the same decades.

Fig. 8.4. Early runestones of the ninth century A.D. Source: Randsborg 1980.

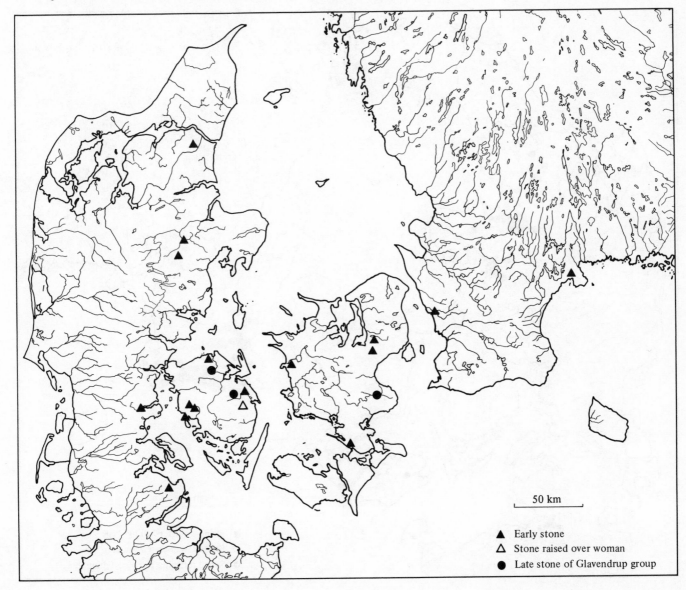

50 km

▲ Early stone
△ Stone raised over woman
● Late stone of Glavendrup group

Burial data

The Viking Age graves are usually simple inhumations, orientated East—West (Randsborg 1980, pp. 121ff.). Some cremations are also known, especially from northernmost Jutland, where they are the usual type of burial and define one of the sub-areas of special burial customs. Some of the inhumations, almost all of them prominent graves of the tenth century, are found in wooden chambers. The chambers allowed for display at the burial and gave room for accompanying goods. However, grave goods are in general very scarce (fig. 8.7). In fact, rich graves almost disappeared in Denmark at the close of the early Iron Age around A.D. 400, and weapon-graves, reflecting prominent males, were already very rare after A.D. 200. It seems that personal ornaments like the jewellery of the women, tended to be more frequent while other categories of valuables were not included in the grave goods and must have been passed on to the next generation at death. In short, the late Iron Age and the Viking Age had a quite 'rational' perception of valuables as they were not squandered in rituals to any degree.

The skeletal material demonstrates a number of aspects relating both to the different life-styles of the two sexes and to the character of the various social groups in Denmark in the Viking period. As predicted, women tended to have a lower life-expectancy than men, a common feature in pre-modern societies with greater risks at childbirth. In a few cases decapitated bodies have been found in inhumation graves, reflecting sacrifices, most probably of slaves killed in connection with the death of their master. The existence of slaves is otherwise difficult to demonstrate in the Viking Age societies,

Fig. 8.5. Runestones of 'after-Jelling' type, *c.* AD 1000. Source: Randsborg 1980.

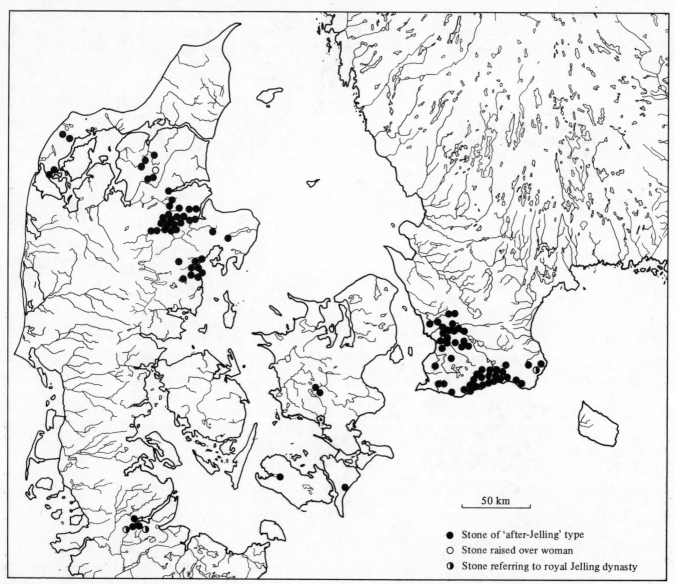

50 km

● Stone of 'after-Jelling' type
○ Stone raised over woman
◑ Stone referring to royal Jelling dynasty

and it is not known to what extent slave-labour had real economic significance in an area which was experiencing a marked population growth.

The ratio between the sexes in cemeteries displays interesting differences at various types of settlement (Randsborg 1980, pp. 81ff.). At the fortresses men were clearly dominant; in fact, women corresponded in number with the group of men above the age of forty. Perhaps it is more surprising that in the towns also men outnumbered women, by about two to one. The town activities, trading and craft production, were mainly male occupations and in Denmark the women were apparently only brought into town to perform services (e.g. weaving). At the landed settlements, however, the sex ratio was in balance.

The cemeteries of the village settlements of the pre-Christian era were made up of graves of uniform type. As mentioned above, inhumations and cremations alike contained only a few insignificant artefacts (fig. 8.7). This was also the case in Christian cemeteries of, for example, the eleventh century, but there the grave goods were even more scanty. In addition, the burials of the Christian period were gathered around (or even inside) the churches, while in pagan times the graveyards were related to the individual settlements or villages.

In the tenth century, at the onset of the state society, we note a number of changes in burial customs, apart from the ones regarding the adoption of Christian ideology and especially Christian institutions. At Stengade on the island of Langeland in West-Central Denmark a cemetery made up of discrete clusters of simple inhumations, probably reflecting single farmsteads or other social units, also held a group of chamber tombs (Skaarup 1976) (cf. fig. 8.7.). This pattern may be seen as a parallel to the distinction between magnate

farms and normal farms in the contemporary village sites. In Central and south-west Denmark we also find small separate cemeteries containing, along with modest graves, conspicuous cavalry burials (fig. 8.8) and female interments in the bodies of carriages (without the wheels) (figs. 8.11 and 8.12). Cavalry graves were also common in North Jutland in the mid-tenth century, but here they were not accompanied by the female carriage-body graves. The latter were paired with male graves containing an axe (plate 8.3) found in provinces of North Jutland other than those with the cavalry graves. The area of the axe and accompanying carriage-body graves also has contemporary runestones (fig. 8.10) (Randsborg 1980, pp. 126ff.).

Before discussing this distribution pattern in detail, it is appropriate to consider separately the two main types of graves, those with riding equipment and weapons, and those with female interments in the body of a carriage. The cavalry graves contained heavy stirrups (plate 8.1), special bits, spurs etc., all meant for cavalry fighting in formations (fig. 8.8). This technique was introduced to north-west Europe by the Hungarians in the early tenth century and seems to have been imitated by King Harald and later by his son and grandson in the campaigns against England. In addition the burials included weapons and sometimes even a horse. Some of the cavalry graves were rich, like the ship-grave at Ladby in North Funen

Fig. 8.6. Runestones of 'after-Jelling' type in Scania.

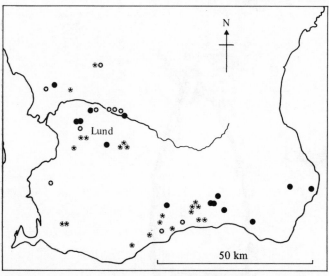

● Stone raised over father or husband ✳ Stone raised over brother etc.
○ Stone raised over *fælle*

Fig. 8.7. Distribution of wealth in three cemeteries as measured by the number of different artefacts in the graves.

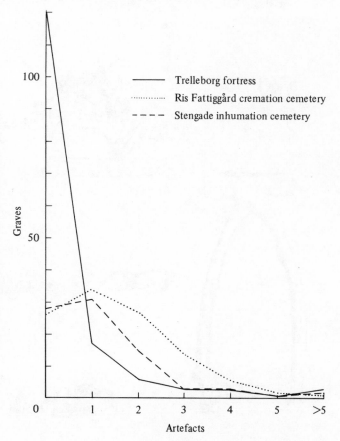

(plate 8.2), others were poorer, but in all of them the standard equipment was uniform. They belong to the early and especially the middle part of the tenth century and the distribution covers West and Mid Denmark (fig. 8.9). A closer look at the scatter reveals that it forms a belt around the Jelling province, about 75–125 km from the political centre of the state. In the South (in Jutland) the graves are found at the Danevirke walls on the German border. In Mid and North Denmark they are placed around Jelling in the same belt as the royal fortresses, Trelleborg on West Zealand, Fyrkat (plate 8.4) and Aggersborg in North Jutland (cf. fig. 8.1). It seems clear that the fortifications and the heavy-weapon graves define the border of the West Danish state of A.D. 950, within which we find the political centre, the towns, the runestones etc. As mentioned, weapons were extremely rare in Danish graves after A.D. 200. Their sudden occurrence in the tenth century, combined with the 'crescent'-shaped distribution, reflects a new social organisation. In the traditional society

Fig. 8.8. Contents of cavalry grave from Kasmusmølle, South Jutland: tenth century A.D. Source: Brøndsted 1936.

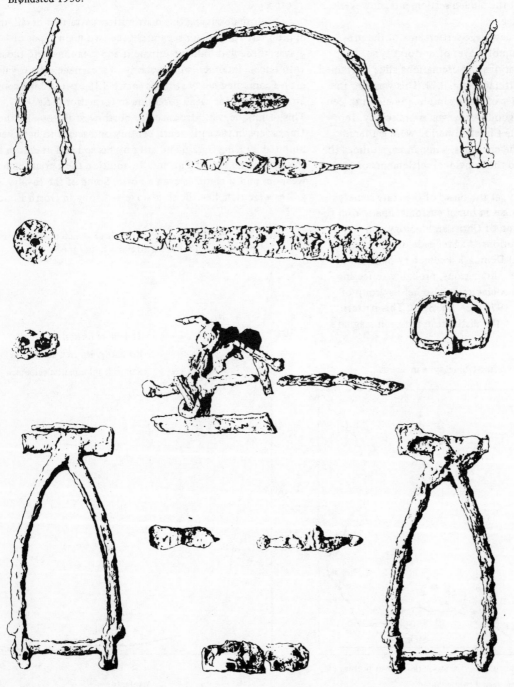

weapons were simply passed on to the heir at the death of the owner. Consequently the cavalry personages did not owe their particular status to the local group, but must be regarded as servants of the state and the king. They obviously had military duties like the drengs and the captains of warships mentioned on the contemporary and later runestones.

However, runestones, which imply changes in ownership of land, were very rare in the provinces holding cavalry graves and therefore we tend to view these burials as belonging to magnates who were members of long-established local families.

The other groups of conspicuous graves, with the body of a carriage acting as a coffin (figs. 8.11 and 8.12), are also from West and Mid Denmark (fig. 8.10) and are contemporary with the heavy cavalry burials, basically from the middle of the tenth century (Randsborg 1980, pp. 129ff.). They held

very high-ranking women (the mother of King Harald was buried in one), wearing flowing dresses of Byzantine inspiration and in fashion among the contemporary West European upper classes. The dress differed from the traditional woman's garment of the Viking Age in Scandinavia, often equipped with a pair of tortoise-buckles of bronze. Silver and gold jewellery is very rare in Viking graves in spite of its frequency in the hoards of valuables. Seemingly such ornaments were also passed on to the heirs at the death of the owner; they probably belonged to the family fortune.

One of the carriage burials, from Hørning in Jutland, was found in a wooden chamber, above which had been erected a small wooden church. This indicates that the burial was a kind of 'founder's tomb' belonging to a female member of the Jelling state establishment at the time of the official

Fig. 8.9. Cavalry graves with heavy stirrups and fortifications of the tenth century A.D. Source: Randsborg 1980.

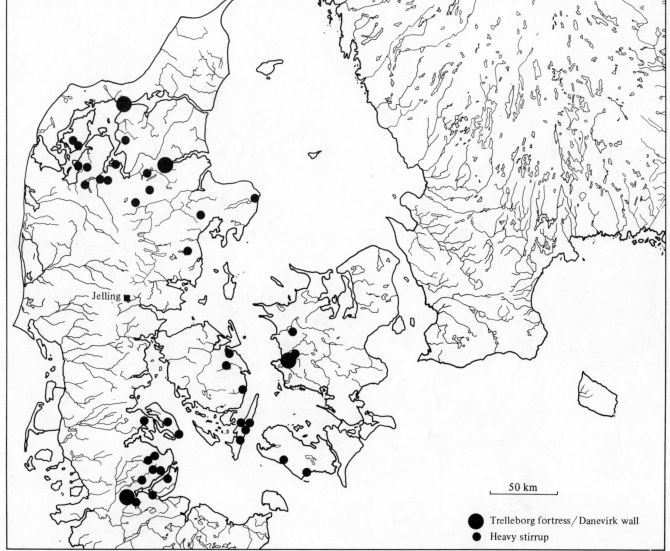

conversion to Christianity (figs. 8.11 and 8.12). A parallel situation is recorded from Jelling itself, where the first wooden church held a chamber-tomb. The chamber contained, apart from remnants of costly garments, some skeletal parts arranged in a way that showed this was not the original grave. They were probably removed from the wooden chamber in the near-by, huge so-called 'Northmound' (thought to contain Thyra, the mother of Harald), which had already been opened and carefully closed in antiquity. In south-west Denmark the carriage graves are found in cemeteries which also have the heavy cavalry graves and do not occur in zones with runestones (fig. 8.10). In North Jutland and in a few other areas these female graves are paired with male interments holding an axe as the only noteworthy grave goods (plate 8.3). These northern carriage-body and axe burials are found in the zones with contemporary runestones which reflect changes in the succession to land. Consequently, these personages from North Jutland may not have been part of the local traditional groups. We assume, of course, as in the Jelling case, that the personages of the highest rank according to burial belonged to the social sphere of the runestones.

A single carriage-body burial has appeared in a Slavonian town-fortress in East Holstein. This woman, perhaps Danish, may have made a political marriage with a local lord. The wife of King Harald came from this land and King Sven, her son, married a Polish princess. Indeed, the relations between the Jelling dynasty and the Slavonian societies in the south-west were very close; many Danish coins have been found in Poland, and at the royal fortress of Fyrkat in North Jutland (plate 8.4) a large cache of southern Polish or Ukrainian rye (probably high-quality seed-corn) was found.

The above observations reveal both the complexity and

Fig. 8.10. Cavalry graves with heavy stirrups, carriage-body graves, and Jelling-type runestones. Source: Randsborg 1980.

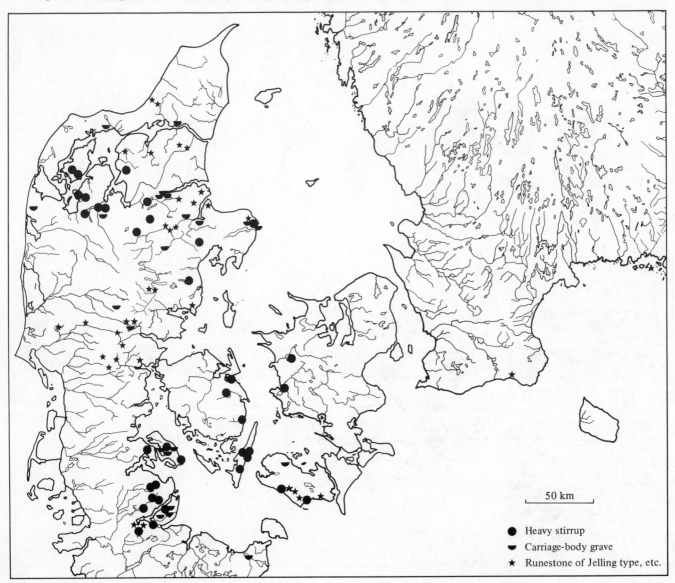

50 km

● Heavy stirrup
◗ Carriage-body grave
★ Runestone of Jelling type, etc.

the planned nature of the socio-political organisation of the West Danish state in the tenth century. A border area (with fortifications) was set up, with the establishment of new military offices, reflected in the heavy cavalry graves (figs. 8.9 and 8.10). The officers were probably of the local traditional establishment. Other personages held a vassal-like status and were given grants of land, the succession to which was marked by the runestones. The wives of the vassals — like those of the royal lineage itself — were given burial in the body of a carriage. In some cases this treatment was also accorded to the females of the cavalry families. However, in the same

decades of the tenth century Christianity was adopted as a state religion by the magnates, and the burial rites and the locations of the graves altered. This leaves the archaeologist with great problems when reconstructing social dimensions from the burial data, although some social information can still be gained from the late runestones.

Conclusions

The methodological difficulties we have had in dealing with the social aspects of the formation of the Danish State highlight a few problems in the research on death. It is very important to enter the study of social dimensions at the level of the local tradition for treatment of the dead. The means that states and other societies use to communicate social status, succession etc. by way of funerary practices and memorial stones cannot be derived from any simple archaeological formula. Social changes are certainly reflected in the burial data, but the appearance of change may take a variety of forms according to the cultural milieu. In spite of these difficulties, in the case of the Viking Age in Denmark we have been helped greatly by the existence of a few written texts.

Fig. 8.11. Hørning (Jutland): stave church over tenth-century burial chamber and mound. Source: Krogh and Voss 1961.

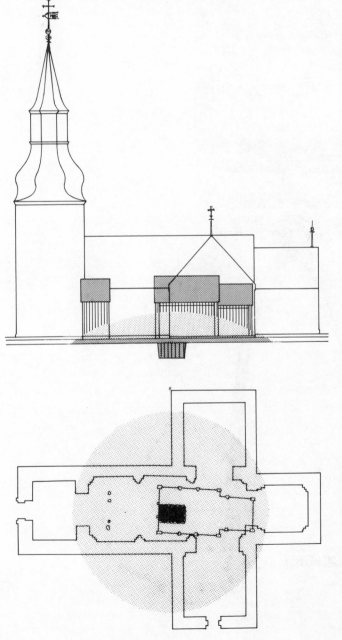

Fig. 8.12. Hørning: carriage-body grave in burial chamber. Source: Krogh and Voss 1961.

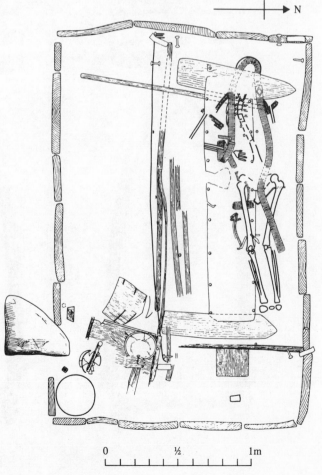

N

0   ½   1m

The integration of various kinds of data has benefited from the application of methods first developed in the study of mute, 'prehistoric' societies.

The study of Viking Age burials and memorial stones has proved to be an important part of the research into the formation of the Viking Age state in Denmark. It has not explained the development, but has outlined crucial points in the complex social, and economic, behaviour in the sequence of societies leading to the early state. It has, hopefully, become clear that the Viking Age data on death do not constitute the amorphous unit that traditional research conceives of, intersected only by the distinction between the conspicuous tombs of chieftains and the graves of the peasantry, and by the problems of the pagan versus the Christian norms of burial. The archaeological remains which represent social processes are complex, but they are structured both by variables of cultural tradition and by the factors, elusive and debatable though they may be, that make societies change.

Plate 8.1. Silver- and copper-decorated stirrups (length 35 cm) from tenth-century cavalry grave at Nr. Longelse, island of Langeland. Photograph by courtesy of the National Museum, Copenhagen.

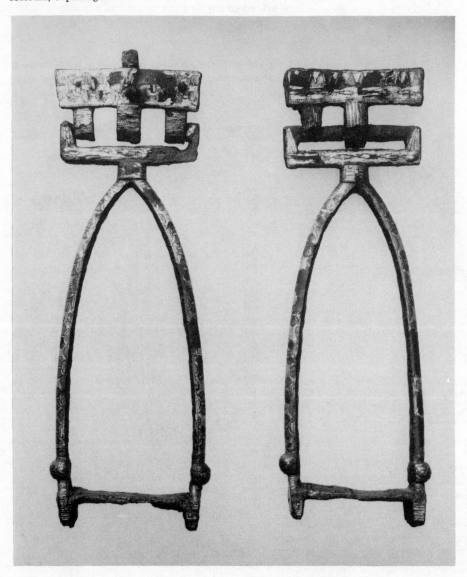

Plate 8.2. Tenth-century boat (and cavalry) grave at Ladby, Funen. Photograph by courtesy of the National Museum, Copenhagen.

Plate 8.3. Axe with silver inlays (length 17.5 cm) from burial chamber in Bjerringhøj, northern Jutland. Photograph by courtesy of the National Museum, Copenhagen.

Plate 8.4. Tenth-century fortress (diam. 144 m) at Fyrkat, northern Jutland. Cemetery lies outside the wall to the left. Photograph by courtesy of the National Museum, Copenhagen.

Chapter 9

Mortuary practices, palaeodemography and palaeopathology: a case study from the Koster site (Illinois)
Jane E. Buikstra

Introduction

For an osteologist, investigating archaic human remains presents a special challenge. Frequently fragmented and poorly preserved, such ancient skeletons require extreme care during archaeological recovery and painstaking effort during reconstruction and analysis. The very rarity which makes such specimens inordinately valuable also places limitations upon the degree to which their attributes may be said to reflect a representative pattern for an extinct population. Overstating the data base is tempting, as the researcher seeks to develop some small new insight concerning ancient life-styles. For instance, in this period of ecological archaeology, there is frequently pressure upon the osteologist to contribute information concerning demographic parameters (e.g. estimates of group size, mortality rates) to models of prehistoric adaptation. Thus encouraged, he may do so, perhaps even enriching the discussion with appropriate qualifying statements with reference to the limitations of the data base. All too often these qualifications are lost as the general models develop, and error is compounded as higher levels of inference are reached.

It is the opinion of this writer that a conservative and critical stance is essential when investigating skeletal samples of small size, such as the series which is reported here. Following this premise, the current study has the following goals: (1) the description of important osteological attributes; (2) the inference of biocultural parameters within the bounds prescribed by the data base; and (3) the critical evaluation of prior models of human adaptation which are based upon contemporary remains.

This paper presents a preliminary evaluation of human remains which predate most skeletal samples from the midwestern United States. This series, excavated between 1969 and 1973 from the Koster site, an open-air, deeply stratified site in west-central Illinois (fig. 9.1), is important in developing a model of Archaic adaptation for the region (Asch, Ford and Asch 1972; Butzer 1977; Cook, T.G., 1976; Houart 1971; Struever and Carlson 1977). The published data from Modoc Rock Shelter, another stratified site in Illinois, will be referred to in this analysis, as will information from Gibson Mound 1 and Klunk Mound 7, bluff-crest cemeteries with Archaic components, also located in west-central Illinois. Emphasis will be placed upon the interpretation of osteological data, primarily in reference to defining the Koster burial programme, palaeodemography, and palaeopathology. Archaeological context will assume importance, particularly in the identification of biases which may affect osteological interpretation.

The initial section of this paper presents a summary of current thought concerning the palaeoenvironmental setting and subsistence settlement system(s) which supported the

Fig. 9.1. Location of middle and late Archaic sites discussed in this paper.

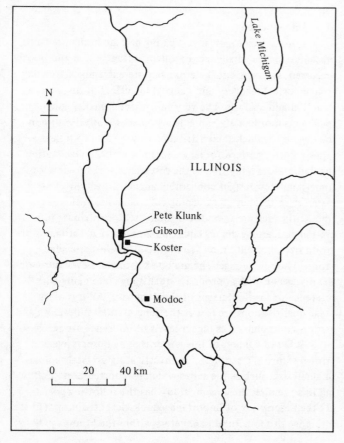

inhabitants of Koster Horizons VI and VII. These horizons have produced the majority of the human remains cited in this study. Following this will be a description of the general research design for human osteological analysis to which this study contributes. The remaining major portion of the paper will be devoted to the three topics indicated in the previous paragraph: mortuary practices, palaeodemography, and palaeopathology.

Koster horizons VI and VII (after Brown *et al.* n.d.; Brown, Bebrich and Struever n.d.)

The organically stained 1.0–1.5 m thick midden of Horizon VI lies approximately 1.5–3 m below the present ground surface at the northern end of the major excavation unit or 'macro-block' at Koster. The depth of this horizon increases as one moves downslope toward the edge of the excavation, owing to the greater rate of colluvial deposition on this portion of the site. Horizon VII is a very lightly stained and diffuse stratigraphic unit immediately underlying Horizon VI. These two horizons are designated Helton Phase by Cook, T.G. (1976), with radiometric dating indicating a time span from about 5900 to 4800 bp.

The presence of a large and diverse tool assemblage, which includes task-specific implements and items of personal adornment, has been combined with data describing a variety of pit features and three house platforms to suggest that the site is best characterised as a base camp during Horizon VI times. Palaeobotanical and faunal remains indicate that the site was occupied during most seasons of the year, thus complementing the artefactual and structural data. Horizon VI strata, as well as other deeper middle Archaic horizons, indicate that the environment during this period was warm and dry, when compared with the climate for horizons immediately pre- and post-dating middle Archaic. It is inferred that the major environmental shift occurred between middle and late, rather than between early and middle Archaic.

Horizon VI/VII occupants are best characterised as hunting and gathering groups who selectively exploited the rich riverine environment of the Illinois River valley as well as the adjacent uplands. A broad range of mussel and vertebrate resources was taken, including waterfowl, turkey, fish and turtle. However, it appears that white-tail deer probably comprised the single most important meat source. Palaeobotanical evidence indicates that, although a wide range of plant resources was available, emphasis was placed upon harvesting hickory-nuts. Archaeologically recovered hickory-nut fragments are as abundant as wood charcoal and, although other nut shells, including acorn, pecan, black walnut, and hazel-nut are present, 90% by weight of the identifiable fragments are hickory. This pattern suggests to the palaeoethnobotanists working on the Koster project that harvesting of the nutritious, easily storable, and seasonally abundant hickory-nut was an optimally efficient adaptation for a hunting and gathering population of inferred small size in this region (Asch, Ford and Asch 1972).

A research strategy for the study of skeletal remains

The investigation of prehistoric behaviour and ecology, a unifying theme of the Koster Research Program, is well suited to human osteological study. Adaptation to the natural environment, genetic and social relationships and social organisation all have an impact on the composition and structure of skeletal series. Skeletal maturation, bony response to chronic and acute developmental upset, and the form and distribution of pathology are important measures of the ability of the human group to deal with the universal problems of nutrition and disease. Demographic information, especially that defining longevity, also measures adaptive efficiency, and is therefore a useful supplement to data derived by the Koster scientists who deal directly with the products of subsistence and extractive-maintenance technology.

Another class of osseous data, inherited morphological attributes, also relates to questions critical to our understanding of the Archaic. Origins of the early Eastern Woodlands Indians may be investigated, as well as patterns of local population interaction and relationship. Such research requires a strategy which emphasises the study of microvariability and microevolutionary change, as well as a careful consideration of those phenotypic attributes chosen to represent genetic information.

Critical to the proper interpretation of inherited and environmentally influenced skeletal attributes is the archaeological context of the burial series. The human biologist, if he is to make accurate statements applicable to the total palaeopopulation, must carefully consider the nature of his sample. Thus, one of the most critical decisions in any research strategy involves the choice of the proper unit for analysis. It has been repeatedly demonstrated through the study of ethnographic records that a single human social group may utilise one or several spatially distinct cemetery areas. Therefore, to assume that any single cemetery comprises a representative sample of prehistoric mortuary behaviour or osseous materials is unwarranted until the inclusive nature of the cemetery is demonstrated. A pleasant by-product of this line of inquiry is the fact that behaviour directed toward the dead provides unique information concerning prehistoric social organisation.

The successful exploitation of osteological data, therefore, requires an inclusive 'bioarchaeological' perspective. Fig. 9.2 illustrates a model research strategy appropriate for this form of study. Numerous archaeological and osteological data classes are collected, synthesised, and directed toward the investigation of the five topics indicated in the centre of the diagram.

Ultimately, Archaic data will be directed toward all five subjects. This preliminary study will focus upon aspects of the first and last items: specifically, the identification of behavioural rules which define the Koster burial programme(s) and an initial test of the hypothesis that the Archaic is characterised by a trend toward increasing adaptive efficiency, using mortality and Harris Line data.

The Koster burial series

This analysis is based upon the sample of human skeletal materials recovered from Archaic cultural horizons at the Koster site between 1969 and 1973. It should be emphasised that Koster is neither exclusively nor primarily a cemetery. Twenty-five individuals are represented in this sample, which is distributed through five horizons (fig. 9.3). Excepting the majority of burials found in Horizons VI and VII and a few infants recovered from deeper horizons, most individuals are represented by broken, redeposited and isolated bones. The Koster sample, therefore, is small, frequently fragmented, and spread through approximately 3000 years of prehistory.

The researcher is now faced with a difficult choice. He may conclude that little, if anything, can be learned from such

Fig. 9.2. Model research strategy appropriate for bio-archaeological study. Figure originally appeared in the *Proceedings of the Southern Anthropological Society*, No. 11 (Buikstra 1977) and is reproduced by permission of the Society.

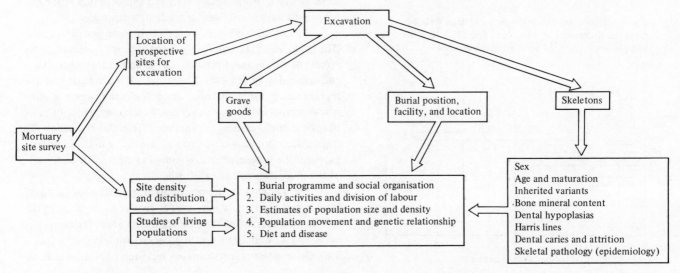

a sparse data base, or he may lump together all burial data and skeletons as a single sample in an effort to 'say something' about the Archaic. In the former approach, of course, one learns nothing. However, in the latter case, failure to take account of sampling biases or to ask whether the 'statistical population' being sampled has any biological or cultural relevance is likely to result in spurious results. This point is critical, since one can in this way assume (and thus create) bio-cultural homogeneity through a time span longer than the more recent Woodland and Mississippian periods combined. The approach suggested here is an alternative strategy: samples will be lumped when it is archaeologically defensible, but in all cases the question of relationship between the sample and the palaeopopulation will be addressed explicitly. In this manner biases will be exposed, and (more importantly) it is suggested that the biases themselves communicate valuable cultural information.

The spatial dimensions of mortuary behaviour
Palaeopathology of Modoc Rock Shelter series

Prior to the excavations at Koster, the only substantial Archaic burial series from a habitation site in Illinois came from Modoc Rock Shelter. Modoc is a stratified site located on the Mississippi River below its confluence with the Illinois (fig. 9.1). Twenty-eight individuals were recovered from strata representing a 3000-year period, broadly paralleling the age of the Koster series (see Cook, T.G., 1976, for a discussion of the temporal correlation between Modoc and Koster occupations). The Modoc series has been reported by Neumann (1967).

According to Neumann's analysis, the Archaic peoples from Modoc show a remarkable amount of bone disease. Noting that 'it was quite surprising to find such a high incidence of bone pathology in a series of this size', Neumann (1967, p. 12) describes numerous cases of striking deformity, including imperfectly healed fractures, a single case of ankylosing spondylitis, and the nearly universal occurrence of degenerative joint disease or osteo-arthritis. The Modoc

skeletons are assumed to be representative of the total population inhabiting the site. Neumann attributes the high frequency of pathology to 'the rugged, difficult mode of subsistence' practised by these hunter-gatherers (1976, p. 12).

Palaeopathology of the Koster series

The burials from Koster Horizon VI, the occupation most comparable in time to the major occupation of Modoc Rock Shelter, also show a striking amount of pathology. Half of the adults show evidence of deformities which would have severely limited their ability to perform a 'normal' round of activities. Included here are cases of pseudarthrosis (fig. 9.4), a necrotic hip with marked dysplasia (fig. 9.5), and an imperfectly healed fracture of the humerus. Arthritic change is also observable in most of the adult individuals. However, before one accepts this as proof of a biologically stressful, rugged *modus vivendi*, one should approach these series with a further set of questions concerning sampling and the biosocial dimensions of mortuary behaviour.

The Koster burial programme

Biases in the structure and composition of burial series can result from both prehistoric disposal modes and archaeological sampling error. The problems of deep-site excavation (discussed in Brown, Bebrich and Struever n.d.) have precluded both total horizon excavation and sampling in a manner which would produce a representative sample of burials. It must be remembered, therefore, that any burial programme designed for Koster presently applies only to those sections excavated prior to 1974. The following discussion, unless otherwise indicated, will consider only those burials from Horizons VI and VII, since these individuals comprise the only sample of even moderate size.

Ethnographic reports (e.g. summaries in Binford 1971; Saxe 1970) repeatedly emphasise the frequency with which human groups structure their burial programmes according to sex, age, or circumstances of death, including chronic disease states. Such structuring frequently includes burial and cemetery locus as well as burial disposition and is commonly reported for groups with hunter-gatherer adaptive strategies.

The identification of intra-site patterning at Koster (Horizons VI–VII) requires that one attempt to eliminate the effects of stratigraphic mixing and random disturbance due to cultural and natural forces. Therefore, all individuals who are represented by isolated bones or small clusters in refuse pits, whose provenance may or may not be a consequence of prehistoric cultural choice, are excluded from this discussion. The distribution and disposition of the remaining individuals do appear to be patterned and to some extent structured by sex of the individual and age at death.

As indicated by Brown, Bebrich, and Struever (n.d.), at least five of the burials were perpendicular to the slope in the north-east quadrant of the site. All of the adult skeletons were male, and all were lying on their backs with legs flexed (fig. 9.6). Other adult males showed a variation of this pattern, and

Fig. 9.3. Histogram indicating the number of skeletons excavated from the Koster site between 1969 and 1973. Horizon assignment and presently accepted dates are also indicated.

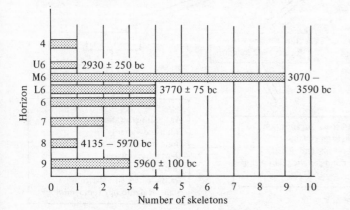

Fig. 9.4. Left elbow of Koster Burial 27 showing arthritic sequelae of traumatic episode. Also present in this individual, but not figured here, was a pseudarthrosis in the midshaft of the left ulna.

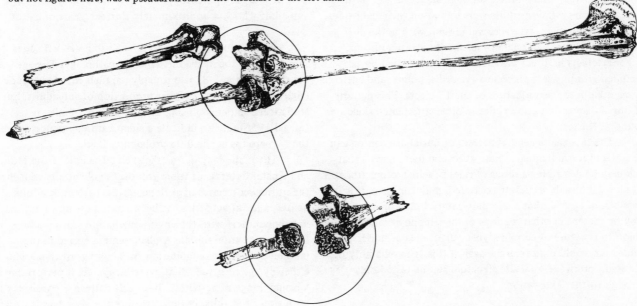

Fig. 9.6. Koster Burial 7 showing burial position typical of adult males.

Fig. 9.5. Koster Burial 7: necrotic hip.

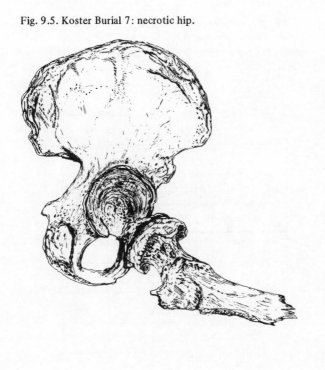

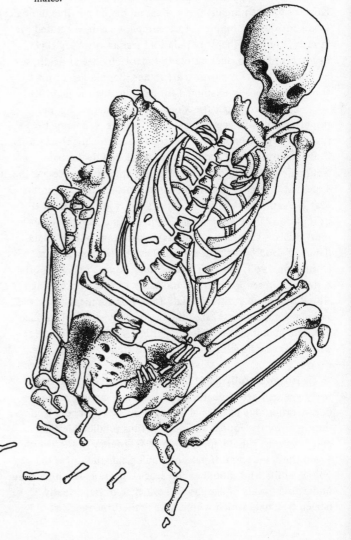

all had their heads turned to the right. Though cranio-caudal orientation was variable, the axes of all skeletons ran south-west to north-east. Sub-adults were buried on their right sides. Within this complex, artefacts were found with both sub-adults and adults. Red ochre or haematite was ubiquitous. Other artefacts in direct association with individual burials included grinding stones, bone awls, drills, points, and antler items used in the manufacture of chert objects. This pattern of burial disposition also applies to other articulated skeletons found at Koster.

The fact that a general pattern of burial disposition can be isolated for individuals found at several loci suggests that one may be describing a series of rules to which other Horizon VI and VII burials, as yet unexcavated, may conform. It is possible, of course, that a complementary burial programme may be present in other sections of the site; however, the ubiquitous nature of certain stylistic attributes of burial behaviour would tend to argue against this. The reliability of the assumption for total site structure can be tested only through further excavation.

Modoc and Koster: prehistoric sampling error

Demographic inferences based upon the Modoc and Koster series require careful evaluation of the possible biological biases introduced by prehistoric sampling error. As stated previously, hunter-gatherer populations frequently bury their dead according to rules defined primarily by age at death, sex, and other skeletally obvious attributes. Population profiles should be carefully examined for inexplicable irregularities.

Considering first the Modoc series, a decidedly 'old' population profile is evident. Fig. 9.7 (after Neumann 1967) illustrates age—sex data for the total series, highlighting those individuals indicated by Neumann to be middle Archaic. Neumann has noted that this does not appear to represent the expected mortality profile for a total social group. He infers that the sample probably represents the results of seasonal occupation of the Modoc rock shelter, principally by older individuals — those who could take advantage of the 'abundance of food [which] was readily available' near the site (Neumann 1967, p. 12). Thus, he does assume that the burial series is representative of the mortality of those occupying the site. Based upon pathology data from this admittedly skewed sample, Neumann recreated the biologically stressful Archaic life. The high incidence of osteo-arthritis (degenerative joint disease) is one form of pathology consistently cited in this regard.

However, fully half the Modoc individuals were over forty years of age at death. Since in *Homo sapiens* bony degeneration due to normal ageing processes generally begins during or by the fourth decade, it is thus predictable that osteo-arthritis should appear in high frequency in the sample. From the standpoint of palaeopathological study, it is the young adults who should excite special interest. All individuals under forty years of age showed evidence of imperfectly healed traumata which would have limited the range of

activities these individuals could perform (after Neumann 1967). The only pathology-free skeleton is the youngest, a sub-adult who was approximately thirteen years of age at death.

As mentioned previously, the Koster VI—VII series resembles Modoc in the incidence of pathology. The age—sex distribution (fig. 9.8) also roughly parallels that for Modoc (fig. 9.7). Koster has a higher proportion of sub-adults, but a statistical comparison using the Kolmogorov-Smirnov test (Siegel 1956) fails to indicate a significant difference between the two groups at the 0.05 probability level.

Thus, one may define the skeletal samples from Modoc and Koster in terms of three groups: (1) old adults who show the normal correlates of skeletal ageing; (2) young adults whose range of activities has been limited owing to unfortunate encounters with the environment; and (3) sub-adults. In this way, the total middle Archaic sample buried in the midden of these two habitation sites consists of those who, either by age or by accident, were incapable of performing a 'normal' range of activities. Since this pattern is consistent for both sites, it is unlikely that intra-site sampling bias is responsible for it. A consideration of other Archaic burial loci is necessary.

Fig. 9.7. Frequency distribution of Modoc skeletons by age and sex. Source: Neumann 1967.

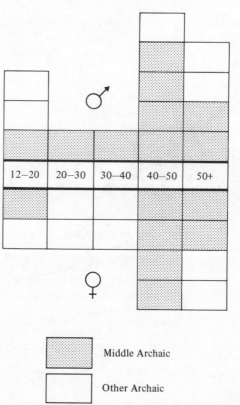

Middle Archaic

Other Archaic

Inter-site mortuary variability

It is obvious that for Koster Horizon VI not all of the dead were buried in the midden. It is impossible to reconcile the low burial density of this horizon with the occupational density indicated by the thick, black, debris-laden soil. The bluff crests overlooking the site are logical locations for additional cemeteries. Given the presence of diagnostic Archaic artefacts within Woodland burial mounds located on these bluff crests, one might suspect the presence of additional Archaic skeletons here. Though such burials were not identified upon excavation and are therefore not available for study, a series with more precise cultural affiliation is available from a similar topographic situation 10.5 km distant. Across the Illinois River and north of Koster (fig. 9.1) a primarily middle Woodland mound group called Gibson has been excavated by the writer and Gregory Perino. The southernmost mound, Mound 1, was found to have an underlying Archaic cemetery component. Diagnostic artefacts found with the burials suggest that the site is broadly contemporaneous with Koster Horizon VI (Cook, T.G., 1976). Though this does not imply that the Gibson and Koster VI–VII series comprise the same biological population or social group, it may perhaps be instructive to examine Gibson Mound 1 as an alternative track of the middle Archaic burial programme.

The frequency distribution by sex and age at death for the Gibson burials (fig. 9.9) indicates that most of the population consists of young and middle-aged adults, none of whom show signs of striking pathology or arthritic change. A comparison of the frequency distribution by age with that for the Koster midden series emphasises the complementary nature of the two samples (fig. 9.10). The Kolmogorov-Smirnov test indicates that the difference between the two distributions is

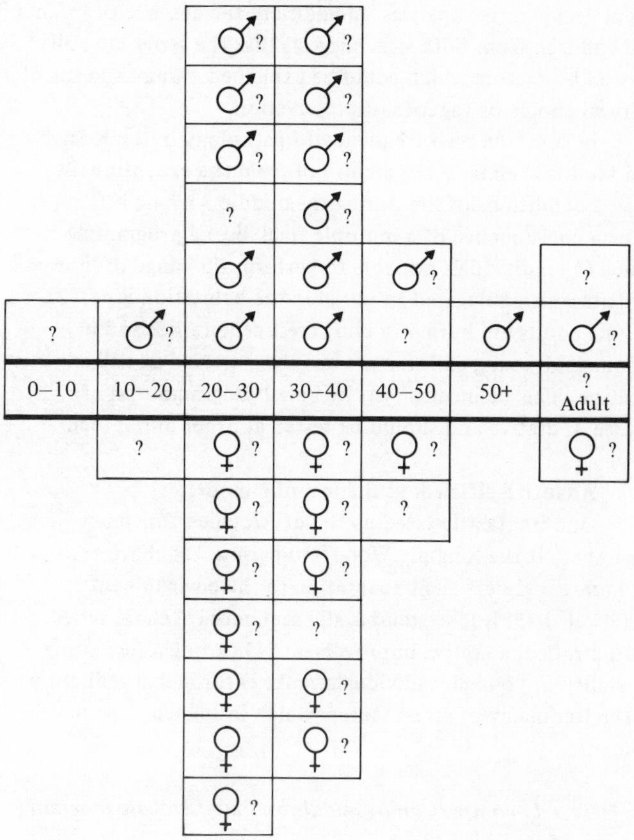

Fig. 9.9. Frequency distribution of Gibson Mound 1 Archaic component by age and sex.

Fig. 9.8. Frequency distribution of Koster skeletons from Horizons VI and VII by age and sex.

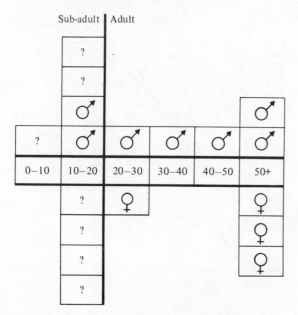

Fig. 9.10. Histogram showing age distribution of burials from Gibson Mound 1 and Koster Horizons VI and VII.

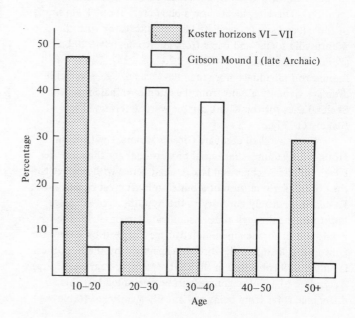

statistically significant at the 0.05 probability level. This illustrates the fact that neither cemetery by itself is a sample sufficiently complete for demographic reconstruction. These spatially distinct cemeteries appear to be alternative tracks in a single burial programme, and should be combined in subsequent comparative analysis. In addition, the absence of infants and children from both sites suggests that the series are still skewed by factors which could be explained either in terms of cultural choice or vagaries of preservation.

In sum, the high frequency of pathology in the Koster and Modoc skeletal series stems not from the exceptionally rugged conditions of life during the middle Archaic but appears to be a consequence of a multiple track burial programme in which (1) individuals not able to perform the range of 'normal' adult tasks are relegated to burial in the habitation area; (2) normal adults are buried in bluff crest cemeteries; and (3) infants and young children are possibly interred in still another location. This delineation of the burial programme is, of course, tentative and should be tested at other burial loci.

Adaptive efficiency: the test of a model

One frequently cited model of Archaic subsistence suggests that the long pre-Woodland period was characterised by increasingly efficient adaptation to the environment (Caldwell 1958). If so, temporally sequential skeletal series should reflect adaptive improvement (1) through decreasing mortality in younger individuals; and (2) through a reduction in the frequency of stress factors which influence bone development.

Test 1: comparison of middle and late Archaic mortality profiles

The first comparison will be made using the Gibson and Koster samples to represent middle Archaic series and a very late Archaic sample from a sub-mound context. The late Archaic sample is from Klunk Mound 7 (see fig. 9.1 for location). This site, located on a bluff crest about 1 km north of the Gibson site is associated by the excavator with the 'Kampsville focus' and dates from approximately 920 bc (Perino 1968; Crane and Griffin 1963, p. 233). The test is limited to individuals more than ten years of age, since children are virtually absent from the middle Archaic series. Skeletal ages for the Klunk sample were determined by Blakely (1971).

First, we shall compare Gibson Mound 1 with Klunk Mound 7, assuming that burial programmes are the same between middle Archaic and late Archaic series with respect to the criteria for inclusion of a burial in bluff-crest cemeteries. Results are entirely contrary to the hypothesis of adaptive improvement through time. As indicated in fig. 9.11, the maximum difference in cumulative age distribution curves for Gibson and Klunk in the direction specified by the hypothesis is only 0.079 (observed in the thirty- to forty-year age group). According to a Kolmogorov-Smirnov one-tailed test this difference is far from being statistically significant (table 9.1).

The deviation between cumulative distributions is far more prominent in the *opposite direction* to the 'adaptive improvement' hypothesis. According to a Kolmogorov-Smirnov two-tailed test the maximum deviation in the opposite direction (0.251, observed in the ten- to twenty-year age group) almost attains statistical significance at the 0.05 probability level.

However, it is possible that Klunk Mound 7 represents an inclusive cemetery of a late Archaic group, in which case its skeletal series should be compared with the combined Gibson and Koster series. Comparison of the Klunk series with a synthetic series based on the combined Gibson-Koster series does result in considerably closer agreement of cumulative age distribution curves. Of course, there is no justification for simply adding the Gibson and Koster series together. What we have done is to assume (1) that $x\%$ of the total burial population is missing from the Gibson mound and (2) that this $x\%$ was selected according to the rules for inclusion in Koster midden. For any percentage of x whatsoever, the synthetic cumulative distribution resembles the Klunk curve more closely than does the Gibson curve. In fact as x, the percentage assumed to be missing, increases from 0 to 47%, the cumulative distribution curves become increasingly similar. If the missing fraction were 47% of the middle Archaic population, then the middle and late Archaic cumulative curves would differ by a maximum of 0.059 (fig. 9.11). At this percentage level, the synthetic middle Archaic distribution and the late Archaic distribution show a remarkable resemblance.

In sum, these mortality statistics lend no support to a hypothesis of increasing adaptive efficiency in the Archaic. However, more cemetery samples are needed in order to control for variation in the spatial dimensions of burial programmes.

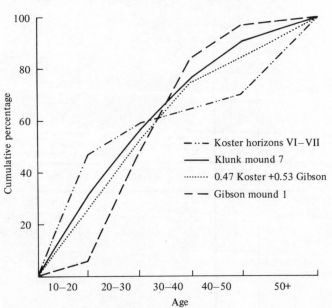

Fig. 9.11. Simulated age distributions for Archaic series.

Legend:
- — ··· — Koster horizons VI–VII
- —— Klunk mound 7
- ········ 0.47 Koster +0.53 Gibson
- — — Gibson mound 1

Table 9.1. *Comparison of mortality figures by age for middle and late Archaic series.*

Series compared	Kolmogorov-Smirnov test used	Maximum difference between cumulative distribution curves	Critical value for difference (0.05 level)[a]
Gibson Md. 1 (n = 32) v. Klunk Md. 7 (n = 166)	One-tailed test of hypothesis that Gibson series is younger than Klunk series	0.079 (for prescribed direction; in 30–40 year age group)	0.236
	Two-tailed test, i.e. no preferred difference	0.059 (in 10–20 year age group)	0.263
Synthetic middle Archaic series (0.53 Gibson + 0.47 Koster midden) v. Klunk Md. 7	–	0.059 (in 10–20 year age group and 40–50 year age group)	–

[a]Based on large-sample approximation (Siegel 1956).

Test 2: Harris Line radiographic analysis of skeletal development

Another approach to evaluating the hypothesis concerning adaptive efficiency is through the study of skeletal development. Assuming increased adaptive efficiency through time, we would expect a reduction in the frequency of stress which influences bone development. Harris Lines, which apparently result from processes of growth renewal following systemic upset, are radio-opaque lines within bone tissue that are frequently used by biological anthropologists as markers of acute stress episodes (cf. Cook, this volume). For instance, Cassidy (1972) working with the Indian Knoll Archaic series reports that the lines tend to be regularly spaced. She infers from this that episodic nutritional upset may have been a regular part of the annual cycle for certain Archaic groups. It seems appropriate, therefore, to evaluate Harris Line frequencies in our Illinois Archaic samples.

Tibiae, femora and radii from the Koster, Gibson, and Klunk series were X-rayed using standard radiographic technique (100 mA, 0.60 sec, 58–63 kV). All adolescents and adults were evaluated. Our standard required that a radiopacity extend at least one-third the transverse diameter of the bone in order to be recorded as a positive occurrence. Since maximum line count was consistently recorded for the femora, maximum femoral counts were selected to represent each individual. These counts were then grouped by five-line intervals and segregated by age of the individual at death and by sex.

When we compare the middle Archaic individuals with the late Archaic series we find similar line counts, with the modal frequencies for each age–sex category being identical for the two populations. Periodicity, defined here as a regular

spacing of three or more lines, occurred in slightly lower frequency for the more recent series. However, the difference was not statistically significant. Thus, we can identify *no* trend of increased or decreased line formation in these two temporally distinct Archaic populations. Certainly, such tests should be extended to include other local and more distant samples. However, at the present time, our data concerning both mortality and acute non-terminal stress are consistent and are taken to indicate stable or equivalent biological adaptations during the middle and late Archaic periods.

Conclusion

Reported here are the preliminary results of a regionally based study which illustrate the importance of the spatial dimension of mortuary behaviour and its effect upon the study of prehistoric human biology. Skeletal series excavated from Koster and Modoc Shelter middens apparently represent a specialised track of middle Archaic burial programmes consisting of individuals incapable of performing a 'normal' range of adult activities either because of age or pathology. Data from Koster and other Archaic cemeteries of southwestern Illinois thus indicate that skeletal information may be misinterpreted if the osteologist does not consider cultural factors which may have affected the composition of his sample. Clearly, the human biologist studying prehistoric remains must be careful not to isolate himself from the source of his data, the mortuary site, or he may generalise too quickly and thus ignore the very variability which will allow him to make precise, predictive statements concerning prehistoric populations.

The hypothesis of increasing improvement in Archaic subsistence adaptations was subjected to preliminary testing using recently acquired data from the Koster site together

with previously published information. Comparison of middle
and late Archaic mortality profiles and Harris Line frequencies
failed to identify temporal trends in adaptive efficiency. This
contradicts conclusions of previous workers whose results
have been biassed by a failure to recognise the spatial dimension of mortuary behaviour.

Acknowledgements

I wish to express my appreciation to all those connected
with the Koster project, especially those who have laboured at
the site itself. The Department of Anthropology of Indiana
University has kindly consented to my study of the Archaic
skeletons from Klunk site. I also wish to thank my laboratory
assistant Tracy Rudd for her able assistance with the illustrations and with osteological analysis.

This research has been funded directly by the Northwestern University Archeological Program and the National
Science Foundation (Grant GS 42142).

Chapter 10

**Mortality, age-structure and
status in the interpretation
of stress indicators in prehistoric
skeletons: a dental example
from the Lower Illinois Valley**
Della Collins Cook

Introduction

In recent years, many scholars have used developmental
aspects of the human skeleton as sources of information about
the biological success of prehistoric populations. A wide
variety of indicators of disturbed or retarded development
have been examined, including long-bone length in children
(Johnston 1962, 1968; Walker 1969; Y'Edynak 1976;
Merchant and Ubelaker 1977; Cook 1979), growth-arrest lines
(Wells 1967; McHenry 1968; Cook 1979), dental asymmetry
(O'Connell 1976; Perzigian 1977) and disturbances of enamel
development (Brothwell 1963; Clement 1963; Schultz and
McHenry 1975; McHenry and Schultz 1976; Rose 1977; Cook
and Buikstra 1979). Findings in such studies are evaluated in
either of two ways: with respect to standards developed from
modern advantaged populations, or by comparison of two or
more prehistoric groups.

A careful look at both these means of evaluation is in
order. Studies that relate subsistence, population density and
other ecological factors to the frequency of stress indicators in
prehistoric skeletons commonly assume that the effect of mortality on these frequencies is either negligible, as when the
dead are compared with standards based on the living, or constant, as when differing archaeological cultures or horizons are
compared. It is unlikely that either assumption is warranted.
What we often refer to as archaeological 'populations' are
samples of the living population who buried them, but the

sampling procedure is a special one. The central fact about archaeological skeletal collections is that they are dead. It is hardly a novel proposition that people who die are not healthy, but the consequences of this fact for the interpretation of stress indicators in prehistoric skeletons have not been generally appreciated.

A skeletal collection is a *mortality sample* of the living population from which it came. The frequency of a stress indicator in such a sample will reflect: (1) the frequency of the indicator in the living population; (2) the age structure of the indicator in the living population as it interacts with age-specific death rates; (3) the interaction between causes of death and the frequency of the indicator; and (4) differential effects of aspects of the mortuary programme, for example distinctions based on age, status, and cause of death (Binford 1971), on inclusion in the sample. There is reason to expect that most of the stress indicators used to evaluate the biological success or adaptedness of prehistoric populations will be affected by the latter three factors. The utility of a stress indicator in evaluating biological success is generally based on the observation that the indicator is more frequent in living individuals with a history of malnutrition or disease; hence one might generally expect higher frequencies in individuals dying at an early age than in those who survive.

Unfortunately, the literature on stress indicators in living populations provides little direct information on these factors. Well-controlled comparisons of survivors with those dying of a particular condition are uncommon, particularly where childhood causes of death are concerned. Where mortality-sample materials have been used to construct developmental standards, for example the Schour and Massler dental standards (Cameron and Sims 1974, pp. 33, 72) and the Stevenson standards for epiphyseal closure (Stevenson 1924), the effects of causes of death have been largely ignored. Where they have been recognised they have generally been seen as a necessary evil rather than a variable deserving independent treatment.

A few exceptions to this generalisation appear in the literature on malnutrition and growth in disadvantaged populations. McGregor and his co-workers (1961) compared survivors with children dying before the age of seven in a retrospective study of longitudinal-growth data from a Gambian population suffering from heavy malarial infestation and seasonal malnutrition. Children who died showed modest retardation in height with respect to survivors. Similarly, an interaction between size at birth, dental defects, and survival has been reported in children from a severely malnourished Guatemalan community (Mata, Kronmal, Urrutia and Garcia 1976; Sweeney, Cabrera, Urrutia and Mata 1969).

Just as the living and the dead in a given population can seldom be expected to correspond in the frequency of stress indicators, so the dead from populations differing in the pattern of causes of death are likely to be dissimilar.

An example suggesting the potential magnitude of this effect can be found in an examination of causes of death in individuals one to four years of age in the United States in

1940 and 1960 (Schapiro, Schlesinger and Nesbitt 1968, pp. 183–200, 341). Table 10.1 presents a summary of mortality-rate data for *Seventh Revision – International Classification of Diseases* categories, which I have grouped according to their probable relationship with growth variables. The two decades between 1940 and 1960 saw a decline in childhood mortality from 297 per 100,000 to 106 per 100,000, as well as the intro-

Table 10.1. *Mortality rates per 100,000 in children 1 to 4 years of age, U.S. population, grouped according to probable effect on growth. Source: Schapiro, Schlesinger and Nesbitt 1968, pp. 183–200, 341.*

	1940	1960	
No likely effect on growth			
Accident	49.6	30.7	
Appendicitis	6.9	0.3	
Acute upper respiratory infection	2.3	0.9	
Meningitis except meningeococcal, tuberculous	3.8	2.6	
Total		62.6	34.5
Mixed effects on growth			
Infective, parasitic diseases except T.B.	50.1	6.8	
Influenza, pneumonia	63.5	14.9	
Gastritis, duodenitis, enteritis, colitis	30.6	3.3	
Vascular affecting central nervous system	1.4	0.9	
Bronchitis	3.5	1.9	
Other respiratory	2.3	1.9	
Other digestive system	12.0	2.4	
Genito-urinary	4.4	0.9	
Other circulatory	3.3	1.3	
Other nervous system	9.0	3.4	
Total		180.1	37.7
Probable effect on growth			
Congenital malformation	10.4	12.3	
Rheumatic fever and chronic rheumatic heart disease	1.8	0.2	
Polio	–	0.9	
Blood, blood-forming organs	2.0	1.6	
Allergic, endocrine, metabolic, nutritional	4.4	1.8	
Malignant neoplasms	9.5	10.6	
Tuberculosis	12.9	0.7	
Total		41.0	28.1
Residual		13.0	5.5
Total, all causes		296.7	105.8

duction of a number of effective therapies against infectious diseases. How is this change reflected in the representativeness of growth variables in these two samples?

Causes of death which might be expected to show *no* relationship to growth variables, principally accidents and acute infections, account for 21% of deaths in 1940 as against 33% in 1960. Causes which might be expected to show *mixed* relationship to growth variables, principally through the inter-action of nutritional failure with mortality due to infectious disease (Scrimshaw 1966), account for 61% of deaths in 1940 and 36% in 1960. Major causes of death in this group are infectious and parasitic diseases other than tuberculosis, influenza and pneumonia, and gastro-intestinal infections. Causes of death in which long-term growth failure might be expected in most cases account for 14% of deaths in 1940 and 27% in 1960. Clearly *neither* of these mortality samples is likely to reflect accurately growth and development in the corresponding living population, and, equally clearly, the degree of growth disturbance is unlikely to be similar in the two. Further, one would expect these problems to be compounded were the comparison to extend to groups differ-ing radically in subsistence base or ecology rather than in medical care (Dunn 1968).

As this discussion suggests, it is naive to assume that frequency of developmental disturbances in a mortality sample directly reflects the experience of the living population. How-ever, the factors that cause this complexity in the interpretation of frequencies of stress indicators can provide useful infor-mation about prehistoric health and disease — if we focus our attention on the interactions discussed above, rather than on the simpler interpretations that characterise most work in this area. An analysis of enamel defects in individuals from the Pete Klunk mound group, a middle Woodland period cemetery, illustrates this approach.

Social and ecological aspects of Middle Woodland

The Pete Klunk mound group is one of three adjacent, multi-component mortuary sites overlooking a large middle Woodland period village at Kampsville, Calhoun County, Illinois. Two of these sites, the Pete Klunk and the Gibson mound groups, have been completely excavated (Perino 1968, 1973*b*; Buikstra 1976). The well-preserved skeletal collections from these two mound groups have been the subject of a wide variety of investigations. Currently housed at Indiana Univer-sity, the Pete Klunk series includes the remains of approxi-mately 370 individuals assignable to a middle Woodland component (Hunter 1968; Blakely 1971; Buikstra 1976) dated at ad 175 ± 75 (Crane and Griffin 1963).

The middle Woodland period in eastern North America has long been of great interest to archaeologists because of the widespread appearance of a cultural efflorescence called Hope-well. Hopewellian manifestations include large sedentary villages, elaborate earthworks, extensive and far-reaching trade networks, and mounded cemeteries showing evidence for social stratification. Early workers suggested that this efflor-

escence must have been based on the cultivation of maize. While there are isolated finds of maize in Hopewellian and earlier sites in eastern North America, and gourds and various commensal plants appear to have been cultivated, present evi-dence suggests that cultivated foods played a relatively minor role (Ford 1974; Asch and Asch 1977). In western Illinois, middle Woodland subsistence seems to have been based on intensive harvesting of wild food sources, including such seed plants as *Chenopodium* and *Iva*, nuts and acorns, deer, mussels, fish and waterfowl (Struever 1968; Munson, Parmalee and Yarnell 1971; Struever and Vickery 1973; Whatley and Asch 1975). This picture of a mixed, relatively high-protein diet is supported by osteological comparisons with later, maize-dependent groups (Stout 1978; Cook 1979).

The mortuary programme for middle Woodland is extremely varied. Social distinctions apparent in the Gibson and Klunk series have been documented by Buikstra (1976). She found that inclusion in the central feature or other log and limestone structures within mounds, body preparation as evi-denced by disarticulation, and grave furnishings showed con-sistent patterns of differential access by age and sex. The status distinction used below is based on her analysis. All burials in central features, burials on the ramps and peripheries of central features, and burials in log or limestone-covered sub-floor pits are considered high status. These individuals are distinct from the remaining burials in their arthritis patterning (Tainter 1973*b*), in the trace element content of their ribs (Szpunar 1977), and in stature (Buikstra 1976), suggesting substantial differences in activity patterns and nutrition. They do not appear to have been genetically distinct from the low-status portion of the middle Woodland component (Buikstra 1976, 1977).

Enamel development

Disturbances of enamel development provide in many ways an ideal stress indicator for use in archaeological materials. Teeth are generally better preserved than other tissues and are relatively easily recovered for both young and old individuals. Enamel is laid down in a regular pattern of incremental bands beginning at the cusp tip and moving outward. Evidence for developmental disturbance in enamel can be assigned to narrow age intervals. Because enamel is not subject to remodelling, this record of developmental disturbances is not modified during the later life of the individual, although the information may be lost through attrition or tooth loss. For this reason gross and microscopic disturbances of enamel development have attracted a great deal of attention as stress indicators in prehistoric skeletons. Both gross defects of the tooth surface — hypoplastic lines — and microscopic alterations of internal structure — pronounced striae of Retzius and prism defects — have been examined. The microscopic is the better of these two levels of observation because wear and erosion can erase surface features, and because surface hypoplasia is most fre-quently seen in the cervical regions of teeth, whatever the developmental age of the enamel.

Methods

As part of a larger study of indicators of developmental disturbance in the Klunk series, sections of first permanent molars were prepared from the 232 individuals with this tooth present. Of these 212 had enamel. In the remaining cases the enamel had been lost through wear. Maxillary first molars were sectioned if possible. Teeth were cast, cleaned, embedded in epoxy resin, and cut on a low-speed diamond saw (Buehler Isomet) in the plane of the mesial cusps. Teeth were then mounted with epoxy on glass slides and sectioned. Sections were thinned to 100–150 microns and polished using a petrographic polisher-grinder (Buehler Minimet) modified to accept specimens mounted on slides. Sections were etched using 0.1 N hydrochloric acid to develop prism features.

Previous studies of microscopic defects have quantified defects across a fixed number of equal-interval increments along the dentino-enamel junction. This method was rejected for two reasons. First, since age structure of defect frequency is its focus, this study includes both individuals with incompletely formed teeth and individuals in whom the cusp is worn away. A fixed-interval scoring system is needed if infants and older adults are included in the sample. Second, teeth differ markedly in size. The length of intact dentino-enamel junctions measured on the maxillary buccal cusp or the mandibular lingual cusp varied from 4.0 to 7.0 mm in this series. Teeth differ in size largely as a result of differences in the timing of the beginning and ending of enamel formation (Moss and Moss-Salentijn 1977) rather than as a result of differences in rate of formation. Dividing large and small teeth into a number of scoring intervals based on the average length of the period of enamel formation (Rose 1977; Massler, Schour and Poncher 1941) results in intervals that differ greatly, both in amount of enamel included and in developmental period. The scoring system used here is thus based on frequency per millimetre rather than frequency per developmental interval. Sections were examined at 40×. Striae of Retzius were observed under transmitted light and assigned to millimetre intervals using a 2.5 mm eyepiece reticle. Intervals were measured from the cusp tip at the dentino-enamel junction where this feature was present. Where it was worn away measurement was begun at the cemento-enamel junction. In this case the most cervical interval was assigned the modal value for length of intact teeth, 6 mm. Striae of Retzius were evaluated under polarised light at 40×. Each field was then searched for pathological bands at 400×. This scoring method follows Rose (1977) in most details except for the definition of intervals along the dentino-enamel junction. Age and sex were determined using standard osteological techniques. Manuscript inventories compiled by K.B. Hunter and J.E. Buikstra on file at Indiana University were reassessed against the skeletal material. Age and sex distributions of the teeth used in this study appear in table 10.2.

Enamel is formed as a series of layers of more or less equal thickness, the incremental bands. These are formed initially at the cusps of the teeth and are arranged concentrically from this point to the cemento-enamel junction, with later bands intersecting the enamel surface. At the cusp they intersect the dentino-enamel junction obliquely; at the cemento-enamel junction they are nearly parallel to the dentino-enamel junction. Striae of Retzius are pronounced incremental bands that appear brown under transmitted light. They may be more mineralised, equally mineralised, or commonly less mineralised than the surrounding enamel (Rose 1977; Molnar and Ward 1975; Yaeger 1976; Soggnaes 1956). In this study incremental bands that were pigmented adjacent to the surface of the enamel or that were not distinct in degree of pigmentation from adjacent bands were considered artefactual, in that materials used here show substantial postmortem staining. Pathological bands or Wilson bands are incremental bands that show structural alterations in the enamel prisms. As in Rose's work on prehistoric Illinois materials, distorted structure bands were the type most commonly encountered (Rose 1977). Bands of the types defined by Rose are analysed here as a single variable. Examples are shown in plate 10.1.

Age of occurrence of enamel defects

The enamel of the first permanent molar begins to form at birth or shortly before, and is completed by two and a half to three years of age. The frequency of striae of Retzius and pathological bands in this tooth thus reflects disturbances in development in the first three years of life. The one-millimetre zones used in scoring defects here can be related to finer age distinctions through use of the specimens themselves to create an internal age standard. In all children aged six months or over the dentino-enamel junction was at least two millimetres long. The third zone is formed by twelve months of age, the fourth by twenty-four months, and the fifth and sixth by thirty-six months. Portions of the fifth one-millimetre zone had formed in some children eighteen months of age. In this sample zones one to three correspond to the first year of life, zones four and sometimes five to the second year of life, and five, six, and seven, if present, to the third. This standard is population specific because tooth size varies across human populations.

The mean frequency of enamel defects per complete one-millimetre zone in the 212 individuals included in this study is presented in fig. 10.1. Skeletons recovered from limited-access contexts within the mortuary programme at Klunk are tabulated separately from individuals recovered from low-status contexts. Striae of Retzius are relatively infrequent in zones one and two corresponding to the first six months of life and sometimes to a portion of the prenatal period. Distinct neonatal lines were not common in this sample. The frequency of striae increases in zone three, reflecting events occurring between six and twelve months of age, and reaches a peak in zone four. Frequencies decline in zone five and six. Striae of Retzius are thus most common in enamel that forms between six and twenty-four months of age. Other studies of enamel defects in prehistoric skeletons have related

Table 10.2. *Age, sex, and status distribution of 232 permanent first molars from the middle Woodland component of the Pete Klunk mound group.*

Age groups	Birth–2	3–11	12–19	20–34	35–49	50+
	Enamel present					
Sex: Male	0	0	5	23	25	14
Female	0	0	9	29	26	18
Indeterminate	31	21	9	1	1	0
Status: High	12	7	10	27	21	18
Low	19	14	13	26	31	14
	No enamel remaining, all categories					
	0	0	0	0	7	13
Total	31	21	23	53	59	45

their distribution to age at weaning (Rose 1977; Schultz and McHenry 1975). It does not seem probable that middle Woodland mothers weaned their children as early as these data would suggest. A number of explanations of the distribution observed here are plausible, for example supplementation of milk with other foods beginning between six and twelve months, increasing calorie deficiency beginning at this age on a diet of milk alone, increasing opportunity for infection as children become more mobile, and so on. However, it is un-

known to what degree the various portions of the enamel in various teeth register disturbances in development, and a local factor may thus be present. Some support for this possibility can be found in the fact that the two studies of enamel defects cited above used canines as their data source. The canine crown develops for a longer period of time than the first molar. If the middle portion of the enamel is more prone to register enamel defects than the occlusal or cervical portions, the differences in distribution can be readily explained without

Fig. 10.1. Frequency of striae of Retzius and pathological bands in 212 permanent first molars. Number of defects is tabulated by complete one-millimetre band for all individuals in the sample, combining age and sex categories.

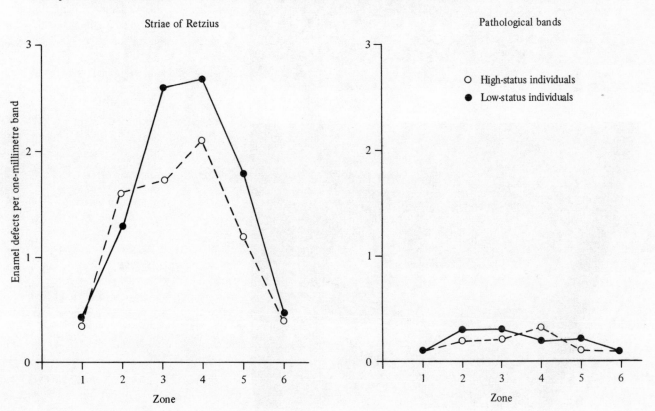

Plate 10.1. Examples of enamel defects

A. Striae of Retzius in an individual aged 50 or more at death, 11–C35–30, zone 4. Magnification 40 ×. Defects of this severity were un-common in adults. In this and the other photographs on this page dentin is labelled d, enamel is labelled e, tooth surface is labelled s, and striae of Retzius are labelled r. All 40 × fields are approximately 1.15 mm by 0.80 mm in size. In this specimen a number of regular incre-mental bands that show post-mortem staining from the surface of the tooth are visible below the s.

B. Striae of Retzius in an individual aged 18 to 25 months at death, 11–C35–36, zones 2 and 3. 40 ×. Extremely dark bands like the group of three in the centre of this view were uncommon in adults.

C. Striae of Retzius in an incompletely calcified first permanent molar from an individual aged 13 months at death, 11–C34–5, zone 3. Only the more pronounced of the many striae present are labelled. Voids in the section result from poor preservation of incompletely calcified enamel. The marked rectangle in this 40 × photograph is shown at 400 × in D.

D. View of striae of Retzius and a stria that also shows distorted prism structure (ds), a category of pathological band. Such bands were common only in children less than three years of age at death.

E. Pronounced striae of Retzius in zones 3 and 4 in an individual aged 18 to 20 months at death, 11–C40–51. 40 ×. Zones 1 and 2, the deepest and earliest formed enamel (e) beneath the cusp in this view, are quite uniform. The marked rectangle crosses an extremely dark stria that is visible as two distinct striae as it proceeds toward the tooth surface. At the tooth surface it terminates in a depression visible as a hypoplastic line in the unworn occlusal surface. A greatly magnified view of the area enclosed in the rectangle appears in F.

F. View of striae of Retzius and a stria that also shows distorted prism structure. Portions of the pathological band shown here are classified as showing structureless enamel (sb), a rare category of pathological band.

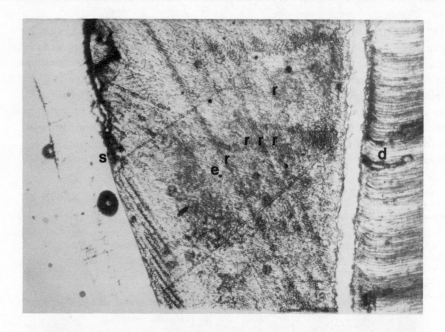

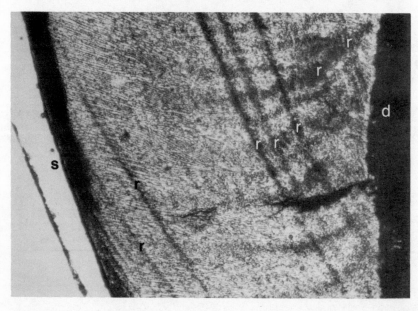

C

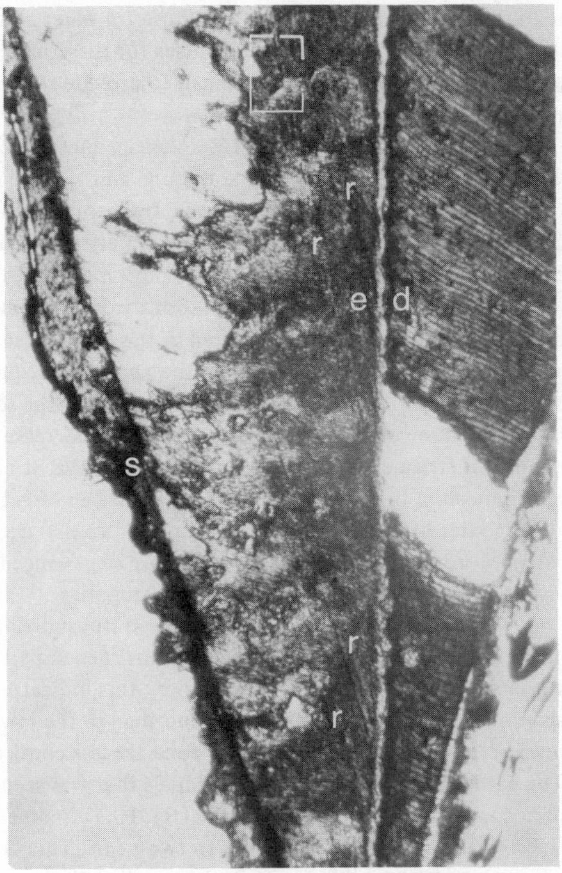

D

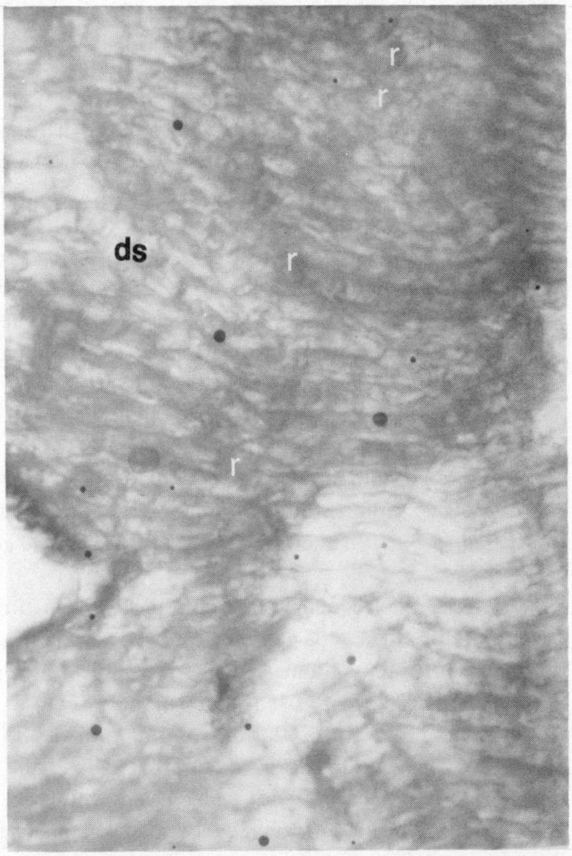

E

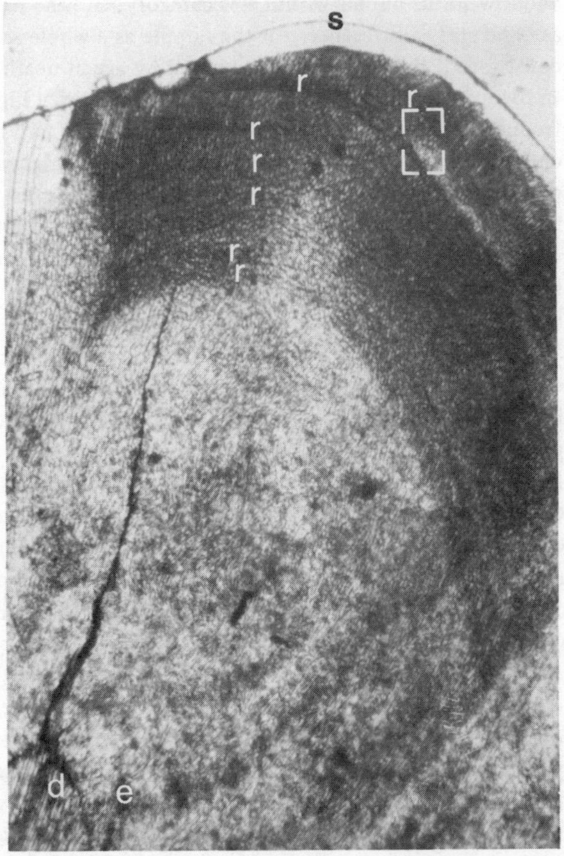

F

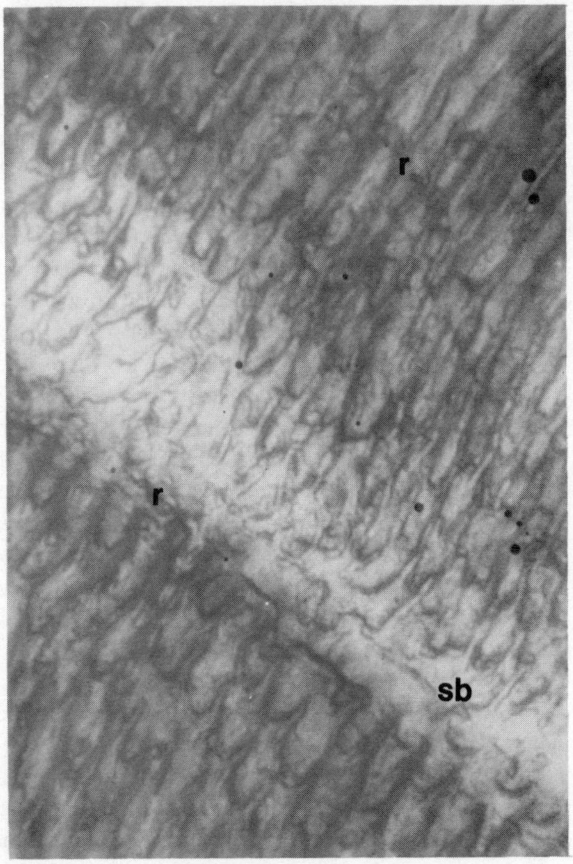

postulating radical differences in age at weaning or some other aspect of child rearing.

Individuals identified as high status and low status, according to presence in limited access aspects of the mortuary programme, differ in the frequency and the distribution of striae of Retzius. The peak in frequency is later in the high-status group, and frequencies in zones three, four and five are much lower than in the low-status group. It would appear that high-status individuals experienced less stress during early childhood and experienced stress somewhat later than did low-status individuals. Distribution by sex was also examined. Frequency of striae in males and females was virtually identical for all six zones.

Pathological bands are relatively rare in both groups. The high- and low-status groups do not differ consistently in the frequency of pathological bands per zone. No distinct peak is visible in either group, although frequencies for the middle zones are somewhat higher than those for the cervical and occlusal zones.

As with the frequency distribution of striae of Retzius, the elevated frequency of pathological bands in the second, third and fourth one-millimetre zones may reflect increased stress experienced before twenty-four months of age in middle Woodland children. Again, this distribution is difficult to explain by appealing to various cultural factors in child care, since one would expect later weaning in most hunter-gatherer populations. Rose (1977) found higher band frequencies in the middle portions of permanent canine enamel in somewhat later Illinois material. He suggested that this reflected weaning stress, since this portion of the canine enamel forms at two to three years of age, when one would expect weaning to have occurred. Comparison of his study with the present one suggests that there may be thresholds in the level of stress necessary to produce pathological bands that are specific to regions of the tooth, perhaps reflecting the ageing of the ameloblasts as they progress from the occlusal to the cervical portions of the enamel. Correlation of striae of Retzius and pathological bands from tooth to tooth in the same individual is necessary before this inference can be tested further.

Age at death and enamel defects

We have seen that the distribution by zone and the frequency of enamel defects differ in high- and low-status groups at Pete Klunk when individuals of all ages are considered together. How are these differences related to age at death? To what extent does survival to a given age reflect differences in stress experienced during the first three years of life? Are we justified in combining, as is usual in studies of this kind, frequencies across age categories, in order to compare status groups?

Mean frequencies of striae of Retzius and pathological bands per one-millimetre zone are presented for six age groups in fig. 10.2. Points for age and status categories in which fewer than eight individuals had intact enamel for a particular zone are omitted. For this reason the graphs for children younger

than three end with zone four, and those for older adults are lacking zones one and two. Frequencies for these missing points are based on samples too small to provide stable estimates.

The frequency of striae of Retzius declines smoothly with increasing age. Changes in zones one and two are relatively slight. For zones three and four, frequencies in adults over thirty-five years of age are approximately half those for children under twelve. This is true for both high-status and low-status groups, and the few deviations from this pattern in one status category are not mirrored in the other. Clearly, age at death has an important effect on the apparent frequency of this stress indicator. Taking the perspective of the scholar interested in measuring stress, we see that the decrease in frequency of striae of Retzius with age indicates that stress experienced in the first three years of life has an effect on survival in later life. This effect is not confined to the age category in which these stress episodes are experienced, but is visible fairly consistently across all age categories.

In each age category high- and low-status individuals differ in the frequency of striae of Retzius. The apparent disturbance in development as measured by this indicator is consistently lower in the high-status group than in the low-status one. Differences in distribution by zone are less consistent. The earlier peak in low-status individuals that was seen in the data combined across age categories (fig. 10.1) is largely confined to the age group from birth to two years. This difference is not due to a difference in the age distribution of high- and low-status burials within this category, and the pattern of age and status differences for the sample as a whole remain consistent if this category is examined by age at death in years. Individuals dying in the first year of life show even higher frequencies of striae of Retzius in zones one and two than do children under three as a whole. Children in the high-status group dying between twelve and twenty-four months of age have higher counts of striae per millimetre than do those in the low-status group, and this is also true for children dying between twenty-four and thirty-six months of age.

Findings for the age distribution of pathological bands are essentially similar. Frequency of bands per millimetre declines relatively smoothly with age. No consistent difference in band frequency distinguishes the high- and low-status groups. Males and females were compared in the same manner for each age group. The frequency and distribution of striae of Retzius and pathological bands in males and females are essentially similar in all age groups. Similar low frequencies of pathological bands have been reported in a sample of 29 adults from the closely related Gibson middle Woodland site (Rose, Armelagos and Lallo 1978).

Age at death is clearly an important variable in these stress indicators. For the data on pathological bands it is possible to argue for a threshold in this age effect at three years. One could exclude individuals younger than three from this sample in order to remove the effect. Such a strategy is not possible for striae of Retzius, and combining by age obscures an interaction between age at death and the distribution by age of this stress indicator.

Analysis of variance provides a convenient way of summarising the effects of age and status on the frequency of striae of Retzius. Enamel zones 3 and 4 were chosen for this analysis because they could be scored in most individuals one year of age and older, and because greatest contrasts in frequency are found in these two zones (fig. 10.2). Table 10.3 presents a one-way analysis of variance in the number of striae of Retzius per zone across the six age categories used previously. High- and low-status individuals are considered separately because the information discussed above suggests that they are different populations with regard to this stress indicator. The effect of age at death on the frequency of striae of Retzius is not significant in the group recovered from limited-access aspects of the Hopewell mortuary system at Pete Klunk, even though the changes with age at death in this

sub-sample follow the same trends that are seen in the remainder of the sample. In the low-status group, however, the effect of age at death is significant for both zones. We cannot account for this difference by appealing to sampling differences. The high- and low-status groups are similar in size and in distribution by age at death. Instead, these results suggest that the effect on later survival of developmental disturbances in the second year of life is more pronounced in the low-status group than in the high-status group. Status as mirrored in mortuary practice reflects differential survival. Social distinctions in middle Woodland had biological importance.

This relationship between status and stress experience can be explored further through an examination of the effect of status on the frequency of striae of Retzius. Again the analysis of variance is applied to zones 3 and 4 (table 10.4). Juveniles and adults are analysed separately in order to lessen

Fig. 10.2. Frequency of striae of Retzius and pathological bands per one-millimetre zone tabulated by age group. Where zones are not plotted, fewer than 10 individuals could be scored for a particular zone. In children younger than 3, missing zones reflect incomplete enamel formation. In adults aged 35 and older, missing zones reflect attrition.

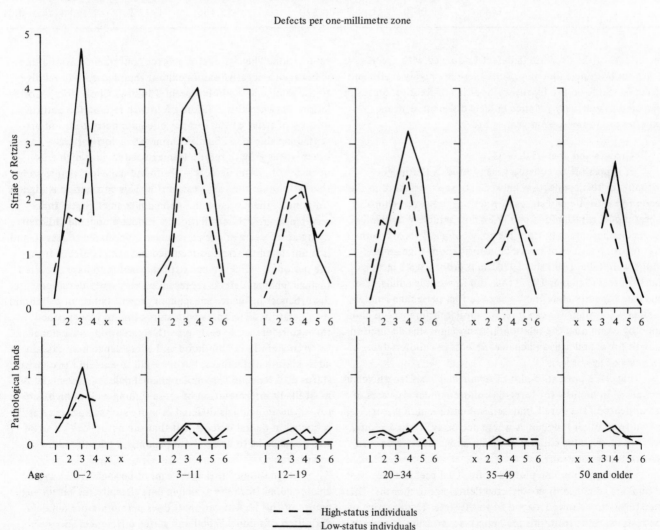

Defects per one-millimetre zone

- - - - High-status individuals
———— Low-status individuals

Table 10.3. *One-factor analysis of variance in number of striae of Retzius per one-millimetre enamel zone across six age categories, sexes combined. Method after Simpson, Roe and Lewontin 1960, pp. 266–71.*

Status	Enamel zone	N	Sum of squares Main effect	Sum of squares Deviations	F	Degrees of freedom	Significance
High	3	75	18.084	194.580	1.282	5, 69	n.s.
	4	84	30.382	371.570	1.276	5, 78	n.s.
Low	3	86	119.815	372.569	5.079	5, 80	p less than 0.01
	4	96	65.275	236.880	4.960	5, 90	p less than 0.01

Table 10.4. *One-factor analysis of variance in number of striae of Retzius per one-millimetre zone across high- and low-status categories, juveniles and adults analysed separately, sexes combined.*

Age group	Enamel zone	N	Sum of squares Main effect	Sum of squares Deviations	F	Degrees of freedom	Significance
Birth to 19	3	70	67.545	276.300	16.623	1, 68	p less than 0.01
	4	68	11.194	181.564	3.946	1, 64	n.s.
20 and older	3	91	3.398	275.734	1.097	1, 92	p less than 0.10
	4	114	252.009	506.228	55.755	1, 112	p less than 0.01

the effects of the decrease in defect frequency with age at death. In both juveniles and adults there is a highly significant effect of status on the frequency of striae of Retzius. Status as mirrored in mortuary practice reflects differential stress experienced in the second year of life.

Growth and enamel defects

It is possible to construct many models that might account for this connection between stress experienced in the second year of life and status distinctions; however, choosing a best model is rather difficult. We know middle Woodland status distinctions only from the archaeological record, but that record provides other useful information. High-status adults were taller (Buikstra 1976), and probably ate more meat protein (Szpunar 1977) than did low-status adults. Was this true for early childhood when the first permanent molar enamel is forming? We can look for similar differences in childhood by examining the relationships among status distinctions, growth for dental age, and enamel defects in children dying at six years of age or less.

Fig. 10.3 presents a plot of femur diaphysis length versus dental age in months for forty-six children under six years of age at death in the Pete Klunk series. Femur length is estimated from other long bones where necessary. Unlike adults, high- and low-status children show no apparent difference in growth for age at death.

The regression line plotted in fig. 10.3 predicts the natural log of conception-corrected dental age in months. This transformation allowed a good fit to the data. The negative of the residual value from this prediction is a measure of growth

retardation. The sign is changed for convenience, so that individuals with negative values exhibit retarded growth relative to the sample as a whole (method follows Cook 1979). Correlations between this measure of growth retardation and frequency of striae of Retzius per one-millimetre zone are presented in table 10.5. Significant negative correlations – in other words growth retardation associated with high frequencies of dental defects – are found only for enamel zones that develop in the first year of life. This correlation is highest for zone 1, the prenatal and neonatal enamel. Stress that resulted in growth retardation in middle Woodland children dying at six years of age or younger is unrelated to status, and it is unrelated to stress as recorded in enamel defects during the period at which we can expect weaning to have occurred. Instead, enamel defects representing very early developmental disturbances influence subsequent growth failure in childhood. Adult stature differences with status cannot be explained through reference to early growth retardation. Nutritional differences in later childhood and adolescence may explain adult stature differences, but they fail to explain the consistent status difference in first-molar enamel defect frequencies. A most likely interpretation of these findings is that high- and low-status individuals differed in acute stress experience as reflected in dental defects, but that the nature of this stress was not such as to bring about prolonged growth failure or retardation.

The nature of this agent cannot be specified in any greater detail from the available data. Despite the rather vague nature of this identification, it does permit a more detailed definition of middle Woodland status differences. Because

Table 10.5. *Correlation of frequency of striae of Retzius with growth retardation in children dying at 6 years of age or younger.*

Enamel zone	Sample size	Pearson's r	Significance of correlation*		
			t	d.f.	probability
1	30	−0.401	2.319	28	p less than 0.005
2	30	−0.220	1.192	28	p less than 0.15
3	25	−0.332	1.690	23	p less than 0.10
4	22	+0.262	1.216	20	not significant
5	17	+0.139	0.545	15	not significant
6	9	−0.225	0.611	7	not significant

*One-tailed probability given.

Fig. 10.3. Plot of femur diaphysis length (vertical axis) by dental age at death (horizontal axis) in 46 children 6 years of age at death or younger in the Klunk series.

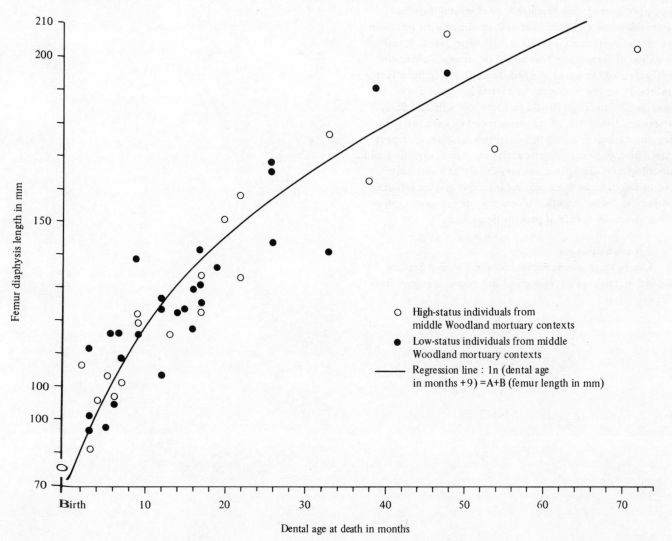

enamel defect frequencies differ with status in both children
and adults, an ascribed, rather than achieved, model for status
distinctions is indicated. One was important for who one was
— not what one had done. While this distinction appears to
have had some nutritional correlates in adults, as reflected in
adult stature and trace-element composition, this nutritional
factor does not appear to have been sufficiently severe to have
resulted in early childhood malnutrition in low-status individuals. Differential exposures to acute disturbances of development is implicated, but we can only speculate as to why high-
status middle Woodland children may have enjoyed fewer
such disturbances than their low-status neighbours.

Implications for stress-indicator studies

This analysis of enamel defects in a middle Woodland
skeletal series has demonstrated both an effect of age at death
on the frequency of the indicator and substantial status differences in the frequency and pattern of defects. These findings
have several broad implications for the interpretation of stress
indicators in general in prehistoric populations. First, comparisons of stress indicator frequencies in skeletal samples
should be age structured. Relatively small differences in the
age composition of such samples — whether resulting from
differential recovery in the field or from differential inclusion
in particular mortuary contexts — may misrepresent actual
population differences or hide useful information about the
age structure of the agent of stress. Second, where the effect
of mortality on the frequency of a stress indicator can be
demonstrated, the dead should be compared with the dead,
not with the living. Use of standards based on survivors, or on
living populations differing in mortality schedules, is inappro-
priate. Third, both osteologists analysing ancient skeletons and
archaeologists reading their analyses should be aware that
social distinctions within a particular sample may be reflected
in biological distinctions that ultimately provide useful information about the nature of prehistoric societies.

Acknowledgement

This research was supported by the National Science
Foundation, Division of Neural and Behavioral Sciences, BNS
77-25310.

BIBLIOGRAPHY

Abel, A. (1939) *Tabeau's Narrative of Loisel's Expedition to the Upper Missouri*, University of Oklahoma Press, Norman

Acsadi, G. and Nemeskeri, J. (1970) *History of Human Life Span and Mortality*, Akadémiai Kiado, Budapest

Albrethsen, S.E. and Brinch Petersen, E. (1976) 'Excavation of a Mesolithic cemetery at Vedbaek, Denmark', *Acta Archaeologica* 47: 1–29

Alexander, J.A. (1979) 'The archaeological recognition of religion: the examples of Islam in Africa and "urnfields" in Europe' in B.C. Burnham and J. Kingsbury (eds.) *Space, Hierarchy and Society. British Archaeological Reports* S59, Oxford

Almagro, A. and Arribas, A. (1963) *El poblado y la necropolis megalíticos de Los Millares*, Instituto Español de Prehistoria del C.S.I.C., Madrid

Andersen, N.H. (1975) 'Die neolithische Befestigungsanlage in Sarup auf Fünen (Danemark)', *Archäologisches Korrespondenzblatt* 5: 11–14

Andersen, S. (1973–4) 'Ringkloster. An inland Ertebølle settlement in Jutland', *Kuml*: 11–108

Angel, J.L. (1975) 'Paleoecology, paleodemography and health' in S. Polgar (ed.) *Population, Ecology and Social Evolution*, Mouton, The Hague

Asch, D.L. (1976) *The Middle Woodland Population of the Lower Illinois Valley: a Study in Paleodemographic Methods. Northwestern University Archeological Program, Scientific Papers*, No. 1, Evanston, Illinois

Asch, D.L. and Asch, N.B. (1977) 'Chenopod as cultigen: a reevaluation of some prehistoric collections from Eastern North America', *Mid-Continental Journal of Archaeology* 2: 3–45

Asch, N.B., Ford, R.I. and Asch, D.L. (1972) *Palaeoethnobotany of the Koster Site: The Archaic Horizons. Illinois State Museum, Reports of Investigations*, No. 24

Ashbee, P. (1966) 'The Fussell's Lodge long barrow excavations, 1957', *Archaeologia* 100: 1–80

Atkinson, R.J.C. (1965) 'Wayland's Smithy', *Antiquity* 39: 126–33

Atkinson, R.J.C. (1972) 'Burial and population in the British Bronze Age' in C. Burgess and F. Lynch (eds.) *Early Man in Wales and the West*, Adams & Dart, Bath

Bailey, G.N. (1978) 'Shell middens as indicators of postglacial economies: a territorial perspective' in P. Mellars (ed.) *Early Postglacial Settlement of Northern Europe*, Duckworth, London

Bakker, J.A. (1976) 'On the possibility of reconstructing roads from the TRB period', *Berichten van de Rijksdienst voor het Oudheidkundig Bodemonderzoek* 26: 63–91

Bakker, J.A. and van der Waals, J.D. (1973) 'Denekamp-Angelslo' in G. Daniel and P. Kjaerum (eds.) *Megalithic Graves and Ritual. III Atlantic Colloquium Moesgård 1969*

Balkwill, C.J. (1976) 'The evidence of cemeteries for later prehistoric development in the Upper Rhine valley', *Proceedings of the Prehistoric Society* 42: 187–214

Barrett, J. (1976) 'Deverel Rimbury: problems of chronology and interpretation' in C. Burgess and R. Miket (eds.) *Settlement and Economy in the Third and Second Millennia BC. British Archaeological Reports* 33, Oxford

Barrett, J. (1980) 'The evolution of later Bronze Age settlement' in J. Barrett and R. Bradley (eds.) *Settlement and Society in the British Later Bronze Age. British Archaeological Reports* 83, Oxford

Barrett, J. and Bradley, R. (1980) 'Late Bronze Age settlement in South Wessex and Cranborne Chase' in J. Barrett and R. Bradley (eds.) *Settlement and Society in the British Later Bronze Age. British Archaeological Reports* 83, Oxford

Barrett, J., Bradley, R., Cleal, R. and Pike, H. (1978) 'Characterisation of Deverel Rimbury pottery from Cranborne Chase', *Proceedings of the Prehistoric Society* 44: 135–42

Bartel, B. (1979) 'A discriminant analysis of Harappan civilisation human populations', *Journal of Archaeological Science* 6: 49–61

Bass, W., Evans, E. and Jantz, R. (1971) *The Leavenworth Site Cemetery: Archaeology and Physical Anthropology. University of Kansas Publications in Anthropology*, No. 2

Bay-Petersen, J. (1978) 'Animal exploitation in Mesolithic Denmark' in P. Mellars (ed.) *Early Postglacial Settlement of Northern Europe*, Duckworth, London

Bell, R.E. (1972) *The Harlan Site, CK-6, a Prehistoric Mound Center in Cherokee County, Eastern Oklahoma. Memoirs of the Oklahoma Anthropological Society*, No. 2

Bendann, E. (1930) *Death Customs: An Analytical Study of Burial Rites*, Kegan Paul, Trench, Trubner & Co., London

Bender, B. and Phillips, P. (1972) 'The early farmers of France', *Antiquity* 46: 97–105

Berry, A.C. (1974) 'The use of non-metrical variations of the cranium in the study of Scandinavian population movements', *American Journal of Physical Anthropology* 40: 345–58

Berry, R.J. (1968) 'The biology of non-metrical variation in mice and men' in D.R. Brothwell (ed.) *The Skeletal Biology of Earlier Human Populations. Symposia of the Society for the Study of Human Biology VIII*, Pergamon Press, Oxford

Binford, L.R. (1962) 'Archaeology as anthropology', *American Antiquity* 28: 217–25

Binford, L.R. (1963) ' "Red Ochre" caches from the Michigan area: a possible case of cultural drift', *Southwestern Journal of Anthropology* 19: 89–108

Binford, L.R. (1964) *Archaeological Investigations on Wassam Ridge. Archaeological Salvage Report*, No. 17. *Southern Illinois University Museum*, Carbondale

Binford, L.R. (1965) 'Archaeological systematics and the study of culture process', *American Antiquity* 31: 203–10

Binford, L.R. (1968) 'Archaeological perspectives' in L.R. Binford and S.R. Binford (eds.) *New Perspectives in Archaeology*, Aldine, Chicago

Binford, L.R. (1971) 'Mortuary practices: their study and potential' in J.A. Brown (ed.) *Approaches to the Social Dimensions of Mortuary Practices. Memoirs of the Society for American Archaeology*, No. 25

Binford, L.R. (1972) *An Archaeological Perspective*, Academic Press, New York, San Francisco and London

Binford, L.R. (1978) *Nunamiut Ethnoarchaeology*, Academic Press, New York, San Francisco and London

Binford, L.R. and Bertram, J.B. (1977) 'Bone frequencies and attritional processes' in L.R. Binford (ed.) *For Theory Building in Archaeology*, Academic Press, New York, San Francisco and London

Binford, L.R., Binford, S.R., Whallon, R. and Hardin, M. (1970) *Archaeology at Hatchery West. Memoirs of the Society for American Archaeology*, No. 24

Binford, L.R. and Chasko, W.J. (1976) 'Nunamiut demographic history: a provocative case' in E.W. Zubrow (ed.) *Demographic Anthropology*, University of New Mexico Press, Albuquerque

Bintliff, J.L. (1977*a*) *Natural Environment and Human Settlement in Prehistoric Greece. British Archaeological Reports* S28, Oxford

Bintliff, J.L. (1977*b*) in Blackman, D. and Branigan, K. 'An archaeological survey of the lower catchment of the Ayiofarango valley', *Annual of the British School of Archaeology at Athens* 72: 13–84

Blakely, R.L. (1971) 'Comparison of the mortality profiles of Archaic, Middle Woodland and Middle Mississippian skeletal populations', *American Journal of Physical Anthropology* 34: 43–53

Blance, B.M. (1960) 'The origins and development of the Early Bronze Age in the Iberian peninsula', Ph.D. dissertation, University of Edinburgh

Bloch, M. (1971) *Placing the Dead*, Seminar Press, London

Bloch, M. (1975) 'Property and the end of affinity' in M. Bloch (ed.) *Marxist Analyses and Social Anthropology*, Malaby Press, London

Boas, F. (1940) *Race, Language and Culture*, Macmillan Company, New York

Bonney, D.J. (1976) 'Early boundaries and estates in southern England' in P.H. Sawyer (ed.) *Medieval Settlement*, Edward Arnold, London

Bosi, R. (1960) *The Lapps*, Thames & Hudson, London

Bouzek, J., Koutecký, D. and Neustupný, E. (1966) *The Knoviz Culture of North West Bohemia. Fontes Archaeologici Pragenses* 10, Prague

Bowen, H.C. and Fowler, P.J. (1978) *Early Land Allotment. British Archaeological Reports* 48, Oxford

Bradley, R. (1978*a*) *The Prehistoric Settlement of Britain*, Routledge & Kegan Paul, London

Bradley, R. (1978*b*) 'Prehistoric field systems in Britain and north west Europe: a review of some recent work', *World Archaeology* 9: 265–80

Bradley, R. (1980) 'Subsistence, exchange and technology: a social framework for the Bronze Age in southern England *c.* 1400–700 bc' in J. Barrett and R. Bradley (eds.) *Settlement and Society in the British Later Bronze Age. British Archaeological Reports* 83, Oxford

Bradley, R. (in preparation) 'Economic growth and social change: two examples from prehistoric Europe'

Bradley, R. and Hodder, I. (1979) 'British prehistory: an integrated view', *Man* 14: 93–104

Braun, D.P. (1979) 'Illinois Hopewell burial practices and social organization: a re-examination of the Klunk-Gibson mound group' in D.S. Brose and N. Greber (eds.) *Hopewell Archaeology: The Chillicothe Conference*, Kent State University Press, Kent, Ohio

Brinch Petersen, E. (1973) 'A survey of the Late Palaeolithic and the Mesolithic of Denmark' in S.K. Kozlowski (ed.) *The Mesolithic in Europe*, Warsaw University Press

Broadbent, N. (1978) 'Prehistoric settlement in northern Sweden: a brief survey and a case study' in P. Mellars (ed.) *Early Postglacial Settlement of Northern Europe*, Duckworth, London

Brøndsted, J. (1936) 'Danish inhumation graves of the Viking Age', *Acta Archaeologica* 6: 81–228

Brøndsted, J. (1939) *Danmarks Oldtid II*, Gyldendal, Copenhagen

Brothwell, D.R. (1963) 'The microscopic dental pathology of some earlier human populations' in D.R. Brothwell (ed.) *Dental Anthropology*, Pergamon Press, Oxford

Brothwell, D.R. and Krzanowski, W. (1974) 'Evidence of biological differences between early British populations from Neolithic to Medieval times, as revealed by eleven commonly available cranial vault measurements', *Journal of Archaeological Science* 1: 249–60

Brothwell, D.R. and Sandison, A.T. (1967) *Diseases in Antiquity*, Charles C. Thomas, Springfield, Illinois

Brown, J.A. (1967) *The Gentleman Farm Site. Illinois State Museum Reports of Excavations*, No. 12

Brown, J.A. (1971a) 'The dimensions of status in the burials at Spiro' in J.A. Brown (ed.) *Approaches to the Social Dimensions of Mortuary Practices. Memoirs of the Society for American Archaeology*, No. 25

Brown, J.A. (ed.) (1971b) *Approaches to the Social Dimensions of Mortuary Practices. Memoirs of the Society for American Archaeology*, No. 25

Brown, J.A. (1975) 'Spiro art and its mortuary contexts' in E.P. Benson (ed.) *Death and the Afterlife in Pre-Columbian America*, Dumbarton Oaks Research Library and Collections, Washington

Brown, J.A. (1976) 'The Southern Cult reconsidered', *Mid-continental Journal of Archaeology* 1: 115–35

Brown, J.A. (1977) 'Current directions in Midwestern archaeology', *Annual Review of Anthropology* 6: 161–79

Brown, J.A. (1979) 'Charnel houses and mortuary crypts: disposal of the dead in the Middle Woodland period' in D.S. Brose and N. Greber (eds.) *Hopewell Archaeology: The Chillicothe Conference*, Kent State University Press, Kent, Ohio

Brown, J.A. (n.d.a) 'Exchange and interaction among Mississippian societies' in S. Williams (ed.) *Reviewing Mississippian Development*, University of New Mexico Press, Albuquerque (in press)

Brown, J.A. (n.d.b) *Spiro Studies V: Burials, Chronology, and Overview*, Stovall Museum of Science and History, University of Oklahoma, Norman (in press)

Brown, J.A., Bebrich, C.A. and Struever, S. (eds.) (n.d.) *Archeological Investigations at the Koster Site, a Progress Report. Northwestern University Archeological Program*

Brown, J.A., Bell, R.E. and Wyckoff, D.G. (1978) 'Caddoan settlement patterns in the Arkansas river drainage' in B.D. Smith (ed.) *Mississippian Settlement Patterns*, Academic Press, New York, San Francisco and London

Brown, J.A., Struever, S., Asch, D.L., Asch, N.B., Bebrich, C.A., Buikstra, J.E., Cook, T.G., Hill, F., Jaehnig, M., Schoenwetter, J. and Vierra, R. (n.d.) 'Preliminary contributions of Koster site research to paleoenvironmental studies of the central Mississippi valley'

Brunton, R. (1975) 'Why do the Trobriands have chiefs?', *Man* 10: 544–53

Buchler, I.A. and Selby, H.A. (1968) *Kinship and Social Organisation*, Macmillan, New York

Buikstra, J.E. (1976) *Hopewell in the Lower Illinois Valley: a Regional Approach to the Study of Human Biological Variability and Prehistoric Behavior. Northwestern University Archeological Program Scientific Papers*, No. 2

Buikstra, J.E. (1977) 'Biocultural dimensions in archaeological study: a regional perspective' in R.L. Blakely (ed.) *Biocultural Adaptation in Prehistoric America. Southern Anthropological Society Proceedings*, No. 11, University of Georgia Press, Athens

Bushnell, D.I. Jr (1920) *Native Cemeteries and Forms of Burial East of the Mississippi. Bureau of American Ethnology Bulletin*, No. 71, Washington

Bushnell, D.I. Jr (1927) *Burials of the Algonquian, Siouan and Caddoan Tribes West of the Mississippi. Bureau of American Ethnology Bulletin*, No. 83, Washington

Butzer, K.W. (1977) *Geomorphology of the Lower Illinois Valley as a Spatial-Temporal Context for the Koster Archaic Site. Illinois State Museum, Reports of Investigations*, No. 34

Caldwell, J.R. (1958) *Trend and Tradition in the Prehistory of the Eastern United States. Memoirs of the American Anthropological Association*, No. 88

Calkin, J.B. (1962) 'The Bournemouth area in the Middle and Late Bronze Age with the "Deverel Rimbury" problem reconsidered', *Archaeological Journal* 119: 107–26

Cameron, J.M. and Sims, B.G. (1974) *Forensic Dentistry*, Churchill Livingstone, Edinburgh

Cancian, F. (1976) 'Social stratification', *Annual Review of Anthropology* 5: 227–48

Caplan, P. (1969) 'Cognatic descent groups on Mafia Island, Tanzania', *Man* 4: 419–31

Carlson, D.S. and Van Gerven, D.P. (1979) 'Diffusion, biological determinism and biocultural adaptation in the Nubian corridor', *American Anthropologist* 81: 561–80

Carneiro, R.L. (1970) 'A theory of the origin of the state', *Science* 169: 733–8

Casparie, W.A., Mook-Kamps, B., Palfenier-Vegter, R.M., Struijk, R.C. and van Zeist, W. (1977) 'The palaeobotany of Swifterbant', *Helinium* 17: 28–55

Cassidy, C.M. (1972) 'A comparison of nutrition and health in pre-agricultural and agricultural Amerindian skeletal populations', Ph.D. dissertation, University of Wisconsin

Chapman, R.W. (1975) 'Economy and society within later prehistoric Iberia: a new framework', Ph.D. dissertation, University of Cambridge

Chapman, R.W. (1976) 'The Bell Beaker problem – a solution?', *Antiquity* 50: 132–5

Chapman, R.W. (1977) 'Burial practices: an area of mutual interest' in M. Spriggs (ed.) *Archaeology and Anthropology: Areas of Mutual Interest. British Archaeological Reports* S19, Oxford

Chapman, R.W. (1978) 'The evidence for prehistoric water control in south-east Spain', *Journal of Arid Environments* 1: 261–74

Chapman, R.W. (1979) ' "Analytical Archaeology" and after – an introduction' in *Analytical Archaeologist: Collected Papers of David L. Clarke*, Academic Press, New York, San Francisco and London

Chapman, R.W. (1980) 'Archaeological theory and communal burial in prehistoric Europe' in N. Hammond, G. Isaac and I. Hodder (eds.) *Pattern of the Past: Studies in Honour of David Clarke*, Cambridge University Press

Chard, C.S. (1974) *Northeast Asia in Prehistory*, University of Wisconsin Press, Madison

Charles-Edwards, T.M. (1976) 'Boundaries in Irish law' in P.H. Sawyer (ed.) *Medieval Settlement*, Edward Arnold, London

Cheverud, J.M., Buikstra, J.E. and Twichell, E. (1979) 'Relationship between non-metric skeletal traits and cranial size and shape', *American Journal of Physical Anthropology* 50: 191–8

Childe, V.G. (1925) *The Dawn of European Civilisation*, Routledge & Kegan Paul, London

Childe, V.G. (1929) *The Danube in Prehistory*, Clarendon, Oxford

Childe, V.G. (1930) *The Bronze Age*, Cambridge University Press

Childe, V.G. (1936) *Man Makes Himself*, New American Library, New York

Childe, V.G. (1956) *Piecing Together the Past*, Routledge & Kegan Paul, London

Childe, V.G. (1957) *The Dawn of European Civilisation* (6th edition), Routledge & Kegan Paul, London

Childe, V.G. (1963) *Social Evolution*, World Publishing Co., Cleveland

Clark, J.G.D. (1967) *The Stone Age Hunters*, Thames & Hudson, London

Clark, J.G.D. (1975) *The Early Stone Age Settlement of Scandinavia*, Cambridge University Press

Clark, J.G.D. (1977) 'The economic context of dolmens and passage graves in Sweden' in V. Markotic (ed.) *Ancient Europe and the Mediterranean*, Aris & Phillips, Warminster

Clarke, D.L. (1977) 'Spatial information in archaeology' in D.L. Clarke (ed.) *Spatial Archaeology*, Academic Press, New York, San Francisco and London

Clement, A.J. (1963) 'Variations in the microstructure of human teeth' in D.R. Brothwell (ed.) *Dental Anthropology*, Pergamon Press, Oxford

Codere, H. (1957) 'Kwakiutl Society: rank without class', *American Anthropologist* 59: 473–86

Cohen, A. (1974) *Two-Dimensional Man*, Routledge & Kegan Paul, London

Coles, J. and Harding, A. (1979) *The Bronze Age in Europe*, Methuen, London

Coles, J. and Taylor, J. (1971) 'The Wessex Culture: a minimal view', *Antiquity* 45: 6–13

Collins, A.E.P. (1976) 'Dooey's Cairn, Ballymacaldrack, County Antrim', *Ulster Journal of Archaeology* 39: 1–7

Cook, D.C. (1976) 'Pathological states and disease process in five Illinois Woodland populations: an epidemiological model', Ph.D. dissertation, University of Chicago

Cook, D.C. (1979) 'Subsistence base and health in prehistoric Illinois Valley: evidence from the human skeleton', *Medical Anthropology* 3: 109–24

Cook, D.C. and Buikstra, J.E. (1979) 'Health and differential survival in prehistoric populations: prenatal dental defects', *American Journal of Physical Anthropology* 51: 649–59

Cook, T.G. (1976) 'Koster: an artifact analysis of two Archaic phases in west-central Illinois' in *Prehistoric Records*, No. 1, *Koster Research Reports*, No. 3. *Northwestern University Archeological Program*, Evanston

Cowgill, G.L. (1975) 'On causes and consequences of ancient and modern population change', *American Anthropologist* 77: 505–25

Crane, H.R. and Griffin, J.B. (1963) 'University of Michigan radiocarbon dates VIII', *Radiocarbon* 5: 228–53

Cunliffe, B. (1978) *Hengistbury Head*, Elek, London

Curtis, E. (1909) *The North American Indians*, vol. 5, Johnson Reprint Company, London

Cybulski, J.S. (1977) 'Cribra orbitalia, a possible sign of anemia in early historic native populations of the British Columbia coast', *American Journal of Physical Anthropology* 47: 31–9

Czarnetzki, A. and Czarnetzki, E. (1971) 'Gebisse aus dem bandkeramischen Gräberfeld bei Niedermerz', *Bonner Jahrbücher* 171: 652–60

Dalton, G. (1977) 'Aboriginal economies in stateless societies' in T.K. Earle and J.E. Ericson (eds.) *Exchange Systems in Prehistory*, Academic Press, New York, San Francisco and London

Daniel, G.E. (1963) *The Megalith Builders of Western Europe*, Penguin Books, Harmondsworth

Daniel, G.E. (1964) *The Idea of Prehistory*, Penguin Books, Harmondsworth

Daniel, G.E. (1967) 'Northmen and Southmen', *Antiquity* 41: 313–17

Daniel, G.E. (1970) 'Megalithic answers', *Antiquity* 44: 260–9

Daniel, G.E. (1975) *150 Years of Archaeology*, Duckworth, London

Darlington, C.D. (1968) *The Evolution of Man and Society*, Oxford University Press

Déchelette, J. (1908) *Manuel d'Archéologie Préhistorique Celtique et Gallo-Romaine*, vol. 1, August Picard, Paris

Deetz, J. (1965) *The Dynamics of Stylistic Change in Arikara Ceramics*, University of Illinois Press, Urbana

Denig, E. (1961) *Five Indian Tribes of the Upper Missouri*: J. Ewers (ed.) University of Oklahoma Press, Norman

Dennison, J. (1979) 'Citrate estimation as a means of determining the sex of human skeletal material', *Archaeology and Physical Anthropology in Oceania* 14: 136–43

Dent, J. (1978) 'Wetwang Slack', *Current Archaeology* 61: 46–50

De Rousseau, C.J. (1973) 'Mortuary site survey and paleodemography in the Lower Illinois valley', paper presented at the 72nd annual meeting of the American Anthropological Association, New Orleans

de Valera, R. (1960) 'The court cairns of Ireland', *Proceedings of the Royal Irish Academy* 60C: 9–140

Doran, J.E. (1973) 'Explanation in archaeology: computer experiment' in C. Renfrew (ed.) *The Explanation of Culture Change: Models in Prehistory*, Duckworth, London

Doran, J.E. and Hodson, F.R. (1975) *Mathematics and Computers in Archaeology*, Edinburgh University Press

Dorsey, J. (1882) 'Omaha sociology', *Bureau of American Ethnology Annual Report* 3: 205–370

Dorsey, J. (1904) *Traditions of the Skidi Pawnee*, American Folklore Society, Boston

Douglass, W.A. (1969) *Death in Murelaga: Funerary Ritual in a Spanish Basque Village. American Ethnological Society Monograph*, No. 49

Dragoo, D.W. (1976) 'Some aspects of Eastern North American prehistory: a review 1975', *American Antiquity* 41: 3–27

Drew, C.D. and Piggott, S. (1936) 'The excavation of Long Barrow 163a on Thickthorn Down, Dorset', *Proceedings of the Prehistoric Society* 2: 77–96

Drewett, P. (1980) 'Black Patch and the later Bronze Age in Sussex' in J. Barrett and R. Bradley (eds.) *Settlement and Society in the British Later Bronze Age. British Archaeological Reports* 83, Oxford

Drucker, P. (1939) 'Rank, wealth, and kinship in Northwest Coast Society', *American Anthropologist* 41: 55–65

Drucker, P. (1955) *Indians of the Northwest Coast*, McGraw-Hill, New York

Dunbar, J. (1880) 'The Pawnee Indians, their history and ethnology', *Magazine of American History* 4: 241–81.

Dunn, F.L. (1968) 'Epidemiological factors: health and disease in hunter-gatherers' in R.B. Lee and I. DeVore (eds.) *Man the Hunter*, Aldine, Chicago

Dunnell, R.C. (1979) 'Trends in current Americanist archaeology', *American Journal of Archaeology* 83: 437–49

Durkheim, E. (1915) *The Elementary Forms of Religious Life*, Allen & Unwin, London

Dyson-Hudson, R. and Alden Smith, E. (1978) 'Human territoriality: an ecological reassessment', *American Anthropologist* 80: 21–41

Earle, T.K. (1978) *Economic and Social Organisation of a Complex Chiefdom: the Halelea District Kuaua'i, Hawaii. Anthropological Papers, Museum of Anthropology, University of Michigan*, No. 63

Eisenstadt, S.N. (1949) 'The perception of time and space in a situation of culture-contact', *Journal of the Royal Anthropological Institute* 79: 63–8

Ellison, A. (1980*a*) 'Deverel Rimbury urn cemeteries: the evidence for social organisation' in J. Barrett and R. Bradley (eds.) *Settlement and Society in the British Later Bronze Age. British Archaeological Reports* 83, Oxford

Ellison, A. (1980*b*) 'Settlements and regional exchange: a case study' in J. Barrett and R. Bradley (eds.) *Settlement and Society in the British Later Bronze Age. British Archaeological Reports* 83, Oxford

Ellison, A. (1980*c*) 'Towards a socio-economic model for the Middle Bronze Age in Southern England' in N. Hammond, G. Isaac and I. Hodder (eds.) *Pattern of the Past: Studies in Honour of David Clarke*, Cambridge University Press

El-Najjar, M.Y., Ryan, D.J., Turner, C.G. and Lozoff, B. (1976) 'The etiology of porotic hyperostosis among the prehistoric and historic Anasazi Indians of southwestern United States', *American Journal of Physical Anthropology* 44: 477–87

Ember, M. (1962) 'Political authority and the structure of kinship in aboriginal Samoa', *American Anthropologist* 64: 964–71

Faull, M.L. (1976) 'The location and relationship of the Sancton Anglo-Saxon cemeteries', *Antiquaries Journal* 56: 227–33

Finklestein, J.J. (1940) 'The Norman site excavations near Wagoner, Oklahoma', *The Oklahoma Prehistorian* 3 (3): 2–15

Flannery, K.V. (1972) 'The cultural evolution of civilizations', *Annual Review of Ecology and Systematics* 3: 399–426

Fleming, A. (1971) 'Territorial patterns in Bronze Age Wessex', *Proceedings of the Prehistoric Society* 37: 138–66

Fleming, A. (1973) 'Models for the development of the Wessex Culture' in C. Renfrew (ed.) *The Explanation of Culture Change*, Duckworth, London

Fletcher, A. (1908) 'The Arikara' in F. Hodges (ed.) *Handbook of American Indians North of Mexico. Bureau of American Ethnology Bulletin* 1: 36–8

Fletcher, A. and La Flesche, F. (1911) 'The Omaha tribe', *Bureau of American Ethnology Annual Report* 27: 17–654

Ford, R.I. (1974) 'Northeastern archeology: past and future directions', *Annual Review of Anthropology* 3: 385–413

Fortes, M. (1953) 'The structure of unilineal descent groups', *American Anthropologist* 55: 17–41

Fowler, M.L. (1969) 'Middle Mississippian agricultural fields', *American Antiquity* 34: 365–75

Frake, C.O. (1956) 'Malayo-Polynesian land tenure', *American Anthropologist* 58: 170–3

Frankenstein, S. and Rowlands, M.J. (1978) 'The internal structure and regional context of early Iron Age society in southwestern Germany', *University of London, Institute of Archaeology Bulletin* 15: 73–112

Frazer, J.G. (1886) 'On certain burial customs as they illustrate the primitive theory of the soul', *Journal of the Royal Anthropological Institute* 15: 64–104

Freeman, J.D. (1972) 'The family system of the Iban of Borneo' in J. Goody (ed.) *The Developmental Cycle in Domestic Groups*, Cambridge University Press

Fried, M.H. (1960) 'On the evolution of social stratification and the state' in S. Diamond (ed.) *Culture and History, Essays in Honor of Paul Radin*, Columbia University Press, New York

Fried, M.H. (1967) *The Evolution of Political Society*, Random House, New York

Friedman, J. (1975) 'Tribes, states and transformations' in M. Bloch (ed.) *Marxist Analyses and Social Anthropology*, Malaby Press, London

Friedman, J. and Rowlands, M.J. (1977) 'Notes towards an epigenetic model of the evolution of "civilisation" ' in J. Friedman and M.J. Rowlands (eds.) *The Evolution of Social Systems*, Duckworth, London

Gallay, M. (1970) *Die Besiedlung der südlichen Oberrheinebene in Neolithikum und Frühbronzezeit. Badische Fundberichte Sonderheft* 12, Staatliches Amt für Ur- und Frühgeschichte, Freiburg

Gerloff, S. (1975) *The Early Bronze Age Daggers in Great Britain. Prähistorische Bronzezeit* 6.2, Munich

Gilbert, R.I. (1975) 'Trace element analyses of three skeletal Amerindian populations at Dickson Mounds', Ph.D. dissertation, University of Massachusetts

Gimbutas, M. (1965) *Bronze Age Cultures in Central and Eastern Europe*, Mouton, The Hague

Gimbutas, M. (1973) 'The beginning of the Bronze Age in Europe and the Indo-Europeans: 3500–2500 BC', *Journal of Indo-European Studies* 1: 163–214

Gluckmann, M. (1937) 'Mortuary customs and the belief in survival after death among the south-eastern Bantu', *Bantu Studies* 11: 117–36

Goldstein, L.G. (1976) 'Spatial structure and social organisation: regional manifestations of Mississippian society', Ph.D. dissertation, Northwestern University

Goldstein, L.G. (1980) *Mississippian mortuary practices: a case study of two cemeteries in the Lower Illinois valley. Northwestern University Archeological Program, Scientific Papers*, no. 4, Evanston, Illinois

Goodenough, W.H. (1955) 'A problem in Malayo-Polynesian social organisation', *American Anthropologist* 57: 71–83

Goodenough, W.H. (1965) 'Rethinking "status" and "role": toward a general model of the cultural organisation of social relationships' in M. Banton (ed.) *The Relevance of Models for Social Anthropology. A.S.A. Monographs*, No. 1, Tavistock, London

Goody, J. (1962) *Death, Property and the Ancestors*, Tavistock, London

Goody, J. (1976) *Production and Reproduction*, Cambridge University Press

Graham, I., Galloway, P. and Scollar, I. (1976) 'Model studies in computer seriation', *Journal of Archaeological Science* 3: 1–30

Greber, N.M.B. (1976) 'Within Ohio Hopewell: analyses of burial patterns from several classic sites', Ph.D. dissertation, Case-Western Reserve University

Greber, N.M.B. (1979) 'Variations in social structure in Ohio Hopewell peoples', *Mid-continental Journal of Archaeology* 4: 35–79

Greene, D.L. (1972) 'Dental anthropology of early Egypt and Nubia', *Journal of Human Evolution* 1: 316–24

Griffin, J.B. (1967) 'Eastern North American archaeology: a summary', *Science* 156: 175–91

Grimes, W.F. (1939) 'The excavation of Ty Isaf long cairn, Brecknockshire', *Proceedings of the Prehistoric Society* 5: 119–42

Gruber, J.W. (1971) 'Patterning in death in a late prehistoric village in Pennsylvania', *American Antiquity* 36: 64–76

Haglund, L. (1976) *Disposal of the Dead among Australian Aborigines: Archaeological Data and Interpretations. (Theses and papers in North-European Archaeology*, No. 5), Institute of Archaeology, University of Stockholm.

Hall, Robert L. (1976) 'Ghosts, water barriers, corn and sacred enclosures in the Eastern Woodlands', *American Antiquity* 41: 360–4

Hall, Roberta L. (1978) 'A test of paleodemographic models', *American Antiquity* 43: 315–29

Hammel, E.A. (1964) 'Territorial patterning of marriage relationships in a coastal Peruvian village', *American Anthropologist* 66: 67–74

Hammond, N., Pretty, K. and Saul, F.P. (1975) 'A Classic Maya family tomb', *World Archaeology* 7: 57–78

Harner, M.J. (1970) 'Population pressure and the social evolution of agriculturalists', *Southwestern Journal of Anthropology* 26: 67–86

Harner, M.J. (1975) 'Scarcity, the factors of production and social evolution' in S. Polgar (ed.) *Population, Ecology and Social Evolution*, Mouton, The Hague

Harris, D.R. (1977) 'Settling down: an evolutionary model for the transformation of mobile bands into sedentary communities' in J. Friedman and M.J. Rowlands (eds.) *The Evolution of Social Systems*, Duckworth, London

Harris, M. (1969) *The Rise of Anthropological Theory*, Routledge & Kegan Paul, London

Harvey, D. (1969) *Explanation in Geography*, Edward Arnold, London

Hassan, F.A. (1978) 'Demographic archaeology' in M.B. Schiffer (ed.) *Advances in Archaeological Method and Theory*, vol. 1, Academic Press, New York, San Francisco and London

Hatch, J.W. (1974) 'Social dimensions of Dallas mortuary patterns', Master's thesis, Pennsylvania State University

Hatch, J.W. (1976) 'Status in death: principles of ranking in Dallas Culture mortuary remains', Ph.D. dissertation, Pennsylvania State University

Hatt, G. (1955) 'Das Eigentumsrecht am gebauten Grund und Boden', *Zeitschrift für Agrargeschichte und Agrarsoziologie* 3: 118–29

Hertz, R. (1907) *Death and the Right Hand* (translated by R. and C. Needham, 1960) Cohen & West, London

Hill, J.N. (1968) 'Broken K Pueblo: Patterns of form and function' in L.R. and S.R. Binford (eds.) *New Perspectives in Archaeology*, Aldine, Chicago

Hillson, S.W. (1979) 'Diet and dental disease', *World Archaeology* 11: 147–62

Hingst, H. (1971) 'Ein befestigtes dorf aus der Jungsteinzeit in Büdelsdorf, Holstein', *Archäologisches Korrespondenzblatt* 1: 191–4

Hodder, I. (1978*a*) 'Social organisation and human interaction: the development of some tentative hypotheses in terms of material culture' in I. Hodder (ed.) *The Spatial Organisation of Culture*, Duckworth, London

Hodder, I. (1978*b*) *The Spatial Organisation of Culture*, Duckworth, London

Hodder, I. (1979) 'Economic and social stress and material culture patterning', *American Antiquity* 44: 446–54

Hodson, F.R. (1970) 'Cluster analysis and archaeology: some new developments and applications', *World Archaeology* 1: 299–320

Hodson, F.R. (1977) 'Quantifying Hallstatt: some initial results', *American Antiquity* 42: 394–412

Hodson, F.R. (1979) 'Inferring status from burials in Iron Age Europe: some recent attempts' in B.C. Burnham and J. Kingsbury (eds.) *Space, Hierarchy and Society. British Archaeological Reports* S59, Oxford

Holden, E.W. (1972) 'A Bronze Age cemetery-barrow on Itford Hill, Beddingham', *Sussex Archaeological Collections* 110: 70–117

Holder, P. (1970) *The Hoe and the Horse on the Plains*, University of Nebraska Press, Lincoln

Holloway, R.R. (1974) 'Buccino: the early Bronze Age village of Tufariello', *Journal of Field Archaeology* 2: 11–81

Houart, G.L. (1971) *Koster: A Stratified Archaic Site in the Lower Illinois Valley. Illinois State Museum, Reports of Investigations*, No. 22

Howard, J. (1965) *The Ponca Tribe. Bureau of American Ethnology Bulletin*, No. 195, Washington

Hughes, J. (1968) 'Prehistory of the Caddoan speaking tribes', Ph.D. dissertation, University of Columbia

Hulst, R. (1969) 'A Bronze Age settlement at Elst, prov. Utrecht', *Berichten van de Rijksdienst voor het Oudheidkundig Bodermonderzoek* 19: 275–81

Hunter, J.R. (1975) 'Glasses from Scandinavian burials in the first millennium A.D.', *World Archaeology* 7: 79–86

Hunter, K.B. (1968) *Preliminary Report on the Hopewellian skeletons from the Pete Klunk site, Calhoun County, Illinois. Illinois Archeological Survey Bulletin*, No. 6

Huntington, R. and Metcalf, P. (1979) *Celebrations of Death*, Cambridge University Press

Indrelid, S. (1978) 'Mesolithic economy and settlement patterns in Norway' in P. Mellars (ed.) *Early Postglacial Settlement of Northern Europe*, Duckworth, London

Jackson, D.A. (1976) 'The excavation of Neolithic and Bronze Age sites at Aldwincle, Northants., 1967–71', *Northamptonshire Archaeology* 11: 12–70

Jacobi, R.M. (1973) 'Aspects of the "Mesolithic age" in Great Britain' in S.K. Kozlowski (ed.) *The Mesolithic in Europe*, Warsaw University Press

Jacobsen, L. and Moltke, E. (1941–2) *Danmarks Runeindskrifter*, Munksgaard, Copenhagen

James, E. (1823) *Account of the S.H. Long Expedition 1819–1820*, London edition

Janssens, P.A. (1970) *Palaeopathology*, John Baker, London

Johnston, F.E. (1962) 'Growth of the long bones of infants and young children at Indian Knoll', *American Journal of Physical Anthropology* 20: 249–54

Johnston, F.E. (1968) 'Growth of the skeleton in earlier peoples' in D.R. Brothwell (ed.) *The Skeletal Biology of Earlier Human Populations*, Pergamon Press, Oxford

Kaelas, L. (1967) 'The megalithic tombs in southern Scandinavia – migration or cultural influence?', *Palaeohistoria* 12: 287–321

Kelley, M.A. (1979) 'Parturition and pelvic changes', *American Journal of Physical Anthropology* 51: 541–6

Kelly, A.R. (1938) *A Preliminary Report on Archaeological Explorations at Macon, Georgia. Bulletin of the Bureau of American Ethnology*, No. 119, Washington

Kendall, D.G. (1963) 'A statistical approach to Flinders Petrie's sequence-dating', *Bulletin of the International Statistical Institute* 40: 657–80

Kendall, M.G. (1948) *Rank Correlation Methods*, C. Griffin, London

King, L. (1969) 'The Medea Creek cemetery (LAn-243): an investigation of social organization from mortuary practices', *Archaeological Survey Annual Report* 11: 23–68, University of California, Los Angeles

King, T.F. (1970) *The Dead at Tiburon: Mortuary Customs and Social Organisation on Northern San Francisco Bay. Northwestern California Archaeological Society Occasional Paper*, No. 2

King, T.F. (1978) 'Don't that beat the band? Non-egalitarian political organization in prehistoric central California' in C.L. Redman, M.J. Berman, E.V. Curtin, W.T. Langhorne, N.M. Versaggi and J.C. Wanser (eds.) *Social Archaeology: Beyond Subsistence and Dating*, Academic Press, New York, San Francisco and London

Kinnes, I.A. (1975) 'Monumental function in British Neolithic burial practices', *World Archaeology* 7: 16–29

Kjaerum, P. (1967) 'The chronology of the passage graves in Jutland', *Palaeohistoria* 12: 323–33

Klindt-Jensen, O. (1957) *Bornholm i folkevandringstiden og forudsaet – nin gerne i tidlig jernalder*, Nationalmuseets Skrifter, Copenhagen

Kristiansen, K. (1979) 'The consumption of wealth in Bronze Age Denmark: a study in the dynamics of economic processes in tribal societies' in K. Kristiansen and C. Paludan-Müller (eds.) *New Directions in Scandinavian Archaeology*, No. 1, National Museum of Denmark, Copenhagen

Kroeber, A.L. (1927) 'Disposal of the dead', *American Anthropologist* 29: 308–15

Krogh, K.J. and Voss, O. (1961) 'Fra hedenskab til Kristendom i Hørning', *Nationalmuseets Arbejdsmark* 1961: 5–34

Kurtz, D.C. and Boardman, J. (1971) *Greek Burial Customs*, Thames & Hudson, London

La Flesche, F. (1889) 'Death and funeral customs among the Omahas', *Journal of American Folklore* 2: 3–11

Lallo, J.W., Armelagos, G.J. and Mensforth, R.P. (1977) 'The role of diet, disease and physiology in the origin of porotic hyperostosis', *Human Biology* 49: 471–83

Lallo, J.W. and Rose, J.C. (1979) 'Patterns of stress, disease and mortality in two prehistoric populations from North America', *Journal of Human Evolution* 8: 323–35

Lambert, J.B., Szpunar, C.B. and Buikstra, J.E. (1979) 'Chemical analyses of excavated bone from Middle and Late Woodland sites', *Archaeometry* 21: 115–29

Lane, R.A. and Sublett, A.J. (1972) 'Osteology of social organization: residence pattern', *American Antiquity* 37: 186–201

Larson, L.H., Jr. (1971) 'Archaeological implications of social stratification at the Etowah site, Georgia' in J.A. Brown (ed.) *Approaches to the Social Dimensions of Mortuary Practices. Memoirs of the Society for American Archaeology*, No. 25

Leakey, L.S.B. (1977) *The Southern Kikuyu before 1903*, Academic Press, New York, San Francisco and London

Levine, H.G. (1977) 'Intra-cultural variability and ethnographic description: a decision-making analysis of funerary behaviour among the New Guinea Kafe', Ph.D. dissertation, University of Pennsylvania

Lévi-Strauss, C. (1976) *Tristes Tropiques*, Penguin, Harmondsworth

Lindquist, S.-O. (1974) 'The development of the agrarian landscape on Gotland during the Early Iron Age', *Norwegian Archaeological Review* 7: 6–32

Lloyd, P.C. (1966) 'Agnatic and cognatic descent among the Yoruba', *Man* 1: 484–500

Longacre, W.A. (1968) 'Some aspects of prehistoric society in East-Central Arizona' in L.R. and S.R. Binford (eds.) *New Perspectives in Archaeology*, Aldine, Chicago

Louwe Kooijmans, L.P. (1974) *The Rhine-Meuse delta: four studies on its prehistoric occupation and Holocene geology. Analecta Praehistorica Leidensia. Publications of the Institute of Prehistory, University of Leiden*, No. 7

Louwe Kooijmans, L.P. (1976) 'Local developments in a borderland – a survey of the Neolithic at the Lower Rhine', *Oudheidkundige Mededelingen uit Het Rijksmuseum van Oudheden Te Leiden* 57: 227–97

Lowie, R. (1954) *Indians of the Plains. American Museum of Natural History Anthropological Handbook*, No. 1

Ludwickson, J. (1975) 'The Loup River Phase and the origins of Pawnee culture', M.A. thesis, University of Nebraska, Lincoln

McGregor, I.A., Billewicz, W.Z. and Thompson, A.M. (1961) 'Growth and mortality in children in an African village', *British Medical Journal* 2, II: 1661–6

McHenry, H.M. (1968) 'Transverse lines in long bones of prehistoric California Indians', *American Journal of Physical Anthropology* 29: 1–17

McHenry, H.M. and Schultz, P.D. (1976) 'The association between Harris lines and enamel hypoplasia in prehistoric California Indians', *American Journal of Physical Anthropology* 44: 507–12

Mackie, E.W. (1977) *The Megalith Builders*, Phaidon, Oxford

Madsen, T. (1977) 'Toftum ved Horsens. Et "Befaestet" anlaeg tilhorende tragtbaegerkulturen', *Kuml*: 161–84

Madsen, T. (1979) 'Earthen long barrows and timber structures: aspects of the Early Neolithic mortuary practice in Denmark', *Proceedings of the Prehistoric Society* 45: 301–20

Mainfort, R.C. (1977) 'The Fletcher site cemetery (20BY 28) Bay County, Michigan: a study of the social dynamics of the contact period', Ph.D. dissertation, Michigan State University

Manby, T.G. (1976) 'The excavation of the Kilham long barrow, East Riding of Yorkshire', *Proceedings of the Prehistoric Society* 42: 111–60

Marsden, B.M. (1974) *The Early Barrow-Diggers*, Shire Publications Ltd, Princes Risborough

Massler, M., Schour, I. and Poncher, H.G. (1941) 'Developmental pattern of the child as reflected in the calcification pattern of the teeth', *American Journal of Diseases of Children* 62: 33–67

Masters, L.J. (1973) 'The Lochill long cairn', *Antiquity* 47: 96–100

Mata, L.J., Kronmal, R.A., Urrutia, J.J. and Garcia, B. (1976) 'Antenatal events and postnatal growth and survival of children in a rural Guatemalan village', *Annals of Human Biology* 3: 303–15

Meggitt, M.J. (1965a) *The Lineage System of the Mae-Enga of New Guinea*, Barnes & Noble, New York

Meggitt, M.J. (1965b) 'The Mae-Enga of the western Highlands' in P. Lawrence and M.J. Meggitt (eds.) *Gods, Ghosts, and Men in Melanesia*, Oxford University Press, New York

Meier-Arendt, W. (1975) *Die Hinkelstein Gruppe*, Walter de Gruyter, Berlin

Meiklejohn, C. (1978) 'Ecological aspects of population size and growth in late-glacial and early postglacial north-west Europe' in P. Mellars (ed.) *Early Postglacial Settlement of Northern Europe*, Duckworth, London

Meillassoux, C. (1972) 'From reproduction to production', *Economy and Society* 1: 93–105

Meillassoux, C. (1973) 'On the mode of production of the hunting band' in P. Alexandre (ed.) *French Perspectives in African Studies*, Oxford University Press

Merchant, V.L. and Ubelaker, D.H. (1977) 'Skeletal growth of the prehistoric Arikara', *American Journal of Physical Anthropology* 46: 61–72

Miles, D. (1965) 'Socio-economic aspects of secondary burial', *Oceania* 35: 161–74

Milisauskas, S. (1978) *European Prehistory*, Academic Press, New York, San Francisco and London

Moberg, C.-A. (1956) 'Till frågen om Sanhållstrukturen; Norden under bronsåldern', *Forvännen* 51: 65–76

Modderman, P. (1970) *Linearbandkeramik aus Elsloo und Stein. Analecta Praehistorica Leidensia. Publications of the Institute of Prehistory, University of Leiden*, No. 3

Molnar, S. and Ward, S.C. (1975) 'Mineral metabolism and microstructural defects in primate teeth', *American Journal of Physical Anthropology* 43: 3–18

Montelius, O. (1885) *Om tidsbestamning inom bronsåldern med särskilt afseende på Skandinavien, Kungl. Vitterhets Historie och Antiquets Akademiens Handlingar* XXX, Akademiens Forlag, Stockholm

Moore, J.A., Swedlund, A.C. and Armelagos, G.J. (1975) 'The use of life tables in paleodemography' in A.C. Swedlund (ed.) *Population Studies in Archaeology and Biological Anthropology: a Symposium. Memoirs of the Society for American Archaeology*, No. 30

Mordant, D. and Mordant, C. (1977) 'Noyen-sur-Seine. Habitat néolithique de fond de vallée alluviale. I. Étude archéologique', *Gallia Préhistoire* 20: 229–69

Morgan, D. (1953) *Jedediah Smith and the Opening of the West*, University of Nebraska Press, Lincoln

Morgan, F. de M. (1959) 'The excavation of a long barrow at Nutbane, Hants', *Proceedings of the Prehistoric Society* 25: 15–51

Morrell, L.R. (1965) *The Texas Site, Carlyle Reservoir, Southern Illinois. University Museum Archaeological Salvage Report*, No. 23

Moss, M.L. and Moss-Salentijn, L. (1977) 'Analysis of developmental processes possibly related to human dental sexual dimorphism in permanent and deciduous canines', *American Journal of Physical Anthropology* 46: 407–14

Müller, S. (1897) *Vor Oldtid*, Copenhagen (German edition: *Nordische Altertumskunde nach Funden und Denkmäler aus Dänemark und Schleswig*. Published in Strasburg 1897–8)

Munson, P.J., Parmalee, P.W. and Yarnell, R.A. (1971) 'Subsistence ecology of Scovill, a terminal Middle Woodland village', *American Antiquity* 36: 410–31

Murie, J. (1916) 'Pawnee Indian societies', *American Museum of Natural History, Anthropological Papers* 11: 542–644

Netting, R.McC. (1972) 'Sacred power and centralization: aspects of political adaptation in Africa' in B. Spooner (ed.) *Population Growth: Anthropological Implications*, MIT Press, Cambridge

Neumann, H.W. (1967) *The Paleopathology of the Archaic Modoc Rock Shelter Inhabitants. Illinois State Museum, Reports of Investigations*, No. 11

Newell, R. (1973) 'The post-glacial adaptations of the indigenous population of the Northwest European plain' in S.K. Kozlowski (ed.) *The Mesolithic in Europe*, Warsaw University Press

Nylén, E. (1974) 'Bronze, Eisen und Gesellschaft. Ein Soziale Umwalzung mit wirtschaftlichem Huntergrund zwischen Bronze- und Eisenzeit in nordischen Raum?', *Die Kunde* 25: 103–10

O'Connell, B.H. (1976) 'Adaptive efficiency in the Lower Illinois Valley: fluctuating asymmetry as a measure of developmental homeostasis', paper presented before the 41st annual meeting of the Society for American Archaeology, St Louis

Okely, J. (1979) 'An anthropological contribution to the history and archaeology of an ethnic group' in B.C. Burnham and J. Kingsbury (eds.) *Space, Hierarchy and Society. British Archaeological Reports* S59, Oxford

Osborn, A.J. (1977) 'Strandloopers, mermaids and other fairy tales: ecological determinants of marine resource utilisation. The Peruvian case' in L.R. Binford (ed.) *For Theory Building in Archaeology*, Academic Press, New York, San Francisco and London

O'Shea, J. (1978) 'Mortuary variability: an archaeological investigation with case studies from the nineteenth century Central Plains of North America and the early Bronze Age of southern Hungary', Ph.D. dissertation, University of Cambridge

Otto, K.-H. (1955) *Die Socialökonomischen verhältnisse bei den stämmen der Leubinger Kultur in Mitteldeutschland. Ethnographisch-archaeologische Forschungen III*, Berlin

Pader, E.-J. (1980) 'Material symbolism and social relations in mortuary studies' in P.A. Rahtz and L. Watts (eds.) *Anglo-Saxon Cemeteries. British Archaeological Reports* 82, Oxford

Paludan-Müller, C. (1979) 'High Atlantic food gathering in Northwestern Zealand, ecological conditions and spatial representation' in K. Kristiansen and C. Paludan-Müller (eds.) *New Directions in Scandinavian Archaeology*, No. 1, National Museum of Denmark, Copenhagen

Pavuk, J. (1972) 'Neolithisches Gräberfeld in Nitra', *Slovenská Archaeológia* 20: 5–105

Peebles, C.S. (1971) 'Moundville and surrounding sites: some structural considerations of mortuary practices' in J.A. Brown (ed.) *Approaches to the Social Dimensions of Mortuary Practices. Memoirs of the Society for American Archaeology*, No. 25

Peebles, C.S. (1972) 'Monothetic-divisive analysis of the Moundville burials: an initial report', *Newsletter of Computer Archaeology* 8: 1–13

Peebles, C.S. (1974) 'Moundville: the organisation of a prehistoric community and culture', Ph.D. dissertation, University of California, Santa Barbara

Peebles, C.S. (1978) 'Determinants of settlement size and location in the Moundville Phase' in B.D. Smith (ed.) *Mississippian Settlement Patterns*, Academic Press, New York, San Francisco and London

Peebles, C.S. and Kus, S.M. (1977) 'Some archaeological correlates of ranked societies', *American Antiquity* 42: 421–48

Péquart, M. and S.-J. (1954) *Hoëdic, deuxième station-nécropole du Mésolithique cotier armoricain*, de Sikkel, Antwerp

Péquart, M. and S.-J., Boule, M. and Vallois, H.V. (1937) *Téviec, station-nécropole du Mésolithique du Morbihan. Archives de l'Institut de paléontologie humaine*, No. 18, Masson, Paris

Perino, G.H. (1968) *The Pete Klunk mound group, Calhoun County, Illinois: the Archaic and Hopewell occupations. Illinois Archaeological Survey Bulletin*, No. 6

Perino, G.H. (1971) 'The Mississippian component at the Schild site, Greene County, Illinois' in J.A. Brown (ed.) *Mississippian Site Archaeology. Illinois Archaeological Survey Bulletin*, No. 8

Perino, G.H. (1973a) *The Koster mounds, Greene County, Illinois. Illinois Archaeological Survey Bulletin*, No. 9

Perino, G.H. (1973b) *The Late Woodland component at the Pete Klunk site, Calhoun County, Illinois. Illinois Archaeological Survey Bulletin*, No. 9

Perino, G.H. (n.d.) *Certain Hopewell and Late Woodland sites in West-Central Illinois. Illinois Archaeological Survey Bulletin*, No. 12 (in preparation)

Perzigian, A.J. (1977) 'Fluctuating dental asymmetry: variation among skeletal populations', *American Journal of Physical Anthropology* 47: 81–8

Petersen, F. (1972) 'Traditions of multiple burial in Late Neolithic and Early Bronze Age England', *Archaeological Journal* 129: 22–55

Petrie, W.M.F. (1899) 'Sequences in prehistoric remains', *Journal of the Royal Anthropological Institute* 29: 295–301

Phillips, C.W. (1936) 'The excavation of the Giants' Hills long barrow, Skendleby, Lincolnshire', *Archaeologia* 85: 37–106

Phillips, P. and Brown, J.A. (1978) *Pre-Columbian Shell Engravings from the Craig Mound at Spiro, Oklahoma*, part 1, Peabody Museum of Archaeology and Ethnology, Harvard University, Cambridge

Piggott, S. (1938) 'The Early Bronze Age in Wessex', *Proceedings of the Prehistoric Society* 4: 52–106

Piggott, S. (1962) *The West Kennet Long Barrow: Excavations 1955–56*, Her Majesty's Stationery Office, London

Piggott, S. (1965) *Ancient Europe*, Edinburgh University Press

Piggott, S. (1973) 'Problems in the interpretation of chambered tombs' in G. Daniel and P. Kjaerum (eds.) *Megalithic Graves and Ritual. III Atlantic Colloquium, Moesgård, 1969*

Piggott, S. and Piggott, C.M. (1944) 'Excavations of barrows on Crichel and Launceston Downs, Dorset', *Archaeologia* 90: 47–80

Pitt Rivers, A. (1898) *Excavations in Cranborne Chase*, vol. 4, privately printed, London.

Polak, B. (1959) 'Palynology of the "Uddeler Meer". A contribution to our knowledge of the vegetation and of the agriculture in the northern part of the Veluwe in prehistoric and early historic times', *Acta Botanica Neederlandica* 8: 547–71

Powell, T.G.E. (1973) 'Excavation of the megalithic chambered cairn at Dyffryn Ardudwy, Merioneth, Wales', *Archaeologia* 104: 1–50

Randsborg, K. (1974) 'Social stratification in Early Bronze Age Denmark', *Praehistoriche Zeitschrift* 49: 38–61

Randsborg, K. (1975a) 'Social dimensions of Early Neolithic Denmark', *Proceedings of the Prehistoric Society* 41: 105–18

Randsborg, K. (1975b) 'Population and social variation in Early Bronze Age Denmark: a systemic approach' in S. Polgar (ed.) *Population, Ecology and Social Evolution*, Mouton, The Hague

Randsborg, K. (1980) *The Viking Age in Denmark*, Duckworth, London

Rappaport, R.A. (1971) 'The sacred in human evolution', *Annual Review of Ecology and Systematics* 2: 23–44

Rathje, W. (1972) 'Praise the gods and pass the metates: a hypothesis of the development of lowland rainforest civilisations in Mesoamerica' in M. Leone (ed.) *Contemporary Archaeology*, Southern Illinois University Press, Carbondale

Rathje, W.L. (1973) 'Models for mobile Maya: a variety of constraints' in C. Renfrew (ed.) *The Explanation of Culture Change*, Duckworth, London

Rathje, W.L. (1979) 'Modern material culture studies' in M.B. Schiffer (ed.) *Advances in Archaeological Method and Theory*, No. 2, Academic Press, New York, San Francisco and London

Reinecke, P. (1904–11) *Altertümer unserer Leidnische Vorzeit*, vol. 5, Römisch-Germanisches Zentralmuseum, Mainz

Renfrew, C. (1972) 'Monuments, mobilisation and social organisation in Neolithic Wessex' in C. Renfrew (ed.) *The Explanation of Culture Change*, Duckworth, London

Renfrew, C. (1973) *Before Civilisation*, Jonathan Cape, London

Renfrew, C. (1974) 'Beyond a subsistence economy: the evolution of social organisation in Prehistoric Europe' in C.B. Moore (ed.) *Reconstructing Complex Societies: an Archaeological Colloquium. Supplement to Bulletin of the American School of Oriental Research*, No. 20, Massachusetts

Renfrew, C. (1976) 'Megaliths, territories and populations' in S.J. De Laet (ed.) *Acculturation and continuity in Atlantic Europe*, De Tempel, Brugge

Renfrew, C. (1977) 'Space, time and polity' in J. Friedman and M.J. Rowlands (eds.) *The Evolution of Social Systems*, Duckworth, London

Renfrew, C. and Sterud, G. (1969) 'Close-proximity analysis: a rapid method for the ordering of archaeological materials', *American Antiquity* 34: 265–77

Richards, A.I. (1950) 'Some types of family structure amongst the Central Bantu' in A.R. Radcliffe-Brown and D. Forde (eds.) *African Systems of Kinship and Marriage*, Oxford University Press

Roche, J. (1966) 'Balance de un siglo de excavaciones en los concheros mesolíticos de Muge', *Ampurias* 28: 13–48

Rose, J.C. (1977) 'Defective enamel histology of prehistoric teeth from Illinois', *American Journal of Physical Anthropology* 46: 439–46

Rose, J.C., Armelagos, G.J. and Lallo, J.W. (1978) 'Histological enamel indicator of childhood stress in prehistoric skeletal samples', *American Journal of Physical Anthropology* 49: 511–16

Rosman, A. and Rubel, P.G. (1971) *Feasting with Mine Enemy: Rank and Exchange among Northwest Coast Societies*, Columbia University Press, New York

Rothschild, N.A. (1975) 'Age and sex, status and role, in prehistoric societies of Eastern North America', Ph.D. dissertation, University of New York

Rothschild, N.A. (1979) 'Mortuary behavior and social organization at Indian Knoll and Dickson Mounds', *American Antiquity* 44: 658–75

Roudil, J.-L. (1978) 'Circonscription de Languedoc–Roussillon', *Gallia Préhistoire* 21: 661–94

Rowe, J.H. (1962) 'Worsaae's Law and the use of grave lots for archaeological dating', *American Antiquity* 28: 129–37

Rowlands, M. (1980) 'Kinship, exchange and regional economies of the later Bronze Age' in J. Barrett and R. Bradley (eds.) *Settlement and Society in the British later Bronze Age. British Archaeological Reports 83*, Oxford

Royal Commission on Historical Monuments (1970) *County of Dorset*, vol. 2, part 3, Her Majesty's Stationery Office, London

Royal Commission on Historical Monuments (1975) *County of Dorset*, vol. 5, Her Majesty's Stationery Office, London

Sahlins, M.D. (1961) 'The segmentary lineage: an organisation of predatory expansion', *American Anthropologist* 63: 322–45

Sahlins, M.D. (1968) *Tribesmen*, Prentice-Hall, Englewood Cliffs

Sahlins, M.D. (1972) *Stone Age Economics*, Aldine, Chicago

Sampson, G.C. (1974) *The Stone Age Archaeology of Southern Africa*, Academic Press, New York, San Francisco and London

Savory, H.N. (1968) *Spain and Portugal*, Thames & Hudson, London

Savory, H.N. (1977) 'The role of Iberian communal tombs in Mediterranean and Atlantic prehistory' in V. Markotic (ed.) *Ancient Europe and the Mediterranean*, Aris & Phillips, Warminster

Saxe, A.A. (1968) 'Explaining Variability in the Disposal of the Dead: Social Relationship Factors', paper presented to the annual meeting of the Society for American Archaeology

Saxe, A.A. (1970) 'Social dimensions of mortuary practices', Ph.D. dissertation, University of Michigan

Saxe, A.A. (1971) 'Social dimensions of mortuary practices in a Mesolithic population from Wadi Halfa, Sudan' in J.A. Brown (ed.) *Approaches to the Social Dimensions of Mortuary Practices. Memoirs of the Society for American Archaeology*, No. 25

Saxe, A.A. and Gall, P.L. (1977) 'Ecological determinants of mortuary practices: the Temuan of Malaysia' in W. Wood (ed.) *Cultural-Ecological Perspectives on Southeast Asia*, Ohio University Centre for International Studies, Athens, Ohio

Schalk, R.F. (1977) 'The structure of an anadromous fish resource' in L.R. Binford (ed.) *For Theory Building in Archaeology*, Academic Press, New York, San Francisco and London

Schapiro, S., Schlesinger, E.R. and Nesbitt, E.L. (1968) *Infant, Perinatal, Maternal and Childhood Mortality in the United States*, Harvard University Press, Cambridge

Schietzel, K. (1965) *Müddersheim: eine Ansiedlung der jüngeren Bandkeramik im Rheinland*, Bohlau Verlag, Berlin

Schiffer, M.B. (1972) 'Archaeological context and systemic context' *American Antiquity* 37: 156–65

Schiffer, M.B. (1976) *Behavioural Archaeology*, Academic Press, New York, San Francisco and London

Schiffer, M.B. (1978) 'Taking the pulse of method and theory in American archaeology' *American Antiquity* 43: 153–8

Schoeninger, M.J. (1979) 'Diet and status at Chalcatzingo: some empirical and technical aspects of strontium analysis' *American Journal of Physical Anthropology* 51: 295–310

Schoolcraft, H.R. (1851) *Historical and Statistical Information respecting the History, Condition and Prospects of the Indian Tribes of the United States*, Philadelphia

Schroeder, H.A. (1973) *The Trace Elements and Man*, Devin-Adair Company, Old Greenwich, Connecticut

Schultz, P.D. and McHenry, H.M. (1975) 'Age distribution of enamel hypoplasia in prehistoric California Indians', *Journal of Dental Research* 54: 913

Scrimshaw, N.S. (1966) 'The effect of the interaction of nutrition and infection on the preschool child' in *Malnutrition in the Pre-school Child*, National Academy of Sciences, National Research Council, Washington

Service, E.R. (1962) *Primitive Social Organisation*, Random House, New York

Service, E.R. (1975) *The Origins of the State and Civilisation*, Norton, New York

Shennan, S. (1975) 'The social organisation at Branč', *Antiquity* 49: 279–88

Shephard, J.F. (1979) 'The social identity of the individual in isolated barrows and barrow cemeteries in Anglo-Saxon England' in B.C. Burnham and J. Kingsbury (eds.) *Space, Hierarchy and Society. British Archaeological Reports S59*, Oxford

Siegel, S. (1956) *Nonparametric Statistics for the Behavioral Sciences*, McGraw-Hill, New York

Sielmann, B. (1972) 'Die frühneolithische Besiedlung Mitteleuropas', in J. Lüning (ed.) *Die Anfänge des Neolithikums vom Orient bis Nordeuropa*, 5a, Bohlau Verlag, Köln

Simpson, G.C., Roe, A. and Lewontin, R.C. (1960) *Quantitative Zoology* (revised edition), Harcourt, Brace & World, New York

Skaarup, J. (1976) *Stengade 11*, Langelands Museum, Rubkøbing

Smith, G. (1974) *Omaha Indians*, Garland Publishing, New York

Smith, I.F. and Evans, J.G. (1968) 'Excavation of two long barrows in North Wiltshire', *Antiquity* 42: 138–42

Soggnaes, R.F. (1956) 'Histological evidence of developmental lesions in teeth originating from Palaeolithic, prehistoric, and ancient man', *American Journal of Pathology* 32: 547–77

South, S. (1979) 'Historic site content, structure and function', *American Antiquity* 44: 213–37

Spence, M.W. (1974) 'The study of residential practices among prehistoric hunters and gatherers', *World Archaeology* 5: 346–57

Sprague, R. (1968) 'A suggested terminology and classification for burial description', *American Antiquity* 33: 479–85

Srejovic, D. (1972) *Europe's First Monumental Sculpture: New Discoveries at Lepenski Vir*, Thames & Hudson, London

Steponaitis, V.P. (1978) 'Location theory and complex chiefdoms: a Mississippian example' in B.D. Smith (ed.) *Mississippian Settlement Patterns*, Academic Press, New York, San Francisco and London

Stevenson, P.H. (1924) 'Age order of epiphyseal union in man', *American Journal of Physical Anthropology* 7: 53–93

Stickel, E.G. (1968) 'Status differentiations and the Rincon site', *Archaeological Survey Annual Report*, 10: 209–61, University of California, Los Angeles

Stout, S.D. (1978) 'Histological structure and its preservation in ancient bone', *Current Anthropology* 19: 600–4

Struever, S. (1968) 'Woodland subsistence-settlement systems in the

Lower Illinois Valley' in L.R. Binford and S.R. Binford (eds.) *New Perspectives in Archaeology*, Aldine, Chicago

Struever, S. and Carlson, J. (1977) 'Koster site: the new archaeology in action', *Archaeology* 30 (2): 93–101

Struever, S. and Houart, G.L. (1972) 'An analysis of the Hopewell interaction sphere' in E. Wilmsen (ed.) *Social Exchange and Interaction. Anthropological Papers, Museum of Anthropology, University of Michigan*, No. 46

Struever, S. and Vickery, K.D. (1973) 'The beginnings of cultivation in the Midwest-Riverine area of the United States', *American Anthropologist* 75: 1197–220

Suchey, J.M. (1975) 'Biological distance of prehistoric central Californian populations derived from non-metric traits of the cranium', Ph.D. dissertation, University of California, Riverside

Sulimirski, T. (1970) *Prehistoric Russia*, John Baker, London

Swanton, J.R. (1911) *Indian Tribes of the Lower Mississippi Valley and Adjacent Coast of the Gulf of Mexico. Bureau of American Ethnology Bulletin*, No. 43, Washington

Sweeney, E.A., Cabrera, J., Urrutia, J., and Mata, L. (1969) 'Factors associated with linear hypoplasia of human deciduous incisors', *Journal of Dental Research* 48: 1275–9

Szpunar, C.B. (1977) 'Atomic absorption analysis of archaeological remains: human ribs from Woodland mortuary sites', Ph.D. dissertation, Department of Chemistry, Northwestern University

Tainter, J.A. (1973*a*) 'The social correlates of mortuary patterning at Kaloko, North Kona, Hawaii', *Archaeology and Physical Anthropology in Oceania* 8: 1–11

Tainter, J.A. (1973*b*) 'Structure and organization of Middle Woodland societies in the Lower Illinois River Valley', Master's thesis, Department of Anthropology, Northwestern University

Tainter, J.A. (1975*a*) 'The archaeological study of social change: Woodland Systems in West-Central Illinois', Ph.D. dissertation, Northwestern University

Tainter, J.A. (1975*b*) 'Social inference and mortuary practices: an experiment in numerical classification', *World Archaeology* 7: 1–15

Tainter, J.A. (1976) 'Social organization and social patterning in the Kaloko Cemetery, North Kona, Hawaii', *Archaeology and Physical Anthropology in Oceania* 11: 91–105

Tainter, J.A. (1977*a*) 'Modeling change in prehistoric social systems' in L.R. Binford (ed.) *For Theory Building in Archaeology*, Academic Press, New York, San Francisco and London

Tainter, J.A. (1977*b*) 'Woodland social change in west-central Illinois', *Mid-continental Journal of Archaeology* 2: 67–98

Tainter, J.A. (1978) 'Mortuary practices and the study of prehistoric social systems' in M.B. Schiffer (ed.) *Advances in Archaeological Method and Theory*, No. 1, Academic Press, New York, San Francisco and London

Tainter, J.A. and Cordy, R.H. (1977) 'An archaeological analysis of social ranking and residence groups in prehistoric Hawaii', *World Archaeology* 9: 95–112

Taylor, W. (1969) *A Study of Archaeology*, Southern Illinois University Press, Carbondale

Terrell, J. (1978) 'Archaeology and the origins of social stratification in southern Bougainville' in *Rank and Status in Polynesia and Melanesia, Essays in Honor of Professor Douglas Oliver. Publications de la Société Océanistes*, No. 39

Thomas, D.H. (1978) 'The awful truth about statistics in archaeology', *American Antiquity* 43: 231–44

Toms, H.S. (1925) 'Bronze Age, or earlier, lynchets', *Proceedings of the Dorset Natural History and Antiquarian Field Club* 46: 89–100

Toynbee, J.M.C. (1971) *Death and Burial in the Roman World*, Thames & Hudson, London

Tringham, R. (1971) *Hunters, Fishers and Farmers of Eastern Europe, 6000–3000 BC*, Hutchinson, London

Trubowitz, N. (1977) 'A statistical examination of the social structure

of Frontenac Island' in R.E. Funk and C.F. Hayes III (eds.) *Current Perspectives in Northeastern Archaeology: Essays in Honor of William A. Ritchie. Researches and Transactions of New York Archaeological Association*, No. 17

Tuck, J.A. (1971) 'An Archaic cemetery at Port au Choix, Newfoundland', *American Antiquity* 36: 343–58

Tylor, E.B. (1871) *Primitive Culture*, John Murray, London

Ubelaker, D.H. (1974) *Reconstruction of Demographic Profiles from Ossuary Skeletal Samples: A Case Study from the Tidewater Potomac. Smithsonian Contributions to Anthropology*, No. 18, Smithsonian Institute Press, City of Washington

Ubelaker, D.H. and Willey, P. (1978) 'Complexity in Arikara mortuary practices', *Plains Anthropologist* 23: 69–74

Ucko, P. (1969) 'Ethnography and archaeological interpretation of funerary remains', *World Archaeology* 1: 262–80

Vandermeersch, B. (1976) 'Les sépultures néandertaliennes' in H. De Lumley (ed.) *La Préhistoire Française, Tome 1: Les Civilisations Paléolithiques et Mésolithiques de la France*, Centre National de la Recherche Scientifique, Paris

van de Velde, P. (1979) 'The social anthropology of a Neolithic cemetery in the Netherlands', *Current Anthropology* 20: 37–58

van Der Waals, J.D. (1977) 'Excavation at the natural levee sites S2, S3/5 and S4', *Helinium* 17: 3–27

van Geel, B. (1978) 'A palaeoecological study of the Holocene peat bog sections in Germany and the Netherlands', *Review of Palaeobotany and Palynology* 25: 1–120

van Gennep, A. (1960) *The Rites of Passage*, University of Chicago Press, Chicago

van Gerven, D.P., Armelagos, G.J. and Rohr, A. (1977) 'Continuity and change in cranial morphology of three Nubian archaeological populations', *Man* 12: 270–7

van Zeist, W. (1967) 'Archaeology and Palynology in the Netherlands', *Review of Palaeobotany and Palynology* 4: 45–65

Vincent, J. (1978) 'Political anthropology: manipulative strategies', *Annual Review of Anthropology* 7: 175–94

Walker, P.L. (1969) 'The linear growth of long bones in Late Woodland Indian children', *Proceedings of the Indiana Academy of Sciences* 78: 83–7

Wedel, W. (1936) *An introduction to Pawnee Archaeology. Bureau of American Ethnology Bulletin*, No. 112, Washington

Weiss, K.M. (1973) *Demographic Models for Anthropology. Memoirs of the Society for American Archaeology*, No. 27

Wells, C. (1964) *Bones, Bodies and Diseases*, Thames & Hudson, London

Wells, C. (1967) 'A new approach to palaeopathology: Harris' lines' in D.R. Brothwell and A.T. Sandison (eds.) *Diseases in Antiquity*, C.C. Thomas, Springfield

Weltfish, G. (1965) *The Lost Universe*, Basic Books, New York

Wendorf, F. (ed.) (1968) *The Prehistory of Nubia*, Southern Methodist University Press, Dallas

Whallon, R. (1968) 'Investigations of Late Prehistoric social organisation in New York State' in L.R. and S.R. Binford (eds.) *New Perspectives in Archaeology*, Aldine, Chicago

Whatley, B.L. and Asch, N.B. (1975) 'Woodland subsistence: implications for demographic and nutritional studies', paper presented before the annual meeting of the American Association of Physical Anthropologists, Denver

Whimster, R. (1977) 'Iron Age burial in southern Britain', *Proceedings of the Prehistoric Society* 43: 317–27

White, L. (1959) *Lewis Henry Morgan. The Indian Journals, 1859–62*, The University of Michigan Press, Ann Arbor

Whittle, A. (1977) *The Earlier Neolithic of S. England and its Continental Background. British Archaeological Reports* S35, Oxford

Wilkinson, R.G. (1971) *Prehistoric Biological Relationships in the Greater Lakes Region. Anthropological Papers, Museum of Anthropology*, No. 43, University of Michigan

Wilks, I. (1977) 'Land, labour, capital and the forest kingdom of

Asante; a model of early change' in J. Friedman and M.J. Rowlands (eds.) *The Evolution of Social Systems*, Duckworth, London

Willey, G.R. (1966) *An Introduction to American Archaeology*, vol. 1, Prentice-Hall, New York

Willey, G.R. and Sabloff, J.A. (1974) *A History of American Archaeology*, Thames & Hudson, London

Wilson, D.M. (1976) 'Introduction' in D.M. Wilson (ed.) *The Archaeology of Anglo-Saxon England*, Methuen, London

Wissler, C. (1922) *The American Indian* (2nd edition), Oxford University Press, New York

Wolf, D.J. (1976) 'A population model for the analysis of osteological materials', Ph.D. dissertation, University of Arizona

Worsaae, J.J.A. (1843) *Danmarks Oldtid oplyst ved Oldsager og Gravhøie*, Selskabet for Trykkefrihedens rette Brug, Copenhagen

Worsaae, J.J.A. (1849) *The Primeval Antiquities of Denmark*, translated by W.J. Thomas, John Henry Parker, London and Oxford

Wright, G.A. (1978) 'Social differentiation in the early Natufian' in C.L. Redman, M.J. Berman, E.V. Curtin, W.T. Langhorne, N.M. Versaggi, and J.C. Wanser (eds.) *Social Archeology: Beyond Subsistence and Dating*, Academic Press, New York, San Francisco and London

Wright, H.T. (1977) 'Recent research of the origins of the state', *Annual Review of Anthropology* 6: 379–97

Yaeger, J.A. (1976) 'Enamel' in S.N. Bhasker (ed.) *Orban's Oral Histology and Embryology*, C.V. Mosby, St Louis

Y'Edynak, G. (1976) 'Long bone growth in Western Eskimo and Aleut skeletons', *American Journal of Physical Anthropology* 45: 569–74

Zentai, T. (1979) 'The sign-language of Hungarian graveyards', *Folklore* 90: 131–40

Zimmerman, W.H. (1978) 'Economy of the Roman Iron Age settlement, Flögeln, Lower Saxony — husbandry, cattle farming and manufacturing' in B. Cunliffe and T. Rowley (eds.) *Lowland Iron Age Communities in Europe. British Archaeological Reports* S48, Oxford

Zipf, G. (1949) *Human Behavior and the Principle of Least Effort*, Addison-Wesley Press, New York

INDEX